1997

HEALTH CARE POLICY IN CONTEMPORARY AMERICA

Issues in Policy History
General Editor: Donald T. Critchlow

# HEALTH CARE
# POLICY
# IN
# CONTEMPORARY
# AMERICA

Edited by
Alan I Marcus and Hamilton Cravens

The Pennsylvania State University Press
University Park, Pennsylvania

This work was originally published as a special issue of *Journal of Policy History* (vol. 9, no. 1, 1997). This is its first paperback publication.


Library of Congress Cataloging-in-Publication Data

Health care policy in contemporary America / edited by Alan I Marcus and
    Hamilton Cravens.
        p.        cm. — (Issues in policy history : #7)
    Includes bibliographical references.
    ISBN 0-271-01740-6 (pbk. : alk. paper)
    1. Medical policy—United States.  I. Marcus, Alan I, 1949– .  II. Cravens,
Hamilton.   III. Series.
RA395.A3H4135  1997
362.1'0973—dc21

                                      97-13457
                                      CIP

# Contents

# Editor's Preface

In the twentieth century, Americans have witnessed a revolution in the medical sciences and technology that continues to accelerate at an extraordinary speed as new advances are announced daily. Yet there has been a constancy to the debate over health policy since President Harry S. Truman, in the aftermath of World War II, urged the establishment of a comprehensive medical system prepaid through Social Security taxes. Truman's proposal for a national health insurance system immediately faced opposition from the American Medical Association and a Congress that concluded that the program would be too political, too expensive, too administratively burdensome, and too detrimental to the nation's economic health. Such complaints would be echoed fifty years later when President Bill Clinton offered a new national health insurance scheme in the early 1990s.

To suggest that the medical sciences have been revolutionized, while the health policy debate continued largely constant in terms of rhetoric, partisan politics, and the substantive issues raised by national health insurance, is not to maintain that it is detrimental that policy lags behind technology, although this might be the case. Instead, the observation that health policy in America remains a perplexing problem reveals the difficulties inherent in establishing a health policy for a nation so diverse in its population—ethnically, socially, and regionally. Indeed, medical advances in science and technology, while creating new problems for policy makers, have the potential for making many of the problems in current health policy moot. For example, new developments in contraception might very well make issues concerning abortion meaningless if pregnancy could be avoided altogether.

The editors of this volume—Hamilton Cravens, an intellectual historian, and Alan Marcus, a historian of technology—bring to this collection the importance of political ideas and technology in understanding health policy in contemporary America. The importance of this volume is that these essays examine issues in health policy beyond the narrow confines of the debate over national health insurance that has dominated much of the literature on the subject. By examining a broad range of issues, including the politicization of medical research, the role of expertise, insurance regulation, deinstitutionalization of the mentally ill, the role of labor in health policy, genetics, health fraud, and the cultural context of the health policy debate, the authors of these essays bring new insights to our understanding of national health policy. In doing so, these essays extend our knowledge of health policy by showing that many of the policy questions remain perennial, even while our cultural concepts—even the definition of what constitutes "health"— change.

The revolution in the medical sciences and technology has reinforced our belief as Americans that we deserve the medical right to good health, thereby setting the cultural context for much of the health policy debate. Although this scientific revolution in medicine and health technology will continue, making profound changes in the length and quality of our lives, health policy will remain as perplexing and controversial as ever. These essays, many of which will elicit strong reaction from readers, will not resolve the health policy debate, but they will allow a deeper understanding of the meaning of health, and policy-related questions, in contemporary America.

> Donald T. Critchlow
> General Editor, Issues in Policy History
> The Woodrow Wilson International
>    Center for Scholars
> Washington, D.C.

ALAN I MARCUS AND HAMILTON CRAVENS

# Editors' Introduction

The sages tell us the world has changed since World War II. Under the G.I. bill, returning veterans were given unprecedented access to higher education and job training. Corporate scientists created an extraordinary number of new products that freed women from domestic toil and enabled them to join the workforce. Television brought visual entertainment and the possibilities of high culture to the most diverse spectrum of persons ever. Widespread prosperity swept the land. Single-family dwellings and suburban living became the rage as Americans truly became a people of plenty.

This postwar explosion left its mark on America. Contemporary Americans are healthier, live longer, and live materially better than their parents and their parents' parents. Opportunity, although not equality, has spread throughout American society. Persons of difference—gender, race, culture, and sexual orientation—have a more nearly equal opportunity now than ever before in the nation's history. In health, the situation is even better. Virtually all childhood diseases are under control, and smallpox is on the verge of being eradicated. Americans live longer and grow taller. They eat healthier and have the safest and cheapest food supply on the planet. Chemicals added to foods or used in food production have increased nutritional content, reduced spoilage, and enhanced taste. America devotes more money to medical and medical-related research than any other nation.

Then why do so many Americans seem so disappointed or uneasy? Prodigious material accomplishments have not brought happiness or even contentment. Some in America might argue that the challenge of abundance has revealed the perils of prosperity. Americans as a group seem continually miserable. Taxes are too high. Political leadership has failed. Personal job satisfaction has fallen. Wages seem as depressed as the people who earn them.

In health and health-related matters, the situation appears even more desperate. Cancer is everywhere. Auto-immune, nervous, and environmental diseases have reached pandemic proportions. Americans have become consumed by their health. Every new report of some potential health benison sets off a mindless and often indiscriminate stampede to adopt and implement that new health "discovery." Medical malpractice suits have reached an all-time high. Americans passionately worry about their health-care benefits and whether the health-care system will sustain them in time of trouble. Those fortunate enough to maintain health benefits fear that freedom to choose their physician is well on its way to becoming a thing of the past. Fear of dying has replaced the joy of living as Americans increasingly despair about their health. Americans exhibit persistent frustration and complain about perpetual helplessness. Some find meaning and empowerment in a refusal to submit to a feeling of helplessness. They find that lashing out invigorates them and provides a potent, albeit brief, sense of satisfaction; these men and women engage in political action, undertake class-action lawsuits, or seek comfort in nontraditional or alternative medicine as ways of taking charge of their fate and overcoming the perceived lack of control.

How did we reach this state? Which is the true America? How has the boon of the last fifty years resulted in such gloom and despair? How did Americans get themselves into this morass? Has a malaise or some such thing infected the body politic?

These are important questions, to be sure, but the most crucial issue is the simple acknowledgment of dissonance itself. Identifying the parameters of the social pathology of the present, defining what is wrong now and what makes it wrong,  points to potential remedies. It is that sense, the sense of perspective, that history can bring. What historians can do is trace differences. They can document changes in perception and reality and show the onset and development of psychopathologies. They provide perspective. And as in the case of this collection of essays in a single field, a certain pattern may emerge.

The essays in this volume show conclusively that with respect to health and health-care policy, the period since World War II is not a unified whole. Two deep divisions emerge. Beginning in the 1950s there emerged a subtle yet critical reconceptualization as the individual rather than the group began to figure prominently as the central policy-planning unit. It was as if the economic and social expansion of the previous decade had provided the resources necessary to tailor policy to individual units of society rather than to society itself. So long as delivery of health and health-care services seemed adequate or better, the new emphasis on the individual did not deflate optimism. It held out the promise that services or policies might be delivered on a more effective and/or more equitable basis. Impatience and a sense of frustration surfaced at times, but that remained the extent of conflict. Not until the very late 1960s and early 1970s did the second fundamental change occur. A palpable sense of limits rendered the individualism of the previous decade into a Malthusian formulation: the greater the access or benefits that any one person received reduced the others accordingly. In this Hobbesian world, a war of all against all for all resulted. Everyone demanded their "fair" share and viewed everyone else as attempting to secure more than what they were entitled and hence were the enemy. Coalitions, if sustainable at all, were viable only for extremely brief periods. The situation was exacerbated by a belief, new to the late 1960s and 1970s, that the future was not necessarily different from or better than the present. To flourish in this heartless world required each individual to save him or herself. A keen and permanent pessimism was the consequence.

Emphasis on the individual as referent negated any sense of deference, even deference based upon knowledge. Each person, no matter how ignorant, owed it to him or herself and posterity to decide for him or herself. In that sense, expertise ceased to exist. To be sure, persons continued to exist who possessed technical skills. But expertise as a cultural manifestation had always required reference to the decisions of others, especially those in possession of the same skills and attributes as those they sanctioned. Expertise suggested a de facto homogeneity in which technique, skill, or knowledge, often objectified as science or the scientific method, guaranteed that all members of that expert group would analyze a phenomenom or problem similarly. Expertise guaranteed consistency of expert and of result.

Such a formulation was antithetical to the new individuated America of the past several decades. It is not surprising, therefore, that traditional notions of expertise have been excised from recent health and health-care policy. Expertise has no place in that world where contemporary health and health-care policy has been and is made. Health policy, and policy in general, reflects and is a creature of cultural parameters and characteristics; public policy reflects cultural values. That really ought to be no shock because the formulators of public policy are the people—the public—not simply abstract and unrepresentative entities. No matter how satisfying—and empowering—it remains to attribute policy formation to impersonal forces and agents, the fact persists that we the people formulate policy. That you or I seem unhappy or furious with a policy choice means that we lack a majority or an effective means to express our majority. But even that does not mean that others have usurped the process; it is not simply a matter of money or control (Steve Forbes's multimillion-dollar failure during the 1996 Republican caucus in Iowa testifies that money does not naturally result in control), although many persons employ both money and control as an explanation for their impotence or anomie and as a way of not facing reality. As Walt Kelly said in his comic strip "Pogo" many years ago, "We has met the enemy and it is us." If Americans truly seek different health or health-care policy, then they need to understand, evaluate, and confront contemporary cultural values. Only in that fashion could policy be erected and made that in some way matches expectations. Only if perception would match reality would the dissonance between them diminish. A sense of commonality might emerge, and that would make for the reinstitution of common sense, a commodity impossible in an era that prizes individuation.

*Iowa State University*

AMY SUE BIX

# Diseases Chasing Money and Power: Breast Cancer and Aids Activism Challenging Authority

Through the 1980s and early 1990s, the course of American health research was increasingly shaped by politically-aggressive activism for two particular diseases, breast cancer and AIDS (Acquired Immunodeficiency Syndrome). Even as national stakes rose, both in dollars spent and growing demands on the medical system, breast cancer and AIDS advocates made government policy-making for research ever more public and controversial. Through skillful cultivation of political strength, interest groups transformed individual health problems into collective demands, winning notable policy influence in federal agencies such as the National Institutes of Health (NIH) and Food and Drug Administration (FDA). Activists directly challenged fundamental principles of both government and medical systems, fighting to affect distribution of research funds and questioning well-established scientific methods and professional values. In the contest for decision-making power, those players achieved remarkable success in influencing and infiltrating (some critics said, undermining) both the politics and science of medical research. Between 1990 and 1995, federal appropriations for breast cancer study rose from $90 million to $465 million, while in that same period, NIH AIDS research rose from $743.53 million to $1.338 billion.[1]

Twentieth-century American medicine had never been separate from politics, as demonstrated in history of cancer research.[2] More than simply extending the old politics of medicine, however, activists' pressure reached a new level of politicization in the last fifteen years. In previous decades, procedures for drug approval and research funding had not commonly elicited detailed public interest or sustained passion. Breast cancer and AIDS activism established FDA and NIH policy as regular topics for media analysis and high-profile public protest. Through activism, policy-making "insiders" (officials and researchers whose claims to expertise were secured by professional acknowledgement) were forced to cede some territory to "outsiders." Breast cancer and AIDS movements affected direction of funding and helped re-write official guidelines for research, testing, and drug approval, even as some scientists complained such changes endangered medical progress. Men and women without specialized education or research credentials found a decision-making place alongside scientists and agency executives. Such a development could not be taken for granted; in the same years, for example, the National Science Foundation was not subject to any parallel public activism which succeeded in pushing broad policy change.

Challenging medical and agency authority was fundamental to AIDS and breast cancer activism, both as a philosophical commitment and as means for turning frustration over lack of medical advance into political mobilization. Activists operated on the assumption that research was primarily driven not by intellectual curiosity, but by the political climate, which could then be manipulated. They approached science and medicine not as disciplines of expertise to be judged on their own professional terms, but as potentially (if not actually) flawed social and political enterprises. Though scientific and medical workers themselves tended to value research as almost ideal objective analysis, activists accused researchers and federal officials of incompetence and unfairness, if not gender bias, racism, and homophobia. In sometimes conspiratorial-sounding language blaming "the system" for literally playing with lives, activists defined research as fair game for public confrontation. Surgeon/activist Susan Love likened the battle for breast cancer funds to past fights over "civil rights and war resistance and the early women's movement," while some AIDS activists adopted Malcolm X's slogan, "By any means necessary."[3]

While observers in recent years have written volumes on breast cancer and AIDS separately, their policy-making significance for the 1980s and early 1990s can be best appreciated by examining them in tandem. Their activism evolved with significant parallels; not coincidentally, since the two causes learned from each other's approaches and cooperated. For both breast cancer and AIDS, activism coalesced around specific population and political subgroups: women and homosexuals respectively; though sexual orientation did not limit AIDS infection, gay groups took leadership in promoting action. In each case, mobilization, protest, and hard-fought campaigns brought public attention and political clout to disease-specific concern, winning activists recognition and policy concessions even as they questioned scientific and government authority.

## Politicization of Women's Health

1980s and early 1990s politicization of breast cancer was closely linked to general history of modern feminist concerns. Through the 1960s, as women organized around explicitly feminist motivations, they began scrutinizing gender dimensions of political, social and economic life, including health care. Under the maxim of "the personal as political," women's health was transformed from individual problems into a mutual concern and impetus for political action.

From its 1969 start, the Boston Women's Health Collective encouraged women to educate themselves about their physical well-being, to become informed health consumers who would refuse to tolerate condescending or inadequate treatment by the medical system. The group's 1974 reference *Our Bodies, Ourselves* described both medical details and women's own health experiences, from childbirth to contraception and more; within a decade, the text sold more than two million copies nationwide. In 1975, concerned parties established the National Women's Health Network to draw attention to female health issues and distribute information. Female-friendly health clinics became important providers of women's medical treatment and also worked to influence policy: rather than waiting for development of new contraceptives, feminist clinics helped promote cervical cap research.[4]

Women's health mobilization also crystallized in response to two medical disasters: the Dalkon Shield, touted as a wonderful new 1970s IUD, turned out to cause miscarriage and pelvic inflammatory disease (some severe cases proving fatal), while the drug DES, once popularly administered to pregnant women in hope of avoiding miscarriage, was linked to cancer and reproductive problems extending even two generations down from users.[5] Frustrated by seeming failure of doctors, lawyers, and politicians to provide information, health care, or compensation, concerned women formed grass-roots organizations such as DES Action to support affected women, raise public awareness, and maintain political, medical, and legal pressure.

By the late 1980s, feminist advocates argued that beyond disastrous products such as DES and the Shield, women's health had been systematically endangered by an entire medical establishment. Health was a gendered issue, critics contended; despite evidence of important medical differences between men and women on such matters as cholesterol levels, researchers often investigated health questions or tested new drugs on male subjects alone. The multi-year Physician's Health Study especially troubled women's advocates; the report relied on an all-male sample of 22,000 doctors and so offered no evidence whether aspirin's cardiovascular benefits held true for females. The project head pointed to inherent constraints such as relative scarcity of older female doctors to complement the male study population, though critics asked why researchers could not draw on nurses or other predominantly female groups. The director maintained female subjects would also have confused results and increased expense of an already difficult project by introducing new scientific factors such as hormonal interactions, a fairly common attitude among researchers. He warned science would suffer if political pressure compelled researchers to alter studies, regardless of appropriateness, to fit a mandated gender balance; drug companies added their own cautions that potential harm to a fetus meant special risk in testing women of childbearing age.[6]

Nevertheless, political forces had acquired momentum. In 1986, Public Health Service (PHS) officials spoke up for greater awareness of women's issues in medical studies, NIH then created policy encouraging all grant applicants to "consider the inclusion of women" and justify any research excluding female subjects. Four years later, however, a General Accounting Office (GAO) analysis confirmed women's suspicions that the new policy had been ineffective, that numerous research proposals still ignored gender considerations. The Congressional Caucus for Women's Issues subsequently introduced Women's Health Equity Act legislation which would, among other measures, create a special OB/GYN program at NIH and enforce rules for including female subjects in research. The Act drew growing attention, and soon House and Senate subcommittees adopted some of its provisions as part of NIH reauthorization. To try regaining credibility and demonstrate good faith on the question of women and research, NIH officials adopted strategy to separate and institutionalize responsibility for female health. In September, 1990, NIH established a new Office of Research on Women's Health, winning praise from Women's Caucus co-chair, Representative Patricia Schroeder, who had previously blamed male-dominated policy for leaving women's health "at risk."[7]

The campaign for women's health united feminist advocates, sympathetic politicians such as Schroeder; individual doctors, scientists and medical researchers also supported the cause and organized groups such as the Society for the Advancement of Women's Health Research. By the 1990s, medical journals featured notable numbers of articles and editorials on the issue, as JAMA put it, whether there was "still too much extrapolation from data on middle-aged white men."[8]

Interest groups made an ever-larger case, arguing that beyond women's underrepresentation in studies, gender bias extended to systematic inequity in federal health funds. For activists, dollars defined commitment; critics complained NIH committed just $778 million to female-specific research within a $6 billion overall budget.[9] The National Women's Health Network pressured politicians to rectify past injustice by immediately investing more money in female medicine.

In 1991, one week after confirmation as first female head of NIH, Bernadine Healy announced the agency was creating a $600 million, fifteen-year Women's Health Initiative to redress history of gendered research imbalance. Healy called this NIH's "awakening to a simple fact... that women have unique medical problems." Explaining that women at or past menopause had been doubly-neglected due to age as well as gender bias, the agency announced plans to concentrate on advancing medical knowledge of older women. As *Science* noted, that choice of focus also did credit to "Healy's political acumen," diverting attention from controversial reproductive topics "such as post-conception... birth control and fetal tissue transplant research."[10]

Healy's announcement, making national news, won approval from women's groups, while NIH reported being flooded by letters and calls expressing "enormous" interest in the new program and praise. The head of NIH's Office of Research on Women's Health commented, "Women's health has risen to the public's consciousness in a way I would not have dreamed...."[11] The Initiative program confirmed the 1980s–1990s transformation of medicine into a gendered policy issue, granting seemingly unquestionable political victory for activists' case that women's health deserved special attention. Initiative research, planned to involve up to 160,000 women, would represent the biggest single clinical trial and research effort in NIH history.

While gratifying women's health activists, that fact met more dubious response from some scientific and medical quarters. The Initiative's giant scale and proposed structure drew criticism: with previous NIH work centering on relatively small-scale investigations proposed by researchers, why should the agency suddenly switch to an enormous undertaking directed top-down? Even while acknowledging that women's medical problems deserved increased support than in previous years, some observers worried the new commitment represented too much too soon, that a sudden financial influx might not be the wisest means of correcting past inequity.

Other researchers expressed concern about initial scientific details, such as plans for overlapping clinical trials on 63,000 women to see how nutrient supplements, exercise, low-fat food regimens, and hormone treatment affected cancer, heart disease, and osteoporosis. Several dozen female epidemiologists worried such a complicated project would be undermined by both technical flaws (sorting out multiple factors) and practical difficulties (unlikelihood of convincing women to continue demanding lifestyle changes over ten or more years of study). In 1993, a formal Institute of Medicine review criticized the Initiative on numerous grounds, though members felt "frustrated with the assignment of assessing an expensive project... already under way." Plans for investigating whether reduced-fat diets could lower breast cancer risk seemed "weakest," unlikely to yield valuable information. The committee also worried NIH had understated trial expenses, allocating under half what could be projected from cost of previous studies. The group recommended that "better designed, smaller, more focused studies" would offer "greater chance of success and probably be less costly" than one huge effort. At the same time, reviewers conceded political reality: canceling the Initiative would be seen to "prove that the government does not really care about women's health." However valid the scientific criticism, the large Initiative satisfied NIH's political needs, addressing feminist demands for funding and research attention.[12]

## Focus on Breast Cancer

Within this context of activism for general women's health research, one particular disease, breast cancer, attracted increasing attention in the 1980s. New organizations were founded to focus public awareness and support concerned women; for example, the Susan G. Komen Breast Cancer Foundation, established in 1982, became known for organizing "Race for the Cure" runs in fifty-eight cities to raise money for research, education, and screening programs. Such groups gathered political strength, mobilizing to get government and public alike to recognize breast cancer as a unique concern and allocate special funds to fight the disease.

In this new political battle for breast cancer research, Susan Love, UCLA Associate Professor of Clinical Surgery and Director of the Revlon/UCLA Breast Center, established visibility and a dual identity as both doctor and political player. Historically, other practitioners, from occupational medicine pioneer Alice Hamilton to pediatrician Benjamin Spock, had combined professionalism with social and political expression. However, Love increasingly defined her medical and activist breast cancer work as inseparable, even as many health professionals still felt uncomfortable positioning themselves to challenge the political and medical order. Love linked her political awakening to her promotion of her 1990 reference book for women concerned about breast cancer; after she tossed off a line proposing a "march topless on the White House" to "make President Bush wake up and do something about breast cancer," she found female listeners ready to take her seriously. Calling this group "fed up... that this virtual epidemic was being ignored,"[13] Love became increasingly vocal about breast cancer being as much a political as medical battle.

Following broader campaigns for women's health research, breast cancer concerns maintained that government and medical authorities had ignored the disease even as it approached epidemic proportion; news commentator Cokie Roberts observed that women's 44,500 breast cancer deaths in 1991 exceeded the total of American soldiers killed in Vietnam.[14] Activists based their work on certain presumptions: without increased federal support, the country would make little progress on breast cancer, but given satisfactory resources, movement leaders promised, the disease could be conquered so modern women's daughters and granddaughters would not experience similar fear of breast cancer. To drive this agenda, Love helped establish the National Breast Cancer Coalition in 1991, linking separate advocacy groups to multiply their political effectiveness and muster parade rallies and other demonstrations of public support. Collecting thousands of signatures in petition drives to the President and Congress demanding more breast cancer research, the Coalition gained access to present its case to both Bill and Hillary Clinton.[15]

Women's push for breast cancer money broke through partisan lines; Republicans such as Marilyn Quayle and Olympia Snowe joined Democrats Mary Rose Oakar and Schroeder. Senators such as Edward Kennedy and Tom Harkin (who lost several relatives to the disease) proved useful allies in Congress. Breast cancer groups also benefitted because their appeal coincided with a unique point in national politics; the 1991 nationally-televised hearings on sexual harassment charges in Clarence Thomas' confirmation as Supreme Court justice had left some Americans with an impression of Congress as insensitive to females' concerns. To mend political fences, some representatives turned to breast cancer funding to demonstrate willingness to listen to women's demands; Senator Arlen Specter, whose image had been especially damaged by harsh cross-examination of Anita Hill, especially highlighted his commitment to fighting breast cancer. Furthermore, in 1992, ongoing fallout over the hearings swept a number of women candidates into Congress; "the Anita Hill class" then established greater female representation on committees and subcommittees where they could speak up for women's health issues such as breast cancer.

As another advantage, no other advocates of specific women's diseases had achieved similarly high political profile by the 1990s, so breast cancer activists did not have to compete with other feminists for money and political consideration. Breast cancer could also be considered politically safe: while a campaign against women's lung cancer would have forced politicians to risk alienating Southern tobacco interests and defy the notoriously tough cigarette lobby, breast cancer did not seem to necessitate major confrontation. As Love acknowledged, advocates had demographics on their side; breast cancer had an image of affecting middle or upper-class Caucasian females, a crucial political constituency. For those reasons, supporting higher breast cancer funding became a way for politicians to exhibit awareness of women's issues. In 1991, government money for studying breast cancer rose $43 million, raising by half the previous level of $90 million; in 1992, funds soared to more than $400 million across various federal agencies. Within the National Cancer Institute (NCI) alone, breast cancer support jumped from $197 million to almost $263 million between 1993 and 1994; to place that in perspective, NCI devoted just over $90 million to lung cancer and under $50 million to prostate cancer in that same period.[16]

Such developments reflected new reality: breast cancer had been established as *the* single most politically compelling part of women's medicine. In fact, politicians and advocates alike often equated feminist health concern with breast cancer issues, a powerful link. Corporate sponsors such as Revlon enlisted in fighting breast cancer, providing research funds and other resources while highlighting their support as showing the female market they took women's issues seriously. Public commitment to breast cancer research became a "safe" yet powerful symbol of sensitivity.

Such a development contrasted sharply with previous American attitudes toward breast cancer; women affected in the early twentieth century had tended to keep the disease a close secret, afraid cancer reflected badly on them personally or simply considering it a private concern. The 1980s–1990s establishment of breast cancer as a public political issue was exemplified by a sign at one rally: "Ask me about our demands to the US Govt." With ability and motivation to translate individual experience into group mobilization, transform concern into "demands," women's activists gave breast cancer new visibility and power to influence government funding decisions.

## Politicization of AIDS

Just as feminist organizations provided both philosophical and practical impetus for activists to demand increasing funding and attention for women's health in general and breast cancer in particular, so AIDS activism reflected mobilization of American's gay community. While the 1960s and 1970s had represented an alternately heady and frustrating period of personal concern and political organization for gays, the 1980s brought what seemed the greatest challenge yet, a devastating and mysterious new disease. By 1981, West Coast doctors treating the gay population started noticing clusters of immune deficiency problems. Physicians and researchers at the Centers for Disease Control (CDC) found unusually frequent reports of rare pneumonia and cancer forms. CDC medical detectives initially had to sort through a variety of possible causes, from chemical poisoning to recreational drug use, and perceived the threat as sufficiently urgent to warrant special studies of what some referred to as "Gay-Related Immune Deficiency" (GRID). However, Reagan-era budget cuts threatened to force CDC staff layoffs, with devastating impact on agency plans and morale. NIH had no coordinated strategy for addressing the new disease, while clinic doctors were literally writing rules as they went along on how to treat the now-renamed "AIDS." Gay aides on Capital Hill tried pressing for increased federal research support. However, NIH representatives and Health and Human Services (HHS) Secretary Margaret Heckler officially assured skeptics that funding for AIDS work was "more than adequate." At various times, budget planners even proposed cuts of 10 percent or more. Meanwhile, between 1983 and 1985, United States AIDS cases jumped from three thousand to sixteen thousand, finally attracting significant national media coverage, especially after announcement of actor Rock Hudson's infection. Though Surgeon General C. Everett Koop began preparing to address the public on the nature and prevention of AIDS, concerned observers detected damning lack of leadership, if not outright sabotage, by the Reagan presidency and federal bureaucracy on research to fight the new fatal illness.[17]

With increasing awareness of AIDS, 1980s gay community leaders mobilized resources for both medical and political efforts. Just as feminists had founded the Boston Women's Health Collective, National Women's Health Network, DES Action, and National Breast Cancer Coalition to call attention to women's health, so gay groups created new AIDS organizations. One West Coast group evolved into the San Francisco AIDS Foundation, while New York leaders established Gay Men's Health Crisis, along with the American Foundation for AIDS Research (Amfar).

The most brazen group, ACT-UP (AIDS Coalition to Unleash Power), had been organized in 1987, largely at New York writer/gay activist Larry Kramer's initiative. Members targeted public figures they believed had expressed insensitive attitudes or failed to show proper commitment to fighting AIDS, from Michael Dukakis and Ed Koch to George Bush and Jesse Helms. Hundreds of ACT-UP supporters took political confrontation to radical heights, designing strategies to draw media attention; most notably disrupting a December, 1989 mass at New York's St. Patrick's Cathedral to condemn church positions on AIDS, condoms, and sex education. Protesters also broke into government hearings, prime-time network newscasts, and political speeches across the country to vent opinions on the AIDS crisis.[18]

Behind such public protest, AIDS activists organized special committees to help care for patients, prepare and distribute preventive public health information, and support research on the disease. As advocates educated themselves about medical details, that sense of knowledge helped some approach health experts on an informed footing, winning professional respect for their seriousness. But the late 1980s proved discouraging; while laboratories turned up apparently hopeful clues to disease mechanisms, converting such findings into practical treatments continued to be difficult and slower than even some experts had predicted. Linking this medical impasse to lack of adequate research funding, frustrated activists blamed government apathy for extending the crisis; Kramer called federal efforts to fight AIDS "murderously slow."[19]

Advocates complained that once developed, medical treatments took longer than necessary to reach desperate patients, due to dragging government regulatory processes. In addition to familiarizing themselves with medical facts, AIDS groups also started learning how NIH and FDA operated, to challenge those authorities more effectively.[20] Incensed with seemingly unconscionable bureaucratic delay in approving new drugs, ACT-UP staged sit-ins at NIH and "die-ins" in front of FDA facilities to dramatize demands.[21] The call for action on a 1994 World AIDS Day poster ran, "Red ribbons are a nice gesture. It's red tape we won't stand for."[22]

FDA drug approval processes had evolved over decades, reflecting various concerns of physicians, pharmaceutical lobbyists, and (infrequently) even the public. Since the 1960s, as the FDA consolidated power and placed highest priority on avoiding thalidomide-style disaster, time elapsing before approval lengthened. Accusing the "snail-like" FDA of having "buried" pharmaceutical companies under "increasingly onerous" and "arbitrar[y]" rules, Tufts analyst Louis Lasagna wrote in 1989, "The FDA prides itself on being the most demanding regulatory agency in the world... remarkably unconcerned about any drug lag...."[23]

Standard procedure before the 1980s allowed corporations, doctors, or other sponsors to register Investigational New Drug applications with the

FDA after conducting basic safety studies on animals. The IND then provided go-ahead for three-stage human clinical testing (with continued animal tests): Phase I small-group clinical pharmacology tests designed to identify any negative side effects; Phase II controlled clinical investigations to evaluate effectiveness; and larger-scale Phase III double-blind work with placebo controls. Products passing all three levels were cleared to file a New Drug Application, with one last review of data to gain final market approval.[24]

But by the late 1980s, AIDS groups such as Treatment Action Group (TAG) and Project Inform subjected established approval procedure to tough new scrutiny. For victims of drastic terminal disease, advocates argued, conventional concerns about side effects and scientifically-measured efficacy were meaningless, while trials comparing new treatments with placebo controls or older drugs inhumanely denied subjects access to promising medicine. While activists fought the system, patients travelled to Mexico to acquire drugs not yet approved in the United States or patronized "black market" clinics which offered a wider range of treatment options than regular doctors.[25]

Late 1980s FDA operations floundered as staff tried to cope with expanding responsibilities under tight Reagan budgets. But 1987 policy changes moved toward accommodating demands of extremely sick patients; under a "treatment IND," doctors could give victims of "immediately life-threatening disease" potentially beneficial medicines which had not yet passed final investigation. Moreover, while the agency insisted on continued vigilance to block potentially dangerous or fraudulent treatments, it agreed to experiment with allowing some patients to bring from abroad medicines not yet approved in America and letting doctors test old drugs for new uses.[26]

The 1991 appointment of pediatrician and law professor David Kessler as new FDA commissioner led the agency to acknowledge and deal more explicitly with AIDS groups' pressure, just as Healy's NIH work both reflected and affected the changing political context of breast cancer concern.[27] Establishing new relationships with informed activists (among others), Kessler moved FDA toward a new image of responsiveness while maintaining responsibility for public safety. An HHS Committee review encouraged the agency to foster more rapid and "dynamic" approval procedures, and Kessler agreed that in "balanc[ing] the need to make drugs available quickly with the need to ensure that patients do not receive unsafe or ineffective products," FDA could afford to swing toward facilitating access for fatal diseases such as AIDS. For such desperate cases, the FDA soon instituted special accommodations for "accelerated approval";

while officials would still require basic safety tests, agency decisions could come before extensive trials proved effectiveness or without waiting for precise application terms to be refined.[28]

Largely in response to such internal and external pressure, FDA's average time before deciding to approve or deny new drug applications dropped 42 percent between 1987 and 1992, from thirty-three months to eighteen, the GAO reported. In December, 1995, the FDA proudly pointed to record speed in approving the new protease-inhibiting AIDS drug saquinavir, just over three months from the manufacturer's first submission. In fact, officials announced, all six anti-AIDS drugs approved in the preceding seven years had come through government review in six months or less.[29]

Early 1990s AIDS activism had not run perfectly smoothly; some advocates expressed resentful sense that public attention had faded away. Critics worried even the gay community was experiencing "compassion fatigue" or "AIDS burnout," while charging leaders let themselves be distracted by other political questions such as repealing the military ban on homosexuals. Nevertheless, AIDS advocates had established their legitimacy, a sense of a right to be involved with policy-making at NIH and FDA, the administration and Congress. In December, 1995, activists gathered at the first White House conference on HIV and AIDS, along with researchers and medical officials, to encourage and pressure Clinton to maintain government's fight against the disease. Meanwhile, the CDC announced AIDS stood as the leading source of fatality for white men twenty-five to forty-four years old, and the third cause for women that age (behind cancer and injury), with 41,930 overall American AIDS deaths reported in 1994.[30]

## Politicizing Numbers, Politicizing Research Money

AIDS and breast cancer advocacy, of course, were not absolutely identical. For example, though women concerned with health issues were able to draw on increased female Congressional representation after 1992, gay groups could not count on having as many "natural" allies come forward in the political establishment. Overall, however, activist development for breast cancer and AIDS displayed significant parallels; in both cases, mobilized organizations transformed a group's specific medical problem into concerns defined as politically crucial. Both AIDS and breast cancer could leave victims feeling powerless, a sense reinforced by consciousness of women's and gays' status as "outsiders." Political activity offered a way to rechannel frustration, away from individual battles against an enemy inside (disease itself), into organized campaigns challenging stubborn outside forces ("the political establishment," "medical system," or both). Even if policy changes and renewed research funding came too late to bring a particular patient/activist any personal medical help, organizations drew the individual into a broader fight, promising their commitment would broadly benefit entire groups of others, even curing or preventing future disease. Both breast cancer and AIDS activists operated from conviction that previous medical funding and research policy had been systematically biased against investigation of "their" disease. Some almost-moralistic undertones insisted government and medical authorities confess previous "injustices," then to be atoned for by generous new spending.

Similarities between AIDS and breast cancer activism should not be surprising. From the late 1980s on, leaders in the two camps studied each other's work, modelling new efforts in light of what had succeeded for the other cause. Breast cancer advocates adopted tactics initiated by AIDS activists and vice versa,[31] cooperating where they saw common need for action. For example, members of Women's Health Action and Mobilization (WHAM!), sharing ACT-UP's aggressive political inclination, joined the 1989 St. Patrick's protest against certain Catholic moral precepts. Each movement developed special fund-raising and public awareness events (from breast cancer-benefit fashion shows, to AIDS-benefit theater, music, and art events). Both causes even acquired shorthand symbols of support: red ribbons for AIDS and pink for breast cancer, fashionable accessories among regular Americans and Hollywood celebrities wishing to display political and philosophical solidarity with activists.

In both cases, AIDS and breast cancer activists achieved certain recognition by White House and Congressional politicians, doctors, FDA and NIH officials even as they harshly criticized government and medical authority. As examples, the 1992 International Conference on AIDS offered a forum to representatives of TAG, one of the groups pushing to reform drug approval,[32] while health agencies arranged for advocates to participate in grant review and research planning.

To support demands, both AIDS and breast cancer activists relied on figures purporting to demonstrate basic inequities in the medical system, but numbers could be disputed. For example, while many scientists, medical experts, and journals agreed with feminists that gender balance in research should be a source of concern, others disputed that severe bias had been as widespread as critics portrayed. A 1991 NCI study noted, for instance, that women, 35 percent of new lung cancer cases, accounted for 33 percent of subjects in lung cancer clinical trials.[33]

AIDS and breast cancer groups also employed numbers for broader

purpose; to emphasize the urgency of increased funding, activists repeatedly stressed how many Americans were threatened by "their" disease.
Such statistics could be challenged; especially in early years of AIDS concern, projections of total infection and relative demographic risk varied
widely, from conservative to apocalyptic. Breast cancer activists' literature, placards and buttons spread the byword that the disease confronted
one in nine American women; one group adopted the slogan "one in nine"
as its name.[34] While easy to remember and politically powerful, the message could be misleading, since the number only held true given assumptions of an 85-year lifespan for women. Furthermore, rather than striking
one in nine at any age, breast cancer in reality exhibited far greater statistical incidence in older women. In projecting younger women as its face,
then, the movement tended to distort relative risks. Activists declared,
however, "If the disease continues to spiral at the present rate, our daughters and granddaughters will have a one in four chance of... breast cancer."[35]

Breast cancer activists deserved credit for tangible progress in public
awareness, both through the movement's own campaigns and the drive
for increased media coverage. By the 1990s, the number of American
women having mammograms rose significantly; up to 65 percent of females past age forty had breast exams.[36] Earlier diagnoses, combined with
better treatment options, were cited as factors in the 4.7 percent decline
in breast cancer deaths between 1989 and 1992; fatality for women age
thirty to fifty-nine dropped eight or nine percent.[37] Clearly, through the
mid-1990s, many important questions about breast cancer remained un-
answered, especially relating to the exact nature of risk factors such as
diet, environment, and genetics. Many doctors testified to need for further investigation; Susan Love stressed the goal of developing practical
tests to screen breasts for cancer on a regular basis, analogous to the way
Pap smears checked for cervical cancer.[38]

As activists turned numbers into a political tool to gain clout, they
established breast cancer funding as a key vote for politicians to show
dedication to women's concern. However, Washington could support only
so many key issues, and defining breast cancer as *the* primary principle
risked in effect shunting aside other female health problems, arguably at
least as serious. Similarly, American women themselves started thinking
of breast cancer as their single greatest health danger, overwhelmingly
out of proportion to actual risk. One study showed 46 percent of women
convinced that breast cancer posed a major threat, though only 4 percent
overall were likely to develop it; by contrast, while 36 percent could be
expected to face heart disease, a mere 4 percent judged cardiac problems

a serious risk.[39] Of course, the very idea of cancer in general had acquired terrible emotional connotations, while some observers contended that breast cancer represented a uniquely terrifying form. Because of the significance attached to breasts in American culture, they argued, the cancer threatened the most vital physical and psychological sense of feminine identity.

Nevertheless, while breast cancer advocates established the issue at the center of women's health politics, drawing cover stories in *Newsweek*, the *New York Times Magazine*, and *Ms.*(among other publications), heart disease remained the primary source of overall female death. Though relatively unnoticed politically, cardiac trouble proved fatal for close to six times more American women than breast cancer. Since the 1950s, Mayo Clinic studies indicated, women's incidence of coronary heart disease rose even as men's rates dropped, while female heart attack fatality passed male death rates. While research had not yet solved many breast cancer questions, risks and treatment of women's heart disease also entailed medical unknowns and issues of gender bias.[40]

Moreover, medical reports emphasized that lung cancer, with increasing incidence and high mortality, actually accounted for more female deaths per year than breast cancer. Comparing 1975–1979 to 1987–1991, lung cancer incidence in women grew 65.3 percent, versus a 2.5 percent rise in men, according to NCI. While smoking had once been predominantly a male habit, discouraged if not forbidden for women, modern social change led female cigarette use to start catching up. Studies since the late 1970s showed teenage girls more likely than boys to experiment with smoking, as an appealing way to control weight or stress; some tobacco company advertising also increasingly targeted young women. Extrapolating from present trends, one PHS official suggested women's cigarette use would pass men's by 2000, reshaping female health risks.[41] While breast cancer medicine offered no miracles by the 1990s, other types such as ovarian cancer also remained notably difficult to detect and colon cancer hard to treat. A 1994 report, "Cancer at the Crossroad," concluded that though the country had invested over $23 billion on general research in twenty-three years since President Richard Nixon's "War on Cancer," relatively little overall progress had been made on the disease.[42]

Such facts served as reminders that while activists had won new consideration for the important breast cancer issue, no comparable political clout had been mustered for other serious diseases in women such as lung cancer or heart disease. Activists such as Love dismissed fear that breast cancer might deplete other research, maintaining health should not be a zero-sum game and that funds could easily come out of "useless government spending." But while an ideal world might offer ample money to study all disease, 1990s political and financial reality, such as renewed attention to balanced budgeting, brought talk of tough review of scientific and medical spending.[43] Nevertheless, through early 1996, breast cancer advocates in Congress had succeeded in largely protecting their gains in funding from the threat of harsh cuts.

Within that political context, those concerned about other diseases felt compelled to try developing new power to keep up with AIDS and breast cancer activism. In 1996, the American Heart Association complained the nation spent $1,700 in research per heart-disease death, versus $39,000 per AIDS fatality. AIDS activists insisted the comparison did not hold, since heart research was well-established while AIDS still involved tremendous unknowns, but the Heart Association announced its intent to engage in letter-writing, marches and other attention-getting tactics which had worked for AIDS politics. But at the same time, AIDS and breast cancer activists declared still more ambitious federal funding goals; the National Breast Cancer Coalition directed supporters to ask Clinton and Congress to "invest $2.6 billion in quality breast cancer research to find a cause and cure, between now and the Year 2000."[44]

Breast cancer and AIDS activism promoted the impression that given past shortfalls in research, any sizable new funding would by definition be money well spent. The politicized drive for specific disease funding sometimes threatened to rush ahead of scientific ideas on how best to use new resources. *Nature* described one version of a 1991 NIH report on planning women's health research as just "a laundry list of needs," calling for "urgent... research" on "every conceivable aspect of a women's life from conception to death" while conspicuously "missing... proposals for scientifically innovative ideas."[45] In other cases, high-profile disease politics led to some detours around established medical system planning, as with the 1993 special $210 million appropriation for breast cancer research allocated not to NIH, FDA or NCI, but the Department of Defense.

Though the devastating impact of AIDS and breast cancer made it difficult to challenge the need for progress, some critics did question the merit of skyrocketing funding. Commenting on perceptions of discrimination against women's health, University of Southern California Norris Cancer Center biostatistician Leslie Bernstein said in 1995 that "the academic world... always had funding to research breast cancer. Less has been spent on studying male-only cancers like prostate cancer and testicular cancer...." One policy analyst (and former breast cancer patient) worried that activist politics meant "micromanagement of science that doesn't result in the best spending..." while Georgetown's cancer center head agreed with concern about "advocacy going overboard."[46]

Love classed such opinion as "backlash" from researchers who resented having to accede to new "taxpayer" new power in directing funding; however, some doubts not so easily dismissed came from individuals sympathetic to women's causes. Columnist Anna Quindlen noted in 1993 that when NCI "now spends more for research on breast cancer than for prostate, ovarian, colo-rectal and liver cancers combined," it showed "something wrong... with how survivor advocacy has driven research dollars... a research agenda that relies so heavily on who makes the most noise." Women's health, she said, would be best served by "a big-picture policy in which, without fear or favor, funding decisions are based on what will yield best results..." determined by science rather than politics.[47]

## Challenging Research and Testing Procedures

Fundamentally, AIDS and breast cancer activists were challenging and politicizing not only funding, but the structure and scientific values of research itself. Under ongoing criticism that NIH had not effectively mandated gender balance in research pools, 1994 agency changes set new guidelines requiring clinical trials to make "valid analysis" of whether the treatment in question affected women and minorities differently than white males. Some scientists resented the policy as imposition of political correctness which would cause delay and add to research cost; a Johns Hopkins biostatistician called it "very foolish and very harsh law that is not in the public's interest." Similarly, for AIDS, some researchers feared that FDA policy change granting more generous access to experimental drugs actually undermined scientific need to acquire knowledge about new medicines. A 1994 FDA review of accelerated approval showed that after treatments such as DDI and DDC became available, manufacturers never completed follow-up research proving effectiveness. While it was one thing for advocates to win political battles, it remained another matter to convince researchers that resulting policy change did not hurt medical progress.[48]

Some AIDS and breast cancer activism explicitly challenged fundamental scientific method such as randomized research trials comparing new promising treatment against placebos or older drugs. AIDS groups objected that random tests might leave some patients stuck with ineffective medicine; a tombstone-shaped poster at one protest read, "I got the placebo." Some FDA officials and researchers feared such objections might end up undermining necessary studies of new AIDS medicine, if "compassionate" or accelerated approval policy offered patients alternate access to experimental drugs without risk of "getting the placebo."[49] Similarly, some women voiced displeasure with randomized controlled testing, as researcher Ann Oakley found in a British study of whether home visits and other support made pregnant women more comfortable and resulted in healthier babies. Midwives in the study, worrying that mothers who really needed help might end up in the control group, tried to subvert randomizing mechanisms by persuading secretaries or otherwise trying to steer certain subjects into the list assigned home visits.[50] Though scientists relied on random clinical trials as a vital scientific method for eliminating bias and so yielding objective results, outside observers did not necessarily value the procedure similarly.

In other cases, breast cancer and AIDS patients actually rejected scientific testing procedures. According to a 1995 report, NCI tests of bone marrow transplants as breast cancer treatment had been undercut because women feared they might be randomly placed in control sections receiving less aggressive therapy. When possible, patients simply chose to avoid enrolling in NCI trials, instead just finding providers willing to give them transplants directly. Worrying that failure to recruit enough subjects might make it impossible to conduct valid tests, the NCI project head hoped physicians might "take a stand and not let this stampede to bone marrow transplant continue"; however, women themselves were expressing reluctance to "be a guinea pig."[51] Similarly for AIDS, some observers suggested that patients had become so infuriated with complex eligibility requirements surrounding research projects that they engaged in "rampant 'lying and cheating' " to be accepted into promising studies. In other cases, subjects might drop out of testing if they suspected they had gotten placebos, or else might share medication with others, adjust dosages as they saw fit, or secretly continue alternate types of treatment. According to one analysis, such individuals could "justify non-compliance with protocols" by adopting a "coercion defense"; if society and science refused to recognize their need for medical support and free choice of treatments, patients bore no obligation to comply with the medical system's rules.[52]

## Challenging Scientific Authority

Beyond questions of research funding and testing procedure, some AIDS and breast cancer activists literally confronted researchers whose perspective did not seem politically acceptable; at a 1994 American Association for the Advancement of Science panel, critics who accused NCI, FDA and the American Cancer Society (ACS) of ignoring links between breast cancer and environmental pollution "exchanged insults with...sceptical scientists."[53]

Some activists' interpretations directly challenged medical system motives. As *Nature* observed in 1991, women's health advocates often put "faith in the belief that disease can be prevented by appropriate behaviour, implying that the behavioural and social sciences are as important as the traditional biomedical sciences in creating a new research agenda... a view that would predicate a change in... NIH... mission."[54] Some breast cancer advocates accused the medical establishment of systematically denying any evidence of nutrition and environmental pollution as causal factors. A 1993 *Ms.* article blamed cancellation of an NCI study on whether low-fat diets could lower cancer rates on clinicians "accumstomed to having a virtual monopoly on the breast cancer research pie." The author, head of the National Women's Health Network's Breast Cancer Committee, accused doctors of favoring high-tech, high-intervention and high-cost chemical and hormonal cancer treatment; changing diet would not give medical interests dollars or prestige, but [i]magine the profits if half the healthy population were put on yet another drug." Another piece accused NCI and ACS of neglecting evidence linking breast cancer to organochlorine contamination, quoting a University of Illinois environmental medicine professor who called "the cancer establishment... myopically fixated on obsolete blame-the-victim theories." In conspiratorial-sounding language, *Ms.* maintained that "a golden circle of power and money," including "mostly male" medical centers, doctors, drug companies, ACS and NCI, pursued mutually-beneficial political and financial interests while rejecting evidence which threatened their control. This inside group could then be defined as the opponent—the *Ms.* cover asked, "Why Did They Dismiss Dietary Fat?"— "they" meaning NCI and other institutions "firmly locked into the myth perpetrated by the modern medical profession" pushing pharmaceutical interests ahead of lifestyle and environmental health concerns.[55]

Breast cancer and AIDS activists did not hesitate to use political clout to force reconsideration of science which did not suit their convictions. In the 1990s, Long Island women detected what seemed unusual clusters of breast cancer in certain counties and focused on water supply contamination as cause. Examining the data, investigators for New York State found no scientific justification for further pursuit; but the Long Island Breast Cancer Coalition, unsatisfied by that decision, won backing from Senator Alfonse D'Amato to push for re-opening the question. At a public hearing convened by the Center for Disease Control (CDC), Long

Island activists expressed conviction that pesticides and toxic waste lay behind area breast cancers. The CDC subsequently found no scientific basis for concern about Long Island breast cancer and pollution, yet thanks to political mobilization, Congress allocated money to undertake a special investigation anyway.[56]

In other cases, advocates challenged what authorities said were rational decisions to end ineffective research. When NIH judged in 1994 that alternate proposals and programs for other cities should supersede New York clinical AIDS trials, Gotham's politicians joined activists and patients in protest. While agency officials insisted the move would shift funding from "mediocre" to "the best science," city doctors maintained that NIH had failed to consider New York's sheer number of AIDS patients and need for fair minority representation in trials. TAG activists called for an independent review of why competing programs ranked ahead of New York's.[57]

As further challenge to authority, activists and medical allies disputed official rulings on the value of ideologically-appealing drugs. In the early 1990s, after the Kenya Medical Research Institute claimed impressive improvement in AIDS patients' immune resistance and health status after oral alpha interferon treatment, some African-American activists became vocal proponents. Though NIH found no scientific support, segments of the African-American community alleged that racism kept federal authorities and the medical system from acknowledging value in African-derived therapy. Members of the National Medical Association, a black doctors' professional group, expressed confidence in oral alpha interferon's efficacy. Surrounded by controversy, NIH re-opened the question in 1992, moving to undertake clinical trials re-assessing the Kenyan treatment.[58] Of course, desperate patients in earlier instances had maintained faith in certain medical options even after expert assessment judged them worthless, as illustrated in the case of Laetrile. By the 1990s, however, the impressive political clout of breast cancer and AIDS could actually persuade government authorities to re-open investigations after first rulings did not serve advocates' political pleasure. Activist pressure even helped win 1996 FDA approval for highly experimental transplant of baboon bone-marrow into an AIDS patient, even as experts warned such animal-to-man tissue grafts risked medical nightmare by facilitating spread of new viruses. One researcher figured officials only agreed since the test was expected almost definitely to fail, with the human system rejecting baboon material,[59] but the incident highlighted how scientific considerations had become negotiable within the highly charged political environment of AIDS.

Questioning of medical authority on breast cancer and AIDS came in a period which also showed broader American skepticism of conventional medicine. According to one 1990 report, over 33 percent of AIDS patients used unorthodox therapies such as acupuncture, imagery, megavitamin doses, and unapproved medicine. A more general 1993 study correspondingly shocked the medical profession, showing one-third of adults supplementing visits to regular physicians with chiropractic care, relaxation technique and other alternative treatments for physical pain (back and headaches) and other problems (anxiety, depression, and insomnia). Such therapy found a home within mainstream health institutions; by end of 1995, the relatively new NIH Office of Alternative Medicine had given out almost $8 million in research support, while Harvard, UCLA, and thirty other medical schools offered classes on unconventional treatments. Alternative medicine's gains came with help from political friends such as Senator Harkin (vitally positioned as chair of the Senate subcommittee with oversight for health, interested himself in bee-sting therapy), succeeding despite harsh criticism from some doctors, researchers, and agency insiders. In 1994, Harkin publicly battled Dr. Joseph Jacobs, former head of the Alternative Medicine office, who charged the senator with "professionally insulting" attempts "to politically intimidate" officials. Brandishing his role as unconventional therapy's political champion, Harkin accused Jacobs of not being properly committed to honest studies of alternate medicine. But for many scientists, the new NIH office and medical courses confirmed fear that non-scientific work was gaining a foothold in respectable institutions, violating the ultimate divide between objectivity and quackery.[60]

For some feminists by the 1990s, the issue of what justified scientific authority had become a powerful philosophical issue. Critics such as Sandra Harding suggested that by definition, science could not be isolated from its historically male-dominated political and social context, so resulting sexist and racist bias undermined the system's supposed objectivity. Though such feminists maintained their analysis was meant to help improve scientific accuracy, some scientists interpreted it as academic-leftist "hostility," hopelessly misguided attacks out to destroy science.[61]

## Conclusion

Breast cancer and AIDS activism had generated high political profile in relatively brief time, drawing support from growing organizational power and aggressive strategy. For AIDS and breast cancer patients, frustration with vicious disease readily translated into protest against government and medical systems; as one woman declared, "Nothing will ever happen to breast cancer unless it is politicized." Activists even influenced public perceptions of risk; though AIDS and breast cancer both undeniably represented terrible problems, their political description as an "epidemic"or "holocaust" which "attacks... brutally and indiscriminately" sometimes threatened to overshadow other serious disease. Convinced that research-establishment bias against women's health and AIDS had shortchanged previous funding, activists harnessed numbers and political power to win significant increases in federal research targeted to "their" diseases.

Both AIDS and breast cancer groups maintained that medical and government narrow-mindedness required them to challenge not just the direction of appropriations, but also established research policies and fundamental scientific values. While scientists considered peer review and controlled testing proven methods for confirming results, critics disdained such rules as bureaucratic nonsense biased to exclude alternate ideas. Even as some researchers complained about endangering the integrity of science, activists took philosophical pride in challenging the system. Advocacy meant defining enemies; unwilling to accept official decisions against politically-appealing treatments, activists turned medical rulings into power games for new battle. By the 1990s, federal officials and doctors had been compelled to address this activist pressure, making some basic change in research procedure, allowing interest groups more chances to comment on policy, and even re-opening decisions which had displeased activists.

While breast cancer and AIDS groups were not the first American organizations to fight for specific medical causes and research money, the 1980s–1990s activism was unique in two respects. First, as those organizations gained political power, they reached for unprecedented influence on government agencies, demanding a voice in distributing research funds, changing policy, and setting research agendas. While in earlier decades the March of Dimes had raised significant sums to fight polio, the group followed mainstream medical opinion on the best direction for using such research funds; by contrast, a 1996 breast cancer petition asked the President and Congress to "mandate that... breast cancer activists help determine how the money gets spent."[62] Second, breast cancer and AIDS activists went beyond other medical causes in posing broad and direct challenges to scientific authority; again, polio groups had not disputed the objective value of research or fought to reverse specific rulings. Breast cancer and AIDS groups did not deny the ultimate value of medicine itself; in fact, they expressed repeated confidence that with significant increases in funding and national commitment, researchers would find better treatments, cures, and preventive measures for such terrible diseases. Yet to achieve such gains, activists contended, the medical community needed to reform its entire approach, even re-considering the value of randomized testing and supposedly "objective" results to accommodate sensibilities of patients and politics.

By the mid-1990s, breast cancer and AIDS activists had won significant power, reviewing and planning research along with scientists and officials. How had advocates achieved such change in so short a time? One doctor argued that "liberal" researchers and agencies had been "sympathetic to the plight" of seriously-ill patients and also "easily intimidated."[63] While that explanation contained elements of truth, it did not fully reflect the power of AIDS and breast cancer activists in taking research to newly politicized heights. In part, these activists may have gained new influence in setting policy precisely because they were able to rally political clout behind such fundamental challenges to scientific method and federal authority. Smaller demands would not have attracted enough public attention to gain political credibility for winning major policy-making concessions, but activists' philosophical and political attacks on the medical system and government agencies resonated with many Americans' broader doubts about authority in the 1980s and 1990s. The activists' critiques alienated some scientists, who resisted what seemed unjustified interference by non-experts who failed to appreciate the value of objective method. But increasing numbers of researchers found some truth in activists' arguments about previous bias in the medical system, leading some doctors, agency officials and politicians alike to decide they could accommodate at least some demands of AIDS and breast cancer groups. By pressing their philosophical and political challenges to scientific and federal authority, AIDS and breast cancer groups won new policy-making authority themselves.

*Iowa State University*

## Notes

1. Figures from the National Cancer Institute and the American Foundation for AIDS Research.

2. Richard A. Rettig, *Cancer Crusade: The Story of the National Cancer Act of 1971* (Princeton, NJ, 1977); James T. Patterson, *The Dread Disease: Cancer and Modern American Culture* (Cambridge, Mass., 1987); and Robert Proctor, *Cancer Wars: How Politics Shapes What We Know and Don't Know About Cancer* (New York, 1995). For a broader look, see Stephen P. Strickland, *Politics, Science, and Dread Disease: A Short History of*

28          DISEASES CHASING MONEY AND POWER

*United States Medical Research Policy* (Cambridge, Mass., 1972); and Victoria A. Harden, *Inventing the NIH: Federal Biomedical Policy, 1887–1937* (Baltimore, 1986).

3. Susan M. Love with Karen Lindsey, *Dr. Susan Love's Breast Book* (Reading, Mass., 1995), 525; and Robert M. Wachter, "AIDS, Activism, and the Politics of Health," *The New England Journal of Medicine* 326, no. 2; January 9, 1992: 129.

4. The Boston Women's Health Book Collective, *The New Our Bodies, Ourselves: A Book By and For Women* (New York, 1984); and Dana M. Gallagher and Gary A. Richwald, "Feminism and Regulation Collide: The Food and Drug Administration's Approval of the Cervical Cap," *Women and Health* 15.2 (1989): 87–97. See also Barbara Beckwith, "Boston Women's Health Book Collective: Women Empowering Women," *Women and Health* 10 (Spring 1985): 1–7.

5. On DES, see Diana Dutton, *Worse Than the Disease* (Cambridge, 1988); for the Dalkon Shield, Morton Mintz, *At Any Cost* (New York, 1985). For detail on DES development and science issues, see Alan I Marcus, *Cancer from Beef: DES, Federal Food Regulation, and Consumer Confidence* (Baltimore, 1994.)

6. Sue Rosser, *Women's Health—Missing from U.S. Medicine* (Bloomington, Ind., 1994); Eileen Nechas and Denise Foley, *Unequal Treatment* (New York, 1994); Kathryn Graff Low et al., "Women Participants in Research: Assessing Progress," *Women and Health* 22.1 (1994): 79–98; Joseph Palca, "Women Left Out at NIH," *Science* 248, June 29, 1990: 1601; and "Is There Still Too Much Extrapolation From Data on Middle-aged White Men?" *JAMA* 263, no. 8; February 23, 1990: 1049–1050. See also Michelle Oberman, "Real and Perceived Legal Barriers to the Inclusion of Women in Clinical Trials," in *Reframing Women's Health*, ed. Alice Dan (Thousand Oaks, Cal., 1994), 266–275.

7. Carol Miller, "Women's Health: A Focus for the 1990s," *Bioscience* 40, no. 11, Dec. 1990: 817; Joseph Palca, "Women Left Out at NIH," and "NIH Adjusts Attitudes Toward Women," *Science* 249, September 21, 1990: 1374. During roughly the same period, the U.S. Public Health Service also created a new Office on Women's Health.

8. "Is There Still Too Much Extrapolation From Data on Middle-aged White Men?" See also Paul Cotton, "Example Abound of Gaps in Medical Knowledge Because of Groups Excluded From Scientific Study," *JAMA* 263, no. 8, February 23, 1990: 1051–1052; and Marcia Angell, "Caring for Women's Health—What is the Problem?" *The New England Journal of Medicine* 329, no. 4; July 22, 1993: 271–272.

9. Kathryn Graff Low et al., "Women Participants in Research: Assessing Progress," *Women and Health* 22.1 (1994): 79–98.

10. Paul Cotton, "Women's Health Initiative Leads Way as Research Begins to Fill Gender Gaps," *JAMA* 267, no. 4, January 22/29, 1992: 469; and "NIH Overwhelmed by Response to Women's Health Initiative," *Science* 252, May 10, 1991: 767.

11. Ibid.

12. Ruth Kirschstein, "From the NIH: Largest US Clinical Trial Ever Gets Under Way," *JAMA* 270, no. 13; October 6, 1993: 1521; Joseph Palca, "NIH Unveils Plan for Women's Health Project," *Science* 254, November 8, 1991: 792; Paul Cotton, "Women's Health Initiative Leads Way as Research Begins to Fill Gender Gaps;" Committee to Review the NIH Women's Health Initiative, Institute of Medicine, *An Assessment of the NIH's Women's Health Initiative* (Washington, D.C., 1993), 90; and David Wheeler, "Women's Health Study Under Fire," *The Chronicle of Higher Education*, November 10, 1993: A9 and A11.

13. Susan M. Love with Karen Lindsey, *Dr. Susan Love's Breast Book*, 518.

14. Cokie Roberts, "One Woman in Nine," *The Washington Post*, February 23, 1992: A19

15. Christine Gorman, "Breast-Cancer Politics," *Time*, November 1, 1993: 74.; and Laura Bell, "Breast Cancer Research Boom," *Chicago Tribune*, August 27, 1995, 6:8.

16. Susan Ferraro, "The Anguished Politics of Breast Cancer," *The New York Times Magazine*, August 15, 1993: 24-27+; and Gina Kolata, "Weighing Spending on Breast Cancer," *New York Times*, October 20. 1993: C14.

17. Randy Shilts, *And the Band Played On* (New York, 1988); and Sandra Panem, *AIDS*

*Bureaucracy* (Cambridge, Mass., 1988).

18. Larry Kramer, "The Plague Years," in *The AIDS Reader*, ed. Nancy McKenzie (New York, 1991), 113-121; Russell Miller, "Act UP Hits the Road," *New York Journal*, September 2, 1991; Eloise Salholz, "Acting Up to Fight AIDS," *Newsweek*, June 6, 1988: 42; and Paul Taylor, "AIDS Guerrillas," *New York Magazine*, November 12, 1990: 65–73. See also Josh Gamson, "Silence, Death, and the Invisible Enemy," *Social Problems* 36 (October 1989): 351–367.

19. Paul Taylor, "AIDS Guerrillas."

20. For more, see Harold Edgar and David J. Rothman, "New Rules for New Drugs: The Challenge of AIDS to the Regulatory Process," in *A Disease of Society*, eds. Dorothy Nelkin (Cambridge, 1991), 84–115.

21. "Protesters Ask for More," *Nature* 345, May 31, 1990: 376. Nor did controversy necessarily end once drugs passed FDA requirements; manufacturers as well as government officials became targets of protest. In the late 1980s, ACT-UP attacked pharmaceutical giant Burroughs Wellcome for reputed price-gouging on its anti-AIDS medication AZT, a year's worth of which was priced at $10,000 in its appearance on the market. Complaining that the drug company was taking profit margins allegedly approaching 80 percent, ACT-UP mounted protests at the firm's headquarters and the New York Stock Exchange, literally dragging floor trading to a halt. While the company insisted that outsiders failed to appreciate the enormous start-up cost of developing such new drugs, it nonetheless cut AZT's selling price roughly 33 percent over the next few years.

22. Stuart Elliott, "Advertising," *New York Times*, December 1, 1994: C11. Ironically, another slogan, "If a murderer kills you, it's homicide... If the FDA kills you, it's just being cautious," came from the opposite end of the political spectrum, an advertisement placed by a conservative anti-regulation foundation. Leon Jaroff, "The Commish Under Fire," *Time*, January 8, 1996: 60. While AIDS activists attacked the FDA's purported slowness in approval from the perspective of dying patients, business groups and conservatives led by House Speaker Newt Gingrich charged the FDA with committing bureaucratic evil through the complexity of its regulatory requirements. Philip J. Hilts, "FDA Becomes Target of Empowered Groups," *New York Times*, February 12, 1995; 1:12; and Connie Mack, "Lift the FDA Roadblock on Experimental Drugs," *New York Times*, February 19, 1995, 4:12.

23. Paul J. Quirk, "Food and Drug Administration," in *The Politics of Regulation*, ed. James Q. Wilson (New York, 1990), 191-235; Peter Temin, *Taking Your Medicine: Drug Regulation in the United States* (Cambridge, Mass., 1980); and Louis Lasagna, "Congress, the FDA, and New Drug Development: Before and After 1962," *Perspectives in Biology and Medicine* 32 (Spring 1989): 322-343. See also James Harvey Young, "Drugs and the 1906 Law"; David Cavers, "The Evolution of the Contemporary System of Drug Regulation Under the 1938 Act"; and Louis Lasagna, "1938–1968: The FDA, the Drug Industry, The Medical Profession, and the Public," all in *Safeguarding the Public: Historical Aspects of Medicinal Drug Control*, ed. John B. Blake (Baltimore, 1970).

24. David A. Kessler, "The Regulation of Investigational Drugs," *The New England Journal of Medicine* 320, no. 5, February 2, 1989: 281–288.

25. Michael Specter, "A Clash of Caution and Urgency," *Washington Post*, October 26, 1987: A15; Martin Delaney, "Patient Access to Experimental Therapy," *JAMA* 261, no. 16, April 28, 1989: 2444, 2447; and Bruce Nussbaum, *Good Intentions: How Big Business and the Medical Establishment are Corrupting the Fight Against AIDS* (New York, 1990).

26. John Iglehart, "The Food and Drug Administration and Its Problems," *The New England Journal of Medicine* 325, no. 3, July 18, 1991, 217–220; and David A. Kessler, "The Regulation of Investigational Drugs."

27. Similarly, in 1995, NCI acquired a new director, Richard Klausner, with an explicit mission, apparently endorsed by NIH, to cut through bureaucracy and so revitalize the agency. Gina Kolata, "New Administrator is 'Not an Administrator,' " *New York Times*, December 12, 1995: B5, B9.

28. John Iglehart, "The Food and Drug Administration and Its Problems;" David A.

Kessler, "The Regulation of Investigational Drugs," 286; "Snipping Away at the Red Tape on Drugs," *U.S. News & World Report*, November 20, 1995: 37; and Philip J. Hilts, "FDA Approves a New Drug to Attack the AIDS Virus," *New York Times*, December 8, 1995: A9.

29. "Snipping Away at the Red Tape on Drugs;" and Philip J. Hilts, "FDA Approves a New Drug to Attack the AIDS Virus." In 1996, however, the FDA faced new challenge with Senate and House moves to force further acceleration in agency procedure. Proposed bills spoke about requiring a four-month deadline for action on drugs to fight life-threatening disease and six months for all other applications; FDA failure to meet such time limits would give an automatic go-ahead to the medicine in question for the United States as long as European or British authority had already approved it. The drive for such legislation drew heavily on pharmaceutical business interests; in hearings, Senator Dan Coats accused the FDA of bearing an "approval bias against companies." Denying such prejudice, Kessler warned that such strict deadlines would lead to a drastic Thalidomide-style mistake one day; but House interests talked about going further, allowing some privatization of the drug review process. ABC Nightly News, February 27, 1996.

30. Frank Rich, "Mary Fisher Now," *New York Times*, May 5, 1995: A17; Patrick Rogers, "Surviving the Second Wave," *Newsweek*, September 19, 1994: 50–51; John Carey, "What Happened to the War on AIDS?" *Business Week*, July 2, 1994: 34; David Dunlap, "A Plea to Clinton to Lead US Efforts Against AIDS," *New York Times*, December 7, 1995: A14; and Philip J. Hilts, "AIDS Death Rate Rising in 25–44 Age Group," *New York Times*, February 16, 1996: A10.

31. J. Gross, "Turning Disease into Political Cause: First AIDS, and Now Breast Cancer," *New York Times*, January 7, 1991: A12.

32. Phyllida Brown, "Activists Home in on Basic Research," *New Scientist*, July 18, 1992: 10.

33. *Science* 251, January 11, 1991: 159.

34. In 1994, over 182,000 American women faced diagnosis of breast cancer, while about 46,000 die from breast cancer per year. The figure "one in nine" was used most commonly in popular discussions, though some breast cancer observers talked about "one in eight" or "one in ten."

35. February, 1996 fundraising letter from the National Breast Cancer Coalition.

36. Complicating the efforts to establish the importance of regular mammograms firmly in women's minds, however, medical organizations and doctors disagreed about the best age to start testing. Claudia Wallis, "A Puzzling Plague," *Time*, January 14, 1991: 48–52.

37. Philip J. Hilts, "U.S. Breast Cancer Deaths Fell Nearly 5 Percent in Three Years," *New York Times*, January 13, 1995: A17. Screening also complicated scientific questions, since new microscopic and molecular diagnostic techniques permitted researchers to find tiny cancer cell clusters, which some researchers suggested might carry a different meaning than full cancer, proving fundamentally harmless. Autopsies done on females age forty to fifty detected tiny breast tumors in 39 percent, "so quiescent [that]... had they been detected while the woman was alive, they would have been labeled as breast cancer" though not fitting the popular image of cancer as a rapidly spreading mass. Researchers expressed concern that as ability to detect smaller tumors increased, practitioners would face the challenge of deciding how aggressively to treat spots which might or might not turn deadly. Gina Kolata, "New Ability to Find Earliest Cancers: A Mixed Blessing," *New York Times*, November 8, 1994: B5, B8.

38. "Confronting Breast Cancer: An Interview with Susan Love," *Technology Review* (May/June 1993): 4748.

39. Jane Brody, "Personal Health," *The New York Times*, March 8, 1995: B6.

40. From the late 1980s on, a number of medical studies found evidence of gender differentials in diagnosis and treatment of heart disease; in general, men complaining of angina or with potentially troublesome indicators were referred for further testing and surgery earlier and more frequently than women with similar or worse conditions. John Z. Ayanian and Arnold M. Epstem, "Differences in the Use of Procedures Between Women

and Men Hospitalized for Coronary Heart Disease," *The New England Journal of Medicine* 325, no. 4, July 25, 1991: 221–225; Marsha Goldsmith, "Heart Research Efforts Aim at Fairness to Women in Terms of Causes, Care of Cardiac Disorders," *JAMA* 264, no. 4, December 26, 1990: 3112–3113; Jonathan Tobin et al., "Sex Bias in Considering Coronary Bypass Surgery," *Annals of Internal Medicine* 107 (1987): 19–25; and Richard M. Steingart et al., "Sex Differences in the Management of Coronary Artery Disease," *The New England Journal of Medicine* 325, no. 4, July 25, 1991: 226–230.

41. Jane Brody, "Cancer Cases Are Up, But the Future Isn't Bleak," *New York Times*, February 1, 1995: B6; Ingrid Waldron, Diane Lye, and Anastasia Brandon, "Gender Differences in Teenage Smoking," *Women and Health* 17.2 (1991): 65–87; and James O. Mason, "A National Agenda for Women's Health," *JAMA* 267, no. 4, January 22/29, 1992: 482.

42. Susan Jenks, "Cancer Experts Set Research Agenda for Women's Health in the 1990s," *Journal of the National Cancer Institute* 83, no. 20; October 16, 1991: 1443–1444; and "Cancer War Has Stalled, A Panel Says," *New York Times*, September 30, 1994: A11. Among other suggestions, the reviewers advocated creating a cabinet-level cancer-coordinating position, investing at least $60 million yearly to translate scientific advances into clinical testing, and terminating government support for tobacco production and sale. See also Daryl Chubin, "Research Missions and the Public: Over-Selling and Buying the U.S. War on Cancer," *Citizen Participation in Science Policy*, ed. James C. Petersen (Amherst, Mass., 1984): 109–129.

43. Susan M. Love with Karen Lindsey, *Dr. Susan Love's Breast Book*, 523–524; "Should the Labs Get Hit?" *U.S. News & World Report* November 6, 1995: 83; and Robert Pear, "For Health Agency, A Fiscal Wake-Up Call," *New York Times*, February 20, 1995: A6.

44. ABC Nightly News, February 27, 1996; and February, 1996 fundraising letter from the National Breast Cancer Coalition.

45. Barbara J. Culliton, "NIH Push for Women's Health," *Nature* 353, October 3, 1991: 383.

46. Monika Guttman, "Chasing Breast Cancer," *USA Weekend*, January 13–15, 1995: 24; and Gina Kolata, "Weighing Spending on Breast Cancer." Similarly, regarding AIDS, two Ohio State University doctors wrote *The New England Journal of Medicine* in 1988 to "question the wisdom of allowing its dramatic nature and the public outcry it generates to dictate public policy in health care funding...." Noting that annual American suicides exceeded the 1988 total of people with AIDS, they called it "unreasonable" for the Alcohol, Drug Abuse, and Mental Health Administration to devote 22 percent of total funds to AIDS-related investigations. Such an emphasis, they worried, might draw researchers away from other vital areas of study or induce some to alter projects to include AIDS patients to win grants. Steven C. Dilsaver and Jeffrey A. Coffman, "Effect of Generous Funding for AIDS Research on General Biomedical Research," *The New England Journal of Medicine* 318, no. 16, April 21, 1988: 1071–1072.

47. Susan M. Love with Karen Lindsey, *Dr. Susan Love's Breast Book*, 523–524; and Anna Quindlen, "Competitive Cancer," *New York Times*, October 31, 1993, 4:17.

48. Stephen Burd, "NIH Issues Rules Requiring Women and Minorities in Clinical Trials," *The Chronicle of Higher Education*, April 6, 1994: A50; and Gina Kolata, "FDA Debate on Speedy Access to AIDS Drugs is Reopening," *New York Times*, September 12, 1994: A13.

49. Harold Edgar and David J. Rothman, "New Rules for New Drugs: The Challenge of AIDS to the Regulatory Process," in *A Disease of Society*, eds. Dorothy Nelkin et al. (Cambridge, 1991), 97; and Ellen Cooper, "Controlled Clinical Trials of AIDS Drugs: The Best Hope," *JAMA* 261, no. 16, April 28, 1989: 2445. Advocates maintained that enough people with AIDS would still sign up for trials, either out of "simple altruism" or to receive "free medical care" and "remain in line for future studies." Moreover, one activist wrote in *JAMA* any policy limiting access to new medicine to impel enough subjects to enter testing would seem like "morally offensive" blackmail to AIDS patients, even if researchers emphasized that such tests were crucial to the noble goal of assuring scientific progress.

Martin Delaney, "Patient Access to Experimental Therapy."

50. Ann Oakley, "Who's Afraid of the Randomized Controlled Trial? Some Dilemmas of the Scientific Method and 'Good' Research Practice," *Women and Health* 15.4 (1989): 25–53.

51. Gina Kolata, "Women Rejecting Trials for Testing A Cancer Therapy," *New York Times*, February 15, 1995: A1 and B7; Kara Smigel, "Women Flock to ABMT for Breast Cancer Without Final Proof," *Journal of the National Cancer Institute* 87, no. 13, July 5, 1995: 952-955; and James Mathews, "NCI Survey Explores the MD's Perspective on ABMT Trials," *Journal of the National Cancer Institute* 87, no. 20, October 18, 1995: 1510–1511. Some medical experts indicated that the cure rate for all forms of life-endangering cancers might improve to as much as 75 percent within ten years, but such promise was endangered because just two to three percent of adult cancer patients participated in clinical testing to help investigate and establish better treatment. Jane Brody, "Personal Health," *New York Times*, November 16, 1994: B8. Brody noted that low enrollment could also be traced to doctors who discouraged patients from joining trials (out of fear of complicated regulations and loss of control over the case), as well as practical problems for potential subjects (lack of transportation or child care, for example.)

52. John D. Arras, "Noncompliance in AIDS Research," *Hastings Center Report*, September/October 1990: 24–32.

53. "Conflict Grows Over Breast Cancer Strategy," *Nature* 368, March 3, 1994: 7.

54. Barbara J. Culliton, "NIH Push for Women's Health."

55. Susan Rennie, "Breast Cancer Prevention: Diet Vs. Drugs," Ms., May/June, 1993: 39–40, 42; Liane Clorfene-Casten, "The Environmental Link to Breast Cancer," Ms., May/June, 1993: 54; and Liane Clorfene-Casten, "Inside The Cancer Establishment," Ms., May/June, 1993: 57.

56. Susan Ferraro, "The Anguished Politics of Breast Cancer," 62; and Liane Clorfene-Casten, "The Environmental Link to Breast Cancer," 52-56.

57. Felicia R. Lee, "U.S. Cuts AIDS Research Grants in New York City," *New York Times*, November 8, 1994: A1, B10.

58. Susan Katz Miller, "Faith in 'False Cure' Leads to Renewed Trials," *New Scientist*, November 7, 1992:7.

59. Christine Gorman, "Are Animal Organs Safe for People," *Time*, January 15, 1996: 58–59.

60. Roger Hand, "Alternative Therapies Used by Patients With AIDS," *The New England Journal of Medicine* 320, no. 10, March 9, 1990; David M. Eisenberg et al., "Unconventional Medicine in the United States," *The New England Journal of Medicine* 328, no. 4, January 28, 1993: 246–252; Robin Wilson, "Unconventional Cures," *The Chronicle of Higher Education*, January 12, 1996: A15–A16; and Tom Carney, "Politics, Science Colliding in Feud," *Des Moines Register*, December 4, 1994: 1B and 3B.

61. See Sandra Harding, *The Science Question in Feminism* (Ithaca, NY, 1986); and Paul R. Gross and Norman Levitt, *Higher Superstition: The Academic Left and Its Quarrels With Science* (Baltimore, 1994). Gross and Levitt also targeted radical environmentalism, Afrocentrism, AIDS activism, animal rights, and postmodern literary theory as sources of "open hostility... toward the assumption, which one might have supposed universal among educated people, that scientific knowledge is reasonably reliable...." For a critique of Gross and Levitt, see Taner Edis and Amy Sue Bix, "Bashing the Science Bashers: Review of Higher Superstition: The Academic Left and Its Quarrels With Science"; *Skeptical Inquirer* 19.2 (March/April, 1995): 46–48.

62. February, 1996 fundraising letter from the National Breast Cancer Coalition.

63. Robert M. Wachter, "AIDS, Activism, and the Politics of Health," *The New England Journal of Medicine* 326, no. 2, January 9, 1992: 129.

## ALAN I MARCUS

# Sweets for the Sweet:
# Saccharin, Knowledge, and the Contemporary
# Regulatory Nexus

In 1977, the United States Congress forbade the Food and Drug Admin-istration to outlaw use of the food additive saccharin as an artificial sweet-ener for a period of three years. Subsequent legislation extended the con-gressional ban. It remains in effect today. Congress's saccharin action neatly represented late twentieth-century federal regulatory policy. The process had become decidedly antibureaucratic and ultimately democratic. Forces both for saccharin's prohibition and for its continued use outlined and debated their positions in public, letting their arguments contend in the marketplace of ideas. Following the conduct of this de facto national plebi-scite, duly elected representatives weighed the respective cases and se-lected the course that their constituents seemed to favor.

This ultimately rationalist scenario lies at the heart of contemporary regulatory policy. The public sphere has emerged as the regulatory locus as decisions are manufactured either by the public or in public. No regu-latory agency, no legally constituted administrative body created expressly to make regulatory decisions, fabricated the saccharin decision, a tacit demonstration of the power of the new regulatory nexus. That the re-puted regulatory agency, the FDA, asked, even begged, Congress as a public representative institution to usurp the agency's legal prerogative further confirms the nature of the new regulatory policy.

In this milieu, each substance is evaluated on a case-by-case basis. Pre-cedent becomes an untenable intellectual construct, although the term continues to appear in the public record. "Precedent" is persistently in-voked but only as nothing more than a tactical defense of any advocacy. The new regulation thus transforms the view and role of laws. Laws have become "guidelines" when persons want to violate or circumvent them, or "bludgeons" when persons demand immediate, definitive action.

This new policy makes several presumptions. It takes regulation in public as sensible or logical, an activity in which persons doing the judging possess the material necessary to make judgments. Surely saccharin was extensively studied; it may be the most heavily investigated food additive of all time. But that assumption about quantity of information and judgment undercuts the idea of controversy, which rests at the heart of the need to establish a public regulatory policy. Quite baldly, if something is controversial, it suggests that there may well be more than one fashion of interpreting the data or even that the data worth interpreting may be under question. Existence of controversy may also indicate that there is more than one type of question and that the relevancy of a question depends on who asks it. All this devolves to mechanisms to resolve controversies. Would the best way to adjudicate these differences in perspective and perception be a simple vote? Are these differences weighed and should they be weighed? Is there an agreement on what constitutes data or evidence? If no area of agreement exists, on what basis does such a comparative measuring take place? Does and should the majority rule?

These assumptions have become the crucial underpinnings of late twentieth-century American regulation. The saccharin decision resonates today and frames the contemporary regulatory milieu. Alar, silicone breast implants, bovine growth hormone, cloned vegetables, interspecies genetic transfers, and even cigarettes fall under its sway. But the saccharin decision itself laid bare the kind of regulatory policy, including food regulation, that actually had been taking place sub rosa for years. Saccharin was the first indisputable public acknowledgment that at its most basic level federal food regulation was often arbitrary, not the product of rational, reproducible impartial determinations. Regulation constituted instead a negotiation between as many persons and forces as were willing to participate. Each person or force had its own individual perspective or sense of perception. The role of factual consensus, dressed as science, was at best indeterminate, at worst irrelevant, almost universally impossible to achieve. Any quest to accomplish it certainly hampered attempts to convince others of the merits of a case. Dramatizing the consequences of particular acts proved the most effective means to galvanize and mold opinion. Terms of debates always masqueraded as furthering the public interest, but disagreement raged as to what the public interest was; if all parties had agreed, there would have been considerably less room for debate. As a consequence of this lack of an agreed-upon adjudication device—the nature of the public interest—or technique—indisputable scientific data—discussion about the public interest was simply a charade, merely a convention. This charade was further disguised by the trumpeting of a new regulatory concept, "risk versus benefit" regulation. What constitutes damage to health is in many cases indeterminable, as is the converse of the question: What benefits health? Often no one knows what the costs in fact were or might be or what the benefits were or might be; since the information upon which these costs and benefits were to be computed were not known or were in dispute, the figures that resulted incorporated those speculative, ultimately fatal limitations. Benefit and risk were not absolutes regardless of how much persons might want or pretend them to be. They were guesses, camouflaged as certainty (or statistical certainty, surely an oxymoron) and thus fobbed off as unassailable.[1] In the case of saccharin, for instance, long-enacted legislation demanded that the drug immediately be taken off the market because of the possibility that saccharin caused cancer or speeded its development. In this new regulatory world, legal absolutes no longer existed, even as they remained technically in force. A sense that recommendations and suggestions have supplanted law marked modern regulation. For saccharin, cancer fears were countered by and balanced against the artificial sweetener's purported role in weight loss. But several groups challenged saccharin as a weight-loss benison and argued that its use simply masked unhealthy eating habits; they disputed the mechanisms by which humans lost weight and wondered whether saccharin consumption would be offset by increased caloric intake. Others argued that the non-nutritive substance did not cause cancer at all or that it posed no harm in the amount humans consumed in food.

This series of antagonistic contentions constituted the debate's particulars, but its essence revolved around the question of the government's responsibility in the social sphere. What was government's role and limits? What was the role of the individual? What was the relationship of the individual to the government? These debates often made strange bedfellows. Very often those very same persons who wanted to keep government out of the bedroom also wanted to put government in the food supply. Conversely, many of those arguing most strenuously for reproductive choice demanded that government restrict dietetic choice.

Food regulation had not always been that way. In its late nineteenth-century inception, food regulation was the province of self-styled experts, scientists charged with analyzing foods to prevent unscrupulous or unknowing persons from adulterating or contaminating the American food supply. Government and the public placed their faith and future in the hands of persons who claimed special training to act as guardians for the public interest. Their charge was relatively clear-cut. They were to stop deceptions—paying for one thing and getting another—and to protect the population from hazards. That work was done by themselves; regulators conducted the research necessary to prove something adulterated or injurious to health. This approach was supposed to be unequivocal, but sometimes scientists disagreed. Never were these debates conducted in public. Scientists acted for the public within the regulatory agency or professional organizations. Their special knowledge made them the only reputable decision makers and therefore public airings of questions would be at best superfluous and at worst pernicious.[2]

By the 1920s, industry recognized the utility of scientists in translating nature's laws into profitable commodities and they began to employ scientists in large numbers to create and develop new products. These new industrial scientists proved no different from their regulatory counterparts. Both groups attended the same schools and received the same degrees. As significant, both received their positions by virtue of their ability as scientists. Their scientific credentials provided them the same frame of reference as their regulatory counterparts; they both possessed a methodology that was claimed to produce unambiguous and reproducible results to scientific questions, such as those posed by regulatory issues. Not only would their method produce an indisputable determination, but it also seemed to transform persons mastering the method. Persons so reared seemed to develop personalities shaped by the demands of science; they presumably brooked no dishonesty or speculation.

These assumptions made regulatory and industry scientists virtually indistinguishable and converted regulation into a partnership. Regulatory and industry scientists shared as scientists similar perspectives, similar abilities, and similar goals. Regulation took for granted a close relationship among the partners. Industrial and university scientists provided research protocols upon which their proposed substance was to be judged. Regulatory law did not charge industry scientists with proving or guaranteeing safety but only with demonstrating that the product in question was not likely to be harmful. Contemporaries deemed this streamlined bureaucratic procedure to provide a substantial margin of safety because scientists, by definition impartial and objective, generated the studies showing that a substance caused no apparent injury. Regulatory scientists did not test products to trip up violators but rather scrutinized industry scientist-generated research protocols. As law made regulation an indisputably scientific issue, it at once acknowledged industry's scientific transformation and forced the few odd persons, such as manufacturers of patent and over-the-counter medicines, who had cast their lot with advertisers (the new market-forming and market-manipulating experts), to embrace that transformation if they hoped to secure FDA approval.[3]

A new notion of the nature of food accompanied the new regulatory synthesis. Food stopped being simply the sum of its constituents and became instead something manufactured to whatever specifications scientists and manufacturers chose. Biological plasticity characterized the new view. It could be grown in virtually any size and shape, as with hybrid corn, or animals could be configured to maximize meat production while minimizing care and feeding, such as with artificial hormones, antibiotics, or a urea-corncob-based diet.[4] Food processors also adopted this model, especially after World War II. Flavor enhancers, emulsifiers, and spoilage retardants seemed to be panaceas that would increase corporate profits, lower consumer prices, and not hamper the product. Chemical means to improve product shipping, life span, appearance, taste, mixability, and nutritional content proliferated as manufacturers sought to increase demand by creating an explosive number of new products and then by fitting each product in a unique way to have it secure a corresponding market niche.[5]

The cascade of chemically enhanced products engendered concern. To maintain a safe food supply and to keep unscrupulous or incompetent persons out of the food business, government acted in a time-honored fashion as coordinator and convenor and called a series of meetings to discuss the matter. The FDA and other involved agencies established forums through which consumers could voice concerns and industry and university scientists could erect additional safeguards to protect the public interest.[6]

Neither these meetings or their initial outcomes, which included tighter controls and passage of new legislation, seemed to place an undue burden upon any participant. Legislation formed the backbone of the regulatory synthesis. Scientists from all walks of life came together and responded to consumer fears and possible health threats after analyzing the data and deciding the scientifically valid course. Regulatory agencies and Congress implemented these products of science, which appeared to provide Americans with considerable margin of safety. Everyone served as partners. Each favored scientifically determined legislation, which guaranteed protection of the food supply.

Premarket clearance for food additives gained considerable scientific backing and became de facto FDA regulation well before passage of a new food-additives law in 1958. Industry scientists needed to prove food additives safe to FDA scientists before their companies could use the chemicals to enhance products. This new regulation required industry to devote additional resources to having a substance approved for use, but food-design companies generally accepted the plank as within the spirit of the established partnership. The FDA's method to examine and regulate additives already in the food supply, but that had not undergone premarketing approval, likewise continued the partnership spirit. The agency conducted a de facto scientific plebiscite; it compiled a list of additives already integrated into the food supply and asked industry and other scientists which ones they understood to be safe. Those Generally Regard As Safe (GRAS), those receiving the scientists' collective blessing, remained unregulated. Industry was required to demonstrate safety for those substances that failed the scientific plebiscite.

One final plank marked the food additive law of 1958. It prohibited use as an additive of any substance in any quantity that was shown to cause cancer in humans or animals. Proposed by Congressman John Delaney (D-N.Y.), industry and FDA scientists initially objected to the Delaney clause but were ultimately persuaded by the argument that scientists considered it redundant. No material that caused cancer would or should ever pass the "injurious to health" provisions of long-established regulatory law and receive FDA approval, they reasoned. The Delaney clause merely expressed that sentiment in another way and as a consequence added nothing to the new law.[7]

As a substance long integrated into the American food supply without any apparent problems, saccharin quickly found a place on the GRAS list, where it remained for well over a decade. The nature of regulation, but not regulatory law, changed profoundly during that period. Consensus, administered through the mechanism of scientific consensus, had undergirded the industry-regulatory partnership. Individuation, especially individual perspective, replaced ideas of consensus. This proved as certain in the scientific sphere as elsewhere. Suspicion, distrust, and contentiousness characterized the new regulatory milieu. Rather than partners, each facet of the regulatory partnership now seemed antagonistic to the interests of each other. Consumers regularly protested against the acts or lack of acts of regulators and industry. Industry deemed regulators out of control and consumers ignorant. Regulators considered industry less than forthcoming and consumers irrational.

Each of these newly contentious groups claimed that its position rested upon scientific evidence. Yet each offered different data to support its views. That each could find scientific determinations to bolster these radically antagonistic perspectives pointed directly to the lack of an agreed-upon mechanism to separate decisively between conflicting claims; scientific institutions no longer possessed the popular cachet to make distinctions that others outside the organizations would naturally accept or accede to. To make such distinctions simply seemed to confirm the obvious: that those coming down on the side of a group were probably beholden to that group and therefore disqualified themselves from any valid decision-making role. Objectivity in scientific determination seemed to have ceased to exist.

As early as 1959, the first evidence of this new milieu could be seen. With great flourish, the FDA announced just before Thanksgiving that the pesticide aminotriazole, a substance thought to cause cancer in laboratory animals, might have contaminated much of the national cranberry crop. The agency then seized the crop to test it for the chemical and although the FDA found most produce uncontaminated, consumer confidence had plummeted so low that Americans generally opted for a cranberryless holiday. That sort of precipitous regulatory action, action necessary as the Delaney clause came to be interpreted, struck regulators and the regulated as extreme. While maintaining their right and obligation to act in that fashion, federal regulators also decided that their maneuver hurt the cranberry industry. Congress even indemnified the growers for their loss.[8]

This nearly apologetic air evaporated over the next decade into a recurring pattern of confrontational politics. Nowhere was the situation more intense than in issues of personal choice. On one hand, a new hedonism, often summed up as "sex, drugs, and Rock 'n Roll" and memorialized by the media's fascination with Haight-Ashbury's hippies, seemed to sweep young America. But so too did a beachboy mentality as thousands of young men and women spent endless summers seeking tan skin and the next great wave. Personal health concerns paralleled the new hedonism and cut a broader path. Americans increasingly sought to secure their health outside conventional means. Megavitamin therapy, chiropractic medicine, and acupuncturists gained considerable popularity and psychobabble, which pronounced everyone OK if everyone simply did their own thing, entered the lexicon. In some instances, people rejected health professionals of all stripes. Periodicals such as *Prevention*, trumpeted the need to seize the initiative, even if it meant a total rejection of the health-care establishment. Allergists, specialists in the ultimate individual disease—a disease unique to the individual in question and often treated with a personalized desensitizing concoction or regimen—sprang up like weeds. The desire to be thin provided booming business for Weight Watchers, an organization that based its weight-loss philosophy on personal testimony, not unlike that found in enthusiastic religion.[9]

Saccharin and cyclamates, the other FDA-approved non-nutritive sweetener, flourished. In the brief period from 1963 to 1967, artificially sweetened soft drinks nearly tripled their market share, growing to more than ten percent. Packets of artificial sweeteners commonly appeared in the coffeeshops that proliferated during the period as well as in individual homes. This mania for thinness—or as the Pepsi Cola commercial reminded "what shape your stomach was in" as a series of slender, swimsuit-clad stomachs paraded across the television screen—met its first challenge in 1969, when Abbott Laboratories provided the FDA with evidence that cyclamates likely caused cancer in laboratory animals. The agency moved swiftly to ban the drug. This ruling had no direct effect on saccharin, but that substance became the sole remaining legal artificial sweetener. [10]

Questions about saccharin's possible role in tumor genesis emerged on the heels of the cyclamate decision. As early as 1971, a Wisconsin Alumni Research Foundation study of mice found that those metabolizing the equivalent saccharin of five percent of their daily diets displayed a slightly higher risk of developing bladder cancer than controls. The FDA followed up those results with a study of its own, which when reported the next year seemed to confirm their earlier determinations. From that moment, the FDA began to equivocate. Its reluctance to ban saccharin led the agency to involve the National Academy of Sciences, which established a special panel to review the saccharin evidence, and to sponsor additional studies aimed at ruling out possible situations previously not considered likely. This strained approach offended at least one senator, Gaylord Nelson (D-Wis.), who in January 1975 asked the General Accounting Office to investigate if the FDA's handling of saccharin conformed to code. [11]

The General Accounting Office issued a stinging rebuke of FDA action a year and a half later. It claimed that the FDA's treatment of saccharin "leaves the unmistakable impression that a group of saccharin defenders were out to beat back saccharin accusers no matter what the cost to logic and scientific impartiality." Nelson concluded that the FDA violated Food and Drug law. The agency disagreed; it maintained that it was pursuing the prudent course and promised to resolve the saccharin question at some future date.

A long-term study by Canadian public health officials in early 1977 forced the agency to act. The Canadian results confirmed and refined the earlier animal studies. Laboratory animals ingesting large amounts of saccharin appeared to have a higher incidence of bladder cancer than saccharin-free controls and that tumor generation was even more pronounced in the second generation of animals exposed to the sweetener. The FDA reviewed the data and announced its plans to ban saccharin "based on science and on requirements of federal law." [12]

It was at that point that saccharin regulation truly began. Industry representatives quickly calculated that an individual would need to consume more than eight hundred cans of artificially sweetened soft drink daily over the course of their lives to receive a saccharin dosage equivalent to that provided the laboratory animals. Industry representatives further contended that the proposed ban was "based on flimsy scientific evidence that has absolutely no bearing on human health." "Specialists in the origins of cancer" discount any assessment of irrelevancy, argued Morton Mintz, a *Washington Post* staff writer, "because they never found a human cancer-causing agent in an amount so small that it might not cause cancer in someone." Mintz's statement did not necessarily exactly reflect the position of all "specialists in the origins of cancer." That group itself was arbitrary, selected and defined precisely according to the criteria that enabled Mintz to categorize them in that fashion. Put another way, what made someone eligible to be considered by Mintz to be a specialist in cancer causation was their position on the threshold question. Anyone suggesting that a threshold limit existed was deemed by Mintz because of that statement to show him or herself not to be an expert on that issue. The idea of a baldly philosophical or political litmus test for expertise was common among proponents of the New Journalism, the journalism of advocacy. This persuasion journalism aimed to change public opinion and to direct public action. It took the expertise of the journalist as informed citizen as the ultimate good and sought to use it to shape or reformulate social action. Mintz was especially adept at this technique. He not only covered FDA matters for the *Post*, but he also wrote books on thalidomide, the Dalkon Shield, and smoking.[13]

Congressional disenchantment with the proposed FDA ban surfaced almost immediately. Congressmen complained that they were "inundated with telephone calls and mail from riled constituents." An estimated one million people wrote their representatives about saccharin during a three-month period. Many angered voters pronounced themselves "fed up with government telling me what I can and what I can't eat. Warn me all you want, but if I want to eat something that you consider inadvisable, it's none of your business!" These men and women argued that the FDA decision "deprived American citizens of a freedom vital to the existence of a democracy, the freedom of choice . . . a matter . . . of life and death." The few persons demanding saccharin's prohibition tried to portray the situation as big business against the people. But saccharin was not "producers versus consumers." The sweetener, noted one observer, "poses a conflict of consumers versus consumer advocates," the latter group reaping considerable prestige and notoriety while professing only to have the common citizens' interests at heart. Even the American Cancer Society weighed in on the side of saccharin and supported efforts to stop the proposed FDA ban. The American Diabetes Association's Heart of America affiliate maintained that diabetics needed saccharin "to enhance their quality of life." They must drink "soda without fear." Diabetic children were especially at psychological risk. Snacking with their peers was mandatory to "their psychosocial development." The American Dental Association predicted that without saccharin to sweeten toothpaste and therefore encourage children to brush frequently, an epidemic of tooth decay would sweep America.

Congressmen responded to the public prosaccharin onslaught by offering no fewer than a dozen different bills in a three-day period to overturn the announced saccharin prohibition. Each congressman justified his bill by targeting the Delaney clause in some fashion. Proposals sought a special Delaney clause exemption for saccharin, modification of the clause to prohibit similar occurrences in the future, or complete abandonment of the clause's provisions. All demanded immediate relief from the cancer clause's inflexibility. The clause reflected, congressmen argued, a simpler scientific time where absolute prohibitions were required because of the insufficiency of then-contemporary analytical, detection, and evaluation methods. Now science had become more sophisticated and could produce rational determinations among risks and benefits.

That a food-additive law failed to incorporate that commonsense approach struck these congressmen as a gross error, which had significant health costs. "No thought has been given to the enormous suffering" that the ban "will impose upon the millions of Americans with heart ailments, weight problems, diabetes and other health problems," complained one congressman. What "is the trade-off here?" he wondered. "We can prevent cancer for people who drink 1,250 cans of diet soda a day. But we cause tens of thousands of other possible deaths by banning a sugar substitute that many people must use for life itself. This is absolute stupidity." Another representative noted that ingesting in a single day even fifty twelve-ounce cans "of pure water would kill a person." His colleague worried about rat–human comparisons and maintained that anyone able to consume enough saccharin-laced diet soda to receive a dosage comparable to that given a rat "probably has a bladder of more strength than any rat." Yet another congressman totaled up the amount of saccharin found in 1,250 cans of soda and complained that an individual would have to eat nearly four pounds of the artificial sweetener each day to approach the dosage given the test rodents. Representative William Tucker of Arkansas also provided statistics. "Just replacing 10 billion cans of diet soft drinks with regular soft drinks would lead to an extra 2 trillion calories and 600 million pounds of fat in America." He called for a saccharin warning label stating that "Canadians have determined that saccharin is dangerous to your rat's health." One congressmen called for congressional action because of the presumed "enormous peer group pressure at high school social functions" on "teenaged diabetics" to consume sugar-sweetened soft drinks to their detriment. Claude Pepper (D-Fla.) thought the ban discriminated against the aged, the largest single diabetic group in America, and opposed it "on behalf of the elderly." Another representative urged action by citing the recent Senate Select Committee on Nutrition report, which claimed a close diet/disease relationship and recommended that Americans cut their caloric intake by forty percent. He also mentioned a series of articles in the *Washington Post* on the disastrous health consequences of obesity as a rationale for continued saccharin usage.

Mechanisms to put aside the proposed FDA saccharin ban varied. One congressman would require the FDA to duplicate and confirm any experiment that showed a substance to cause cancer before it could act. The agency had the option then to ban the substance, attach a warning label, and permit the public to make its own choice or do nothing. Another congressman offered legislation that forbade the FDA to declare anything unsafe "unless tests have proved the additive to be cancer-causing when consumed in normal quantities." His colleague wanted slightly greater protection and substituted "reasonable quantities" in lieu of normality. Another congressman made it the province of the HEW secretary in any case to "weigh potential dangers" against the "benefits that society might derive." The secretary could then continue usage, require labeling announcing potential hazards, or restrict usage only to those with a doctor's prescription. Measuring risks versus benefits was a familiar refrain, but others demanded that the HEW secretary cede this adjudication power to those either more expert or more involved. One congressman demanded that before declaring a substance unsafe the FDA had "to make [an assessment of] the public risks and benefits of a food additive, taking into account the best evidence and expert judgment possible." He chose not to define the parameters of "best evidence and expert judgment." Others showed no such hesitancy. They called on government to make sure that a substance's "benefit outweigh the risks to human health" and would establish a HEW secretary-appointed committee to make that determination. The committee would include three groups of persons: those "qualified by scientific training and experience to evaluate the carcinogenic effect of the food additive"; representatives of the interests of consumers and the food-additive industry, respectively; and "nutritionists, econo-mists, scientists and lawyers." Defining benefits versus risks was also speci-fied. Evaluation criteria in order of importance were to be "first, health risks and benefits; second, nutritional needs and benefits and the effects on the nutritional value, cost, availability, and acceptability of food; third, environmental effects; and fourth, the interests of the general public." Others shifted responsibility on the public. They wanted the FDA only to place a label on the substance reporting the Canadian findings. Only S. I. Hayakawa (R-Calif.) offered a bill that appropriated additional money to study saccharin as a cancer-causing agent. During the three-year time-table of Hayakawa's study, the FDA was prohibited from banning the sub-stance.

Many of these congressional scenarios seem so logical, even reason-able. Each of their authors claimed that his proposal represented the will of the people. "The people have spoken," noted one congressman. "The people recognize" that the Canadian study "does not prove normal doses of saccharin unsafe." The people "believe that no persuasive case has been made that saccharin in normal doses causes cancer in human beings." But upon what was the will of the people based? Certainly not on a prepon-derance of evidence. Neither the people nor their representatives nor anyone else knew the mechanisms or relationships between saccharin and cancer, the validity of animal testing, dosage and thresholds, or co-carci-nogenic relationships. As important, no one knew the benefits or had even attempted to confirm popular assumptions. Only a handful of con-gressmen recognized or acknowledged this profound collective ignorance. No one had studied the relationship among saccharin and weight loss. Did it really lead to a decrease in caloric intake? If the caloric intake remained the same, was high fat or food high in cholesterol substituted for sugar, a complex carbohydrate? How exactly do you quantify the ben-efits of not being subjected to peer pressure or to mental health generally? May not use of saccharin give persons a sense of control over their lives and therefore increase their sense of well-being? Where does a desire for thinness fit in? Did a nation that treasured thinness above potential can-cer risks (and quick solutions to difficult problems) and therefore permit-ted the continued availability of saccharin in fact encourage bulimia or anorexia nervosa in young women? What is the public interest? Is it maxi-mum choice, maximum participation, maximum protection, maximum information, or was there no consensus about what was the public inter-est or even common sense? Was sense itself relative, something not held in common?

These and any number of other meaningful and farcical questions have become institutionalized within and germane to the regulatory nexus. They have become the essence of, the guts of, regulation. The compromise that surfaced within Congress over saccharin set the tone. The FDA understood that its prerogative had been countermanded and agency complicity quickly became total. The FDA not only looked to Congress rather than take dramatic action, but it actually postponed its ban for an additional three months to permit Congress the time necessary to supersede the proposed agency ruling. The matter went to committees chaired by Senator Edward M. Kennedy and Representative Paul D. Rogers. They held hearings, read editorials and statements into the record, asked the Office of Technology Assessment for its opinion, and called numerous witnesses. From this emerged two very similar bills, each of which cleared its house by substantial margins. Differences were easily resolved in conference and Jimmy Carter quickly signed the new saccharin legislation into law.

The saccharin bill prohibited the FDA from removing saccharin from the market for eighteen months. It called for the National Academy of Sciences to summarize what was known about risk-benefit analysis. The academy was to discuss "existing means" to evaluate health risks and benefits and then to see in what types of federal regulation legislation demanded that these two things be compared. The act also asked the academy "to study, to the extent feasible"—a certain acknowledgment that such an endeavor was not possible—saccharin's health benefits. The sweetener would carry a warning label during this period, which stated, "Use of this product may be hazardous to your health. This product contains saccharin which has been determined to cause cancer in laboratory animals." The law made no provisions for additional or new research and apparently abandoned any hope of securing a definitive determination or resolving the then-unresolved situation. It preferred to offer the appearance of regulatory control and thus empower the various congressional constituencies rather than acknowledge its inability to provide a neat or discrete means to decide the matter. By limiting the terms of the agreement to eighteen months, Congress announced its readiness to revisit the matter. But this pretense of involvement was just that. Congress understood it was out of its depth.[14]

Every time the 1977 law has been set to expire, Congress perfunctorily has renewed and extended it. Only approval of aspartame in 1986 decreased public reliance on saccharin and public interest about the compound. Ironically, the FDA had long delayed aspartame approval as several studies and experts linked the substance to brain damage in rats.[15]

That brain damage is not cancer or cancerous provided the FDA the latitude necessary to approve the drug without running afoul of the Delaney clause. The law permitted the agency to use discretion, to decide that it was not injurious or a hazard to health.

That interpretation of hazardness or injuriousness was a relatively recent phenomenon. It was initially put on public view with saccharin. The new regulation reflected rejection of thoughts and hopes of consensus to signify instead the rise of various constituencies and the explicit democratization of what traditionally had been the province of experts—scientists. Now groups could dispute the costs, risks, and benefits of any potential regulation action and often help render the final verdict. It demonstrates on what grounds Congress proved willing to ignore and dismiss its acts and the bureaucratic devices it so carefully nurtured. But has the public acting as a public in public been served? Does the public as public truly act or do only those act who have a monetary or psychological stake in the matter and therefore are by definition not impartial? How does the public know what information exists and what it means? Has majority rule made necessarily good regulatory policy?

*Iowa State University*

## Notes

1. For a detailed study of risk-benefit analysis and its relationships to scientists and scientific inquiry in a single instance, see Alan I Marcus, *Cancer from Beef: DES, Federal Food Regulation, and Consumer Confidence* (Baltimore, 1994).

2. James Harvey Young's *Pure Food: Securing the Federal Food and Drugs Act of 1906* (Princeton, 1989) is the place to begin. See also Peter Temin, *Taking Your Medicine: Drug Regulation in the United States* (Cambridge, Mass., 1980), 27–37.

3. For regulation in the 1920s and after, see Charles O. Jackson, *Food and Drug Legislation in the New Deal* (Princeton, 1970); and James Harvey Young, "Food and Drug Enforcers in the 1920s: Restraining and Educating Business," *Business and Economic History*, 2d series 21 (1992): 119–28.

4. See, for example, Alan I Marcus, "The Newest Knowledge of Nutrition: Wise Burroughs, DES, and Modern Meat," *Agricultural History* 67 (Summer 1993): 66–85, and "The Wisdom of the Body Politic: The Changing Nature of Publicly Sponsored American Agricultural Research Since the 1830s," *Agricultural History* 62 (Spring 1988): especially 21–24; and Temin, *Taking Your Medicine*, 58–88.

5. Suzanne R. White, "Chemistry and Controversy: Regulating the Use of Chemicals in Foods, 1883-1959," Ph.D. diss., Emory University, 1994, 211–36; and Hugh D. Crone, *Chemicals and Society: A Guide to the New Chemical Age* (Cambridge, 1986).

6. White, "Chemistry and Controversy," 254–361; Marcus, *Cancer from Beef*, 17–25.

7. Marcus, *Cancer from Beef*, 34–44; George P. Larrick, "The New Food-Additives Law," *Food Drug Cosmetic Law Journal* 13 (1958): 634–48; Charles Wesley Dunn, "Fundamental Progress of the Pure-Food Law," *Food Drug Cosmetic Law Journal* 13 (1958): 615–33; and "An Act to Protect the Public Health by Amending the Federal Food, Drug, and

Cosmetic Act to Prohibit the Use in Food of Additives Which Have Not Been Adequately Tested to Establish Their Safety" (Public Law 85–929), 71 *U.S. Statutes* (1958): 1784–89.

8. White, "Chemistry and Controversy," 362–99.

9. This volume documents the onset of that sort of thinking. Its essays are a testament to the persuasiveness of that approach. For the 1960s generally, see, for example, William O'Neill, *Coming Apart: An Informal History of the 1960s* (Chicago, 1971); and Morris L. Dickstein, *Gates of Eden: American Culture in the 1960s* (New York, 1987). Also of use is the provocative Christopher Lasch, *The Culture of Narcissism: American Life in an Age of Diminishing Expectations* (New York, 1978).

10. "Government Officially Announces Cyclamate Sweeteners Will be Taken Off Market Early Next Year," *New York Times*, October 19, 1969, 58.

11. 37 *Federal Register* 2437 (1972); and National Academy of Sciences, *Safety of Saccharin and Sodium Saccharin in the Human Diet* (1974). Several persons have written about the regulation of saccharin before the FDA announced its intention to ban the substance. See James Harvey Young, "Saccharin: A Bitter Regulatory Controversy," in Frank B. Evans and Harold T. Pinkett, eds., *Research in the Administration of Public Policy* (Washington, D.C., 1975), 39-49; Richard A. Merrill and Michael R. Taylor, "Saccharin: A Case Study of Government Regulation of Environmental Carcinogens," Elizabeth M. Whelan and William R. Havender, "Saccharin and the Public Interest," and William B. Schultz, "The Bitter Aftertaste of Saccharin," all in *Agriculture and Human Values* 3 (Winter-Spring 1986): 33–73, 74–82, and 83–90, respectively. See also Peter Barton Hutt, "Individual Freedom and Government Control of Food Safety: Saccharin and Food Additives," and Sidney M. Wolfe, "The Conflict Between Individual Freedom and Social Control: Saccharin and Food Additives," both in *Annals of the New York Academy of Sciences* 329 (1979): 221–41 and 242–45, respectively.

12. General Accounting Office, "Need to Resolve Safety Questions on Saccharin," HRD-76—156 (1976); and 42 *Federal Register* 19996, 20000 (1977). See also Frances Cerra, "Questions on Saccharin Are Still Not Resolved," *New York Times*, October 20, 1976, 34.

13. Morton Mintz, "U.S. Will Ban Saccharin," *Washington Post*, March 10, 1977, A-1 and A-11. For Mintz and the New Journalism generally, see Marcus, *Cancer from Beef*, 75–76.

14. *Congressional Record*, 95th cong., 1st sess. (1977): 7022, 7461, 7499, 7639, 7645–46, 7674, 7687, 7697–98, 7705, 7783–84, 7798–99, 7823, 7836, 7923–24, 8063–64, 8067–68, 8104, 8114–15, 8116, 8118, 8381–828383, 8384–8385, 8433, 8615, 8859, 8882–83, 8941, 9061, 9392–94, 9442–43, 9507,9508, 9712–13, 9726, 9817, 9832–33, 9949–50, 10267–69, 10271–80, 10290, 10336, 10341–43, 10538, 10580–81, 10969–70, 12106–07, 12388, 12390, 12715, 12747–50, 13381–82, 15261–62, 15662–64, 16500–01, 17349–53, 1792, 19792, 20483–86, 20742–43, 20941–42, 21156, 21446–61, 22332, 28360, 28582–83, 29253–65, 29371–81, 29389–96, 30013–14, 33970–72, 33917–28, 35382–83, 36971–78, 37145 and 38330–31; and Office of Technology Assessment, *Cancer Testing Technology and Saccharin* (October 1977).

15. Jean Carper, "Aspartame: Has Sugar Met Its Match?" *Washington Post*, July 23, 1981: E–1 and E–19; and "Aspartame: Sweet and Sour," *Washington Post*, July 1, 1983: D–5.

GERALD N. GROB

# Deinstitutionalization:
# The Illusion of Policy

In mid-nineteenth century America the asylum became the foundation of public policy. This ubiquitous institution was regarded as a symbol of an enlightened and progressive nation that no longer ignored or mistreated its severely and chronically mentally ill citizens. The faith in an institutional policy was embodied in a vast and costly system of state mental hospitals that by 1940 had an inpatient population of about 450,000. Despite the presence of serious problems, there was little disposition to call into doubt the wisdom of institutional care and treatment. Even though mental health policy was formulated within a decentralized and divided political system, there was no doubt that a holistic and clear consensus prevailed.

In the decades following the close of World War II, a profound policy transformation occurred. Increasingly the mental hospital began to be perceived as the vestigial remnant of a bygone age. The emphasis was now placed on prevention and the provision of care and treatment in the community. Ultimately, deinstitutionalization became the term used to describe public policy during and after the 1970s. Although this designation seems to suggest a coherent policy, a careful analysis suggests something quite different. Indeed, even as the traditional institutional system was breaking apart, the mental health scene became increasingly fragmented, and what came to be defined as policy was simply the result of a series of incremental and unrelated developments.

What factors were responsible for this remarkable policy transformation? Equally important, what were the consequences of the move away from reliance on institutionalization? The answer to these outwardly simple questions is extraordinarily complex. Indeed, many of the models that purport to explain policy formulation and implementation are simply inadequate when applied to the evolution of mental health policy after 1945. Rather than attempting an exercise in theory, I should like to present an analytic narrative that emphasizes the unpredictability and unanticipated consequences of policy innovation and implementation.

Policy changes rarely occur in a historical vacuum, and mental health is no exception. Of fundamental importance was a change in the character of mental hospitals after 1900. In the nineteenth century the proportion of long-term or chronic cases was relatively low because of the manner in which hospitals were funded. In general, state legislatures provided the capital funds necessary for acquiring new sites and constructing, expanding, and renovating existing physical plants. Local communities, on the other hand, were required to pay hospitals a sum equal to the actual cost of care and treatment of each patient admitted. The system, moreover, did not assume that every mentally ill person would be cared for in a state institution. Laws generally required that only dangerous mentally ill persons had to be sent to state hospitals. Others who could presumably benefit from therapeutic interventions (and thus ultimately be removed from welfare rolls) could, at the discretion of local officials, also be institutionalized. The system, in short, involved divided responsibility. A significant proportion of insane persons, therefore, continued either to live in the community or else were kept in municipal almshouses. Families with sufficient resources could commit their relatives to state institutions, provided they were willing to assume financial liability for their upkeep. States, moreover, had to reimburse hospitals for those patients who had not established legal residency, such as immigrants. The result was a variegated pattern; the majority of chronic cases remained in the community.[1]

As the number of chronic patients increased, however, states slowly began to reconsider their policies. Disillusioned by a system that divided authority, states adopted legislation that relieved local communities of any role whatsoever in caring for the mentally ill. The assumption of those who favored centralization was that local care, although less expensive, was substandard and also fostered chronicity and dependency. Conversely, care and treatment in hospitals, though more costly initially, would in the long run be cheaper because it would enhance the odds of recovery for some and provide more humane care for others.

Although the intent of state assumption of responsibility was to ensure that the mentally ill would receive a higher quality of care and treatment, the consequences in actual practice turned out to be quite different. In brief, local officials saw in the new laws a golden opportunity to shift some of their financial obligations onto the state. The purpose of the legislation was self-evident, namely, to remove the care of the chronic mentally ill from local jurisdiction. But local officials went beyond the intent of the law. Traditionally, nineteenth-century almshouses (which were supported and administered by local governments) served in part as old-age homes for senile and aged persons without any financial resources. The passage of state care acts provided local officials with an unexpected opportunity. They proceeded to redefine senility in psychiatric terms and thus began to transfer aged persons from local almshouses to state mental hospitals. Humanitarian concerns played a relatively minor role in this development; economic considerations were of paramount significance.[2]

As a result, the character of mental hospitals underwent a dramatic transformation after 1900. Prior to that time hospitals had substantial turnover rates even though they retained patients who failed to improve or recover. In the four decades following its opening in the 1840s, the proportion of patients who left the Utica State Lunatic Asylum hovered around 40 percent. In the twentieth century, by way of contrast, the pattern changed markedly as the proportion of short-term cases fell and those of long-term increased. In 1904, 27.8 percent of the total national patient population had been institutionalized for twelve months or less. By 1910 this percentage fell to 12.7, although rising to 17.4 in 1923. The greatest change, however, came among patients hospitalized for five years or more. In 1904, 39.2 percent of patients fell into this category; in 1910 and 1923 the respective percentages were 52.0 and 54.0. Although data for the United States as a whole were unavailable after 1923, the experiences of Massachusetts are illustrative. By the 1930s nearly 80 percent of its mental hospital beds were occupied by chronic patients.[3]

Chronicity, however, is a somewhat misleading term, for the group that it described was actually heterogeneous. The aged (over 60 or 65) constituted by far the single largest component. By 1920, for example, 18 percent of all first admissions to New York State mental hospitals were diagnosed as psychotic because of senility or arteriosclerosis; twenty years later the figure had risen to 31 percent. A decade later, 40 percent of all first admissions were aged 60 and over, as compared with only 13.2 percent of the state's total population. The increase in the absolute number also reflected a change in age-specific admission rates. In their classic study of rates of institutionalization covering more than a century, Goldhamer and Marshall found that the greatest increase occurred in the older category. In 1855 the age-specific first-admission rate in Massachusetts aged 60 and over was 70.4 for males and 65.5 for females (per 100,000); by the beginning of World War II the corresponding figures were 279.5 and 223.0. As late as 1958 nearly a third of all resident state hospital patients were over 65.[4]

The rising age distribution mirrored a different but related characteristic of the institutionalized, namely, the presence of large numbers of patients whose abnormal behavior reflected an underlying somatic etiology. Even allowing for imprecise diagnoses and an imperfect statistical reporting system, it was quite evident that a significant proportion of the hospitalized population suffered from severe organic disorders for which there were no effective treatments. Of 49,116 first admission in 1922 admitted because of various psychoses, 16,407 suffered from a variety of identifiable somatic conditions (senility, cerebral arteriosclerosis, paresis, Huntington's chorea, brain tumors, etc.). Between 1922 and 1940 the proportion of such patients increased from 33.4 to 42.4 percent. In 1946 various forms of senility and paresis accounted for about half of all first admissions.[5]

After 1945 mental hospitals—institutions that had been the cornerstone of public policy for nearly a century and a half—slowly began to lose their social and medical legitimacy. This was hardly surprising. Indeed the prevailing consensus on mental health policy slowly began to dissolve. Developments converged to reshape public policy during these years. First, there was a shift in psychiatric thinking toward a psychodynamic and psychoanalytic model emphasizing life experiences and the role of socioenvironmental factors. Second, the experiences of World War II appeared to demonstrate the efficacy of community and outpatient treatment of disturbed persons. Third, the belief that early intervention in the community would be effective in preventing subsequent hospitalization became popular. Fourth, a faith developed that psychiatry could promote prevention by contributing toward the amelioration of social problems that allegedly fostered mental diseases. Fifth, the introduction of psychological and somatic therapies (including, but not limited to, psychotropic drugs) held out the promise of a more normal existence for patients outside of mental institutions. Finally, an enhanced social welfare role of the federal government not only began to diminish the authority of state governments but also hastened the transition from an institutionally-based to a community-oriented policy.[6]

The popular perceptions of mental hospitals were also shaped by journalistic exposés. In the immediate postwar period journalists and mental health professionals alike published numerous critical accounts of mental hospitals even though their analyses were not always accurate.[7] Admit-

tedly, a decade and a half of financial neglect, due largely to the combined impact of the Great Depression of the 1930s and global conflict of
the 1940s, simply exacerbated already existing severe problems. The depressing state of mental hospitals, however, was as much a function of the
nature of their patients as it was the result of parsimonious or callous
policies. The large number of chronically-ill patients was undoubtedly
the single most significant element in shaping a milieu seemingly antithetical to therapeutic goals.

At this very same time a broad coalition of psychiatric and lay activists
began a campaign to transform mental health policy. The initial success
came in 1946 with the enactment of the National Mental Health Act.
This novel law (which also led to the creation of the National Institute
for Mental Health [NIMH]) made the federal government an important
participant in an arena traditionally reserved for the states. The passage
of the Community Mental Health Centers Act in late 1963 (signed into
law by President Kennedy just prior to his death) culminated two decades
of agitation. The legislation provided federal subsidies for the construction of centers, which were intended to be the cornerstone of a radically
new policy. In short centers were supposed to facilitate early identification of symptoms, offer preventive treatments that would both diminish
the incidence of mental disorders and prevent long-term hospitalization,
and provide integrated and continuous services to severely mentally ill
people in the community. Ultimately, such centers would render traditional mental hospitals obsolete.[8]

Curiously enough the rhetoric and arguments used to justify this departure from the prevailing institutional policy rested on shaky empirical
data. A California study of about 500 patients in three state hospitals in
the 1950s found that most of them were unsuited to treatment in community clinics. The authors concluded by noting "the marked discontinuities
in functions of the participating hospitals and clinics and the difficulties
in initiating outpatient treatment with hospitalized patients shortly after
their admission." They also called attention to "the value of services to
bridge the gap between the traditional functions of hospitals and clinics
for already hospitalized patients."[9] Data collected by Morton Kramer and
his associates at the Biometrics Branch of the NIMH raised more serious
problems. A community policy was based on the expectation that patients could be treated outside of institutions. Underlying this belief were
several assumptions: (1) patients had a home; (2) patients had a sympathetic family or other person willing and able to assume responsibility for
their care; (3) the organization of the household would not impede rehabilitation; (4) the patient's presence would not cause undue hardships for

other family members. In 1960, however, 48 percent of the mental hospital population was unmarried, 12 percent were widowed, and 13 percent were divorced or separated. A large proportion of patients, in other words, may have had no families to care for them. Hence the assumption that patients could reside in the community with their families while undergoing rehabilitation was hardly realistic.[10]

Hailed as the harbingers of a new era, community mental health centers (CMHCs) failed to live up to their promise. Admittedly, appropriations fell far below expectations because of the budgetary pressures engendered by the Vietnam War. More importantly, CMHCs served a different population. They preferred to emphasize psychotherapy, an intervention especially adapted to individuals with emotional and personal problems as well as one that appealed to a professional constituency. Most centers made little effort to provide coordinated aftercare services and continuing assistance to severely and persistently mentally ill persons. Even psychiatrists in community settings tended to deal with more affluent neurotic patients as compared with severely mentally ill persons.[11]

Equally significant, the focus of federal policy shifted dramatically during the 1970s because of a growing perception that substance abuse (particularly drugs and, to a lesser extent, alcohol) represented major threats to the public at large. Beginning in 1968 Congress enacted legislation that sharply altered the role of centers by adding new services for substance abusers, children, and elderly persons. The Congress believed that the act of 1963 had resolved most of the major problems of the mentally ill and that greater attention should be paid to other groups in need of mental health services. As the services provided by centers proliferated, the interests of the severely and persistently mentally ill—clearly the group with the most formidable problems—slowly receded into the background.

The inauguration of Richard Nixon in 1969 altered the political environment. Between 1970 and 1972 his administration worked assiduously to scale back NIMH programs, many of which survived only because of a sympathetic Congress. By 1973, however, the Watergate scandal was preoccupying the attention of White House, and mental health policy issues receded into the background. Nixon's resignation in the summer of 1974 was welcomed by those concerned with mental health policy issues, if only because he was perceived as an opponent of any significant federal role in shaping and financing services. In the months preceding and following Nixon's resignation, Congress undertook a reassessment of the CMHC program. The result was the passage of a mental health law in mid-1975 over President Gerald Ford's veto. Yet this legislation—which expanded the role of CMHCs—never addressed the fundamental issue of providing for the basic human and medical needs of the severely mentally ill.[12]

The accession of Jimmy Carter to the presidency in 1977 introduced a new element of hope. In one of his first acts, Carter signed an executive order creating the President's Commission on Mental Health to review national needs and to make necessary recommendations. Yet the Commission's final report offered at best a potpourri of diverse and sometimes conflicting recommendations. Eventually Congress passed the Mental Health Systems Act a month before the presidential election. Its provisions were complex and in some respects contradictory. Nevertheless, the law suggested at the very least the outlines of a national system that would ensure the availability of both care and treatment in community settings.[13]

The Mental Health Systems Act had hardly become law when its provisions became moot. The accession of Ronald Reagan to the presidency led to an immediate reversal of policy. Preoccupied with both reducing taxes and federal expenditures, the new administration proposed a 25 percent cut in federal funding. More importantly, it called for a conversion of federal mental health programs into a single block grant to the states carrying few restrictions and without policy guidelines. The presidential juggernaut proved irresistible, and in the summer of 1981 the Omnibus Budget Reconciliation Act was signed into law. Among other things, it provided a block grant to states for mental health services and substance abuse. At the same time, it repealed most of the provisions of the Mental Health Systems Act. The new legislation did more than reduce federal funding for mental health; it reversed nearly three decades of federal involvement and leadership. In the ensuing decade the focus of policy and funding shifted back to the states and local communities, thus restoring in part the tradition that had prevailed until World War II. The transfer and decentralization of authority, however, exacerbated existing tensions; federal support was reduced at precisely the same time that states were confronted with massive social and economic problems that increased their fiscal burdens.

Disagreements over national mental health policy received considerable attention. Nevertheless, these disagreements were eventually overshadowed by a far more significant development, namely the acceleration in the discharge of large numbers of severely and persistently mentally ill persons from public mental hospitals. The origins of "deinstitutionalization"—a term that is both imprecise and misleading—

are complex. Indeed, in its origins deinstitutionalization was not a policy mandated by statutory law. On the contrary it was an unforseen outgrowth of a series of federal entitlement programs having little to do with the severely mentally ill. To be sure, deinstitutionalization during and after the 1960s was indirectly sanctioned by the judiciary when federal and state courts began to take up longstanding legal issues relating to the mentally ill. The identification of new legal issues had significant consequences for psychiatrists and the mentally ill. Courts defined a right to treatment in a least restrictive environment; shortened the duration of all forms of commitment and placed restraints on its application; undermined the sole right of psychiatrists to make purely medical judgments about the necessity of commitment; accepted the right of patients to litigate both before and after admission to a mental institution; and even defined a right of a patient to refuse treatment under certain circumstances. The emergence of mental health law advocates tended to weaken the authority of both psychiatrists and mental hospitals, and conferred added legitimacy to the belief that protracted hospitalization was somehow counterproductive and that community care and treatment represented a more desirable policy choice.[14]

Judicial decisions, however significant, merely confirmed existing trends by providing a legal sanction for deinstitutionalization. Some experts recognized the danger and voiced concern.[15] Nevertheless the pattern of discharging patients from mental hospitals after relatively brief length-of-stays accelerated after 1970 because of the expansion of federal entitlement programs having no direct relationship with mental health policy. States began to take advantage of a series of relatively new federal initiatives that were designed to provide assistance for a variety of disabled groups and thus facilitate their maintenance in the community.

The elderly were among the first to be affected by new federal policies. Immediately following the passage of Medicaid in 1965, states began to shift the care of elderly persons with behavioral symptoms from mental hospitals to chronic care nursing facilities. Such a move was hardly the result of altruism or a belief that the interests of aged persons would be better served in such institutions. On the contrary, state officials were predisposed to the use of nursing homes because a large part of the costs were assumed by the federal government. The quality of care in such facilities (which varied in the extreme) was not an important consideration in transferring patients. Indeed, the relocation of elderly patients from mental hospitals to extended care facilities was often marked by increases in the death rate. Moreover, many nursing homes provided no psychiatric care. When Bruce C. Vladeck published his study of nursing homes in 1980, he selected as his book title *Unloving Care: The Nursing Home Tragedy*.[16]

During the 1960s the population of nursing homes rose from about 470,000 to nearly 928,000, largely as a result of Medicaid. A study by the General Accounting Office in 1977 noted that Medicaid was "one of the largest single purchasers of mental health care and the principal Federal program funding the long-term care of the mentally disabled." It also was the most significant "federally sponsored program affecting deinstitutionalization." By 1985 nursing homes had over 600,000 residents diagnosed as mentally ill; the cost of their care was over $10.5 billion, a large proportion of which was paid for by Medicaid. The massive transfer of large numbers of elderly patients who behaved in abnormal ways was not controversial, if only because such individuals posed no obvious threats to community residents. Designed to provide services for the elderly and indigent, therefore, Medicaid (as well as Medicare) quickly became one of the largest mental health programs in the United States.[17]

Other federal programs had an equally profound effect on the nonelderly mentally ill. In 1956 Congress had amended the Social Security Act to enable eligible persons age fifty and over to receive disability benefits. The Social Security Disability Insurance (SSDI) program continued to become more inclusive in succeeding years, and ultimately covered the mentally disabled. In 1972 the Social Security Act was further amended to provide coverage for individuals who did not qualify for benefits. Under the provisions of Supplemental Security Income for the Aged, the Disabled, and the Blind (more popularly known as SSI), all those whose age or disability made them incapable of holding a job became eligible for income support. This entitlement program was administered and fully funded by the federal government; its affiliation with Social Security had the added virtue of minimizing the stigmatization often associated with welfare. SSI and SSDI encouraged states to discharge severely and persistently mentally ill persons from mental hospitals, since federal payments would presumably enable them to live in the community. Those who were covered under SSI also became eligible for coverage under Medicaid. In addition, public housing programs and food stamps added to the resources of mentally ill persons residing in the community.[18]

The expansion of federal entitlement programs hastened the discharge of large numbers of institutionalized patients during and after the 1970s. This trend was reflected in the changing pattern of mental hospital populations. In the decade following 1955 the decline in inpatient populations was modest, falling from 559,000 to 475,000.[19] The decreases after 1965 were dramatic; between 1970 and 1986 the number of inpatient beds in state and county institutions declined from 413,000 to 119,000. Length-of-stays dropped correspondingly; the median stay for all patients was about twenty-eight days, suggesting that public hospitals still had an important role in providing psychiatric services for a highly disabled population. Moreover, schizophrenics accounted for slightly more than a third of all mental hospital admissions, whereas only 19 percent of psychiatric patients treated in general hospitals fell into this category. Indeed, state hospitals remained the largest provider of total inpatient days of psychiatric care; their clients were disproportionately drawn from the ranks of the most difficult, troubled, and violent-prone.[20]

In theory, the combination of entitlement programs and access to psychiatric services outside of mental hospitals should have fostered greater state financial support for community programs. The presumption was that a successful community policy would eventually permit the consolidation of some mental hospitals and closure of others, thus facilitating the transfer of state funds from institutional to community programs. In practice, however, the state mental hospital proved far more resilient than its critics anticipated. Some had powerful support among community residents and employees who feared the dramatic economic consequences that would accompany closure.[21] A shrinking inpatient census, therefore, sometimes led to rising per capita expenditures, since operating costs were distributed among fewer patients. Equally important, there remained a seemingly irreducible group of individuals who were so disabled that institutional care appeared to be a necessity. Using data collected by the NIMH, the authors of one study concluded that there appeared "to be a core of some 100,000 residents for whom there is no alternative to state hospital treatment." On the basis of a careful analysis of the patient population of the Massachusetts Mental Health Center (which had responsibility for the Boston geographic catchment area), two psychiatrists estimated that there were about fifteen persons per 100,000 of population who required "secure, supportive, long-term care in specialized facilities at the regional and state level." If their data were representative there were perhaps 35,000 persons in the United States requiring mental hospital care or its equivalent.[22]

In retrospect, mental health policy changed dramatically after 1965, but not in the manner envisaged by those active in its formulation. After World War II there was a decided effort to substitute an integrated community system of services for traditional mental hospitals. The system that emerged in the 1970s and 1980s, however, was quite different. First, mental hospitals did not become obsolete even though they lost their central position. They continued to provide both care and treatment for the most severely disabled part of the population. Second, community mental health programs expanded dramatically, and inpatient and outpatient psychiatric services became available in both general hospitals and CMHCs. A significant proportion of their clients, however, represented new populations. Finally, a large part of the burden of supporting severely mentally ill persons in the community fell to a variety of federal entitlement programs that existed quite apart from the mental health care system. Since the 1970s, therefore, severely and persistently mentally ill persons have come under the jurisdiction of two quite distinct systems—entitlements and mental health—that often lacked any formal programmatic or institutional linkages.

Whatever its contradictory and tangled origins, deinstitutionalization had positive consequences for a large part of the nation's severely and persistently mentally ill population. Data from the Vermont longitudinal Research Project offered some dramatic evidence that individuals with severe mental illness who were provided with a range of comprehensive services could live in the community. Between 1955 and 1960 a multidisciplinary team initiated a program of comprehensive rehabilitation and community for placement for 269 back-ward patients who were considered to be among the most severely disabled and chronically mentally ill in the Vermont State Hospital. Middle-aged, poorly-educated, and lower class, they had histories of illness that averaged sixteen years, had been hospitalized between one to ten times, and as a group averaged six years of continuous institutionalization. More than 80 percent were single, divorced, separated, or widowed, and were rarely visited by friends or relatives. Their disabilities were characteristic of schizophrenics.

Initially the multidisciplinary team constructed a new inpatient program that consisted of "drug treatment, open-ward care in homelike conditions, group therapy, graded privileges, activity therapy, industrial therapy, vocational counseling, and self-help groups." In the community treatment component, the same clinical team established halfway houses and outpatient clinics, located and placed individuals in jobs, and linked patients to support networks. Periodic follow-up evaluations were conducted over the next twenty-five years. The results indicated that two-thirds "could be maintained in the community if sufficient transitional facilities and adequate aftercare was provided." These results were confirmed by four other longitudinal studies, including Manfred Bleuler's twenty-three year study of 208 patients in Zurich, Ciompi and Muller's thirty-seven year study of 289 patients in Lausanne, Huber and colleagues' twenty-two year study of 502 subjects in Bonn, and Tsuang and colleagues' Iowa study.[23]  Other experiments have confirmed that individuals with severe mental disorders prefer and do better in community settings that dispense economic resources (particularly vocational rehabilitation) and a kind of empowerment that provides a feeling of mastery rather than a sense of dependency.[24]


Under the best of circumstances deinstitutionalization would have been difficult to implement. The multiplication of programs and absence of formal integrated linkages, however, complicated the task of both clients and those responsible for providing care and treatment. Moreover, the decades of the 1970s and 1980s were hardly propitious for the development and elaboration of programs to serve disadvantaged populations such as the severely and persistently mentally ill. The dislocations and tensions engendered by the Vietnam War, the rise of antigovernment ideologies, and an economic system that no longer held out as great a promise of mobility and affluence, all combined to create a context that made experimentation and innovation more difficult. The founding of the National Alliance for the Mentally III (NAMI) in 1979 helped in part to redress the balance. It brought together families of the mentally ill in an advocacy organization that began to play an increasingly important role in the politics of mental health during and after the 1980s.

As a policy, deinstitutionalization was based on the premise that the population found in mental hospitals was relatively homogeneous. The first major wave of discharges came after 1965 and occurred among a group of individuals who had been institutionalized for relatively long periods of time or else had been admitted later in their lives. These individuals were relocated in chronic care facilities or else returned to the community where many made somewhat satisfactory adjustments. In its initial stage, therefore, deinstitutionalization dealt with individuals who had constituted the bulk of the traditional inpatient population. This phase was not controversial nor did it create difficulties since few of these individuals seemed to pose a threat to others.

After 1970 a quite different situation prevailed due to basic demographic trends in the population as a whole and changes in the mental health service system. At the end of World War II there was a sharp rise in the number of births that peaked in the 1960s. Between 1946 and 1960 more than fifty-nine million births were recorded. The disproportionately large size of this age cohort meant that the number of persons at risk from developing severe mental disorders was very high. Morton Kramer warned that large increases were to be expected between 1975 and 1990 "in numbers of persons in high-risk age groups for the use of mental health facilities and correctional institutions, homes for the aged and dependent and other institutions that constitute the institutional population." Moreover, younger people tended to be highly mobile. Whereas 40 percent of the general population moved between 1975 and 1979, between 62 and 72 percent of individuals in their twenties changed residences. Like others in their age cohort, the large numbers of young adult severely and persistently mentally ill persons also moved frequently both within and between cities and in and out of rural areas.[25]

At the same time that the cohort born after 1945 was reaching their twenties and thirties, the mental health service system was undergoing fundamental changes. Prior to 1970 persons with severe and persistent mental disorders were generally cared for in state hospitals. If admitted in their youth, they often remained institutionalized for decades, or else were discharged and readmitted. Hence their care and treatment was centralized within a specific institutional context, and in general they were not visible in the community at large. Although chronically mentally ill persons were always found in the community, their relatively small numbers posed few difficulties and in general did not arouse public concern.

After 1970, however, a subgroup of the severely mentally ill—composed largely of young adults—were adversely affected by the changes in the mental health service system. Young chronically mentally ill persons were rarely confined for extended periods within mental hospitals. Restless and mobile, they were the first generation of psychiatric patients to reach adulthood within the community. Although their disorders were not fundamentally different than their predecessors, they behaved in quite different ways. They tended to emulate the behavior of their age peers who were often hostile toward conventions and authority. The young adult mentally ill exhibited aggressiveness, volatility, and were noncompliant. They generally fell into the schizophrenic category, although affective disorders and borderline personalities were also present. Above all, they lacked functional and adaptive skills.[26]

Complicating the clinical picture were high rates of alcoholism and drug abuse among these young adult chronic patients, which only exacerbated their volatile and noncompliant behavior. Their mobility and lack of coping skills also resulted in high rates of homelessness. Many of them travelled and lived together on the streets, thereby reinforcing each other's pathology. Urban areas in particular began to experience the presence of young adult severely and persistently ill individuals. But even rural states such as Vermont found that their chronic cases were made up of transients who required treatment, welfare, and support services. An APA report on the homeless mentally ill emphasized the tendency of these young persons to drift.[27]

Virtually every community experienced their presence on the streets, in emergency medical facilities, and in correctional institutions. Recent estimates have suggested that perhaps a quarter to a third of the single adult homeless population have a severe mental disorder. Many have a dual diagnosis of severe mental illness and substance abuse. Studies of these individuals found that they "were more likely to experience extremely harsh living conditions." More so than other groups, they suffered from "psychological distress and demoralization " granted "sexual favors for food and money" and were often "picked up by the police and ... incarcerated." They had few contacts with their families; "were highly prone to victimization"; were socially isolated; mistrusted people and institutions; and were resistant to accepting assistance.[28]

At the same time that young adult chronic patients were becoming more prominent, the mental hospital was losing its central position and the traditional links between care and treatment were shattered. Treatment was subsumed under a decentralized and fragmented medical and psychiatric service system that served a varied and diversified client population. Care, by contrast, increasingly came under the jurisdiction of a series of federal entitlement programs which presumed that income maintenance payments would enable disabled persons to live within their community. Indeed, such programs increasingly drove the process of deinstitutionalization, since the release of patients from state institutions to communities meant an implicit transfer of funding responsibilities from states to the federal government.

The combination of a decentralized psychiatric system and the emergence of a young adult chronic population had profound consequences. Before 1965 mental hospitals retained responsibility for the severely mentally ill population. After 1970 a quite different situation prevailed among the new subgroup of young mentally ill adults. Many from this group tended to be pervasive but unsystematic users of psychiatric facilities. They entered and left mental hospitals after brief length-of-stays; they used emergency and psychiatric wards of general hospitals and other inpatient and outpatient facilities; and they could be found as well in correctional and penal institutions. Their high use of services tended to resemble a revolving door. Because of their mobility and restlessness, they moved quickly from one service to another. They proved to be noncompliant; their use of medication was sporadic and inconsistent; their refusal or inability to follow a sustained and rational treatment plan meant that the benefits gained were transient and minimal; and they often had a dual diagnosis of serious mental disorder and substance abuse. Such patients also tended to arouse negative reactions from mental health professionals; chronicity and substance abuse contradicted the medical dream of cure.[29]

Deinstitutionalization was largely irrelevant to many of the young patients who were highly visible after 1970. They had little or no experiences with prolonged institutionalization and hence had not internalized the behavioral norms of a hospital community. To be sure, many of the norms of patienthood in institutions were objectionable, but at the very least they provided individuals with some kind of structure. Lacking such guidance, many young chronic mentally ill patients—especially those with a dual diagnosis—developed a common cultural identity quite at variance with the society in which they lived. The mobility of such individuals, the absence of a family support system, and programmatic shortcomings complicated their access to such basic necessities as adequate housing and social support networks. The dearth of many basic necessities of life further exacerbated their severe mental disorders. Ironically, at the very time that the need for unified, coordinated, and integrated medical and social services were needed to deal with a new patient population, the policy of deinstitutionalization had created a decentralized system that often lacked any clear focus and diffused responsibility and authority.

The outcome of the presidential election of 1980 further exacerbated the problems of the mental health system. However the presidency of Jimmy Carter may be evaluated on other issues, there is little doubt that his administration was seeking to develop more effective policies to deal with some of the unanticipated and undesirable consequences of deinstitutionalization. Stimulated by the President's Commission on Mental Health, the Department of Health and Human Services and a number of constituent groups developed a National Plan for the Chronically Mentally Ill. Released a month after Carter's defeat, the plan focused on the severely and chronically mentally ill. It acknowledged the importance of such programs as SSI, SSDI, Medicaid, and Medicare, and offered a series of incremental recommendations to modify and integrate them within a more effective national system.[30]

The inauguration of Ronald Reagan in early 1981, however, aborted efforts to integrate federal entitlement and disability programs with the mental health system. The new administration wanted to diminish sharply, if not reverse, the growth of federal domestic spending and thus to reduce taxes. The National Plan was shelved and the Mental Health Systems Act repealed. Equally important, there were sustained efforts to limit programs dealing with the dependent and disabled and to eliminate other programs, including public housing. Aside from efforts to convince Congress to alter the federal role in social policy issues, the White House also began to use its administrative authority to implement its political agenda.

A provision in the Disability Amendments legislation of 1980 gave the administration an opening. This act had mandated that the Social Security Administration should review the eligibility of all SSI and SSDI recipients once every three years. By this time Congress had begun to be concerned with the dramatic increase in entitlement expenditures and wanted to guard against potential abuse. In 1980 the presumption was that such reviews would result in a modest saving of $218 million by 1985. At the time that Reagan took office, there were about 550,000 disabled persons receiving assistance under these programs, including the mentally ill. The administration seized upon this clause to deny benefits to thousands of new applicants and to purge thousands of others from the rolls. The mentally disabled were especially hard hit. They accounted for 11 percent of SSDI recipients, but represented 30 percent of those cut. The administration projected a savings of nearly $3.5 billion by 1985, and even larger savings in the future, since the mentally disabled who were receiving benefits were young and therefore would be on the roles for decades. The massive reduction in the eligibility rolls was achieved when the Social Security Administration developed a definition of disability and procedures that were quite at variance with earlier practices as well as with existing definitions of the nature of mental disorder.

When the magnitude of the cuts became evident, a public uproar followed. Testimony by individuals from the General Accounting Office brought into question the entire process, which was patently designed to reduce federal expenditures rather than eliminating ineligible recipients. Congressman Claude Pepper, the venerable champion of the aged and dependent, accused the administration of "cruel and callous policies designed to strike terror into the hearts of crippled people all across America." The actions of Social Security officials and the administration received even more negative publicity when news reports revealed that Sergeant Roy Benavidez, a wounded Vietnam veteran and winner of the Congressional Medal of Honor, had been cut off from receiving disability benefits. Besieged by judicial challenges and under attack by state officials, the administration in mid-1983 yielded to growing public criticism and reversed its policy. The incident, however, suggested the lengths that a Republican administration was prepared to go to achieve their social and political objectives.[31]

A superficial analysis of the mental health scene in the recent past can easily lead to depressing conclusions. The combined presence of large numbers of young adult chronic individuals as well as larger numbers of homeless people undoubtedly reinforced feelings of public apprehension and professional impotence. Indeed, the popular image of mental illnesses and the mental health service system was often shaped by spectacular exposés in the media—visual and printed—that seemed to reveal sharp and perhaps irreconcilable tensions. In them could be seen the conflict between absolutist definitions of freedom and other humanitarian and ethical principles, as well as the concerns that the well-being, if not the very safety, of the community seemed endangered.[32]

The image of deinstitutionalization so often portrayed in the press and on television, nevertheless, represented a gross simplification that ignored a far more complex reality. The popular image of severely and persistently mentally ill adults, using drugs, wandering the streets of virtually every urban area, threatening residents, and resisting treatment and hospitalization, was true but represented only a subgroup of a much larger seriously mentally ill population. Often overlooked were innovative programs that were specifically designed to deal with the severely and chronically mentally ill in the 1970s and 1980s.

Even as the policy of deinstitutionalization was being implemented, psychiatrists and sociologists were emphasizing some of its shortcomings. Bert Pepper, a psychiatrist who directed the Rockland County CMHC, reiterated that there were "overwhelming dimensions of unmet human needs," and that psychiatric services, however important, had to "wait until fundamental problems of shelter and survival" were addressed. Similarly, John Talbott, a psychiatrist at Cornell Medical College, insisted in 1979 that "a reconceptualization of the problem" was required that addressed both the psychiatric and human needs of a severely disabled population. David Mechanic, perhaps the preeminent sociologist of mental health, emphasized time and time again the importance of strategies to integrate mental health services in ways that overcame the barriers associated with decentralized and uncoordinated systems of treatment, care, and financing.[33]

Paradoxically, the presence of flaws in the existing systems was recognized by the NIMH, the federal agency that had played a central role in the passage of the Community Mental Health Centers act of 1963. Employing its relatively broad mandate to sponsor research and related activities, the agency launched a new initiative when it created the Community Support Program in 1977. Modestly financed at the outset with an allocation of $3.5 million and rising to $15 million a decade later, the program involved a federal/state partnership designed to assist in the development of community support programs for adults with severe mental disorders. It consisted of ten distinct components, including housing, income, psychiatric and medical treatment, and support services, most of which had been specified (but never realized) in the regulations governing the original legislation of 1963. The initiative was not intended to support services but rather to encourage states to introduce changes in the mental health system. Although the program was unpopular in the Reagan administration, Congress enacted legislation in 1984 that gave it legal standing. The State Comprehensive Mental Health Services Plan Act two years later built upon this initiative. In 1989 the Community Support Program was redesigned to test the effectiveness of different specific approaches, thus ending its role as a means of encouraging system change.[34]

Some of the initial results in the early 1980s with community support systems programs were encouraging. They served a chronic population; the ten services defined by the NIMH were actually in use; and those with the greatest needs were the beneficiaries. Outward appearances to the contrary, the condition of many severely and persistently ill persons improved during the remainder of the decade as many states attempted to integrate such federal entitlement programs as SSDI, SSI, Medicaid and Medicare with community mental health services. Nevertheless, the impact of these developments was often overshadowed by massive problems posed by homelessness, the presence of individuals who were both severely mentally ill and substance abusers, and an angry and sometimes alienated public fearful that their security was being endangered.[35]

A quite different perspective on community programs became evident during these years. From World War II to the 1960s community mental health had been portrayed in terms of an all-embracing panacea; its supporters employed rhetoric and largely ignored the absence of a body of empirical data that might validate their assertions. Exaggerated claims inevitably prepared the ground for a reaction that threatened to inhibit or undermine efforts to deal with the needs of a severely disabled population. In succeeding decades, by contrast, community care and treatment came to have a quite different meaning. The focus on cure and prevention, although still pervasive, became less significant. The emphasis shifted to the need to limit disability and to preserve function. Moreover, advocates of experimental community programs were more prone to concede that cure, independence, and total integration into normal society was often not achievable, and that many (but not all) severely and persistently mentally ill persons might require comprehensive assistance and services for much of their adult lives. In sum, the challenge was to create a system that provided all of the elements incorporated into traditional mental hospitals, but without the liabilities that accompanied protracted institutionalization.

The integrated and comprehensive community programs created during and after the 1970s provided evidence of the difficulties that lay ahead. To administer a program responsible for a variety of different patients proved a formidable undertaking, especially in view of the need to deal with multiple sources of funding. Nor was it inexpensive or easy to replicate elsewhere the results achieved in any given community. Yet at the very least such programs offered guidelines.

Perhaps the best known of the community mental health care programs was developed in Madison, Wisconsin, by Leonard Stein, Mary Ann Test, and others. Its origins went back to the late 1960s, when efforts were made to combat the negative effects of long-term hospitalization that tended to infantilize patients and reduce them to a state of near total dependency. Initially the emphasis was on psychosocial rehabilitation, which was designed to assist patients to become more independent and thus to leave the hospital and live in the community. Although successful, there was little carryover when patients were returned to the community. Moreover, data from a variety of outpatient treatment experiments indicated that individuals in such programs deteriorated once their involvement ceased. By 1970 Stein and his colleagues had launched the first phase of a program designed to prevent hospitalization. Out of this emerged the Training in Community Living project. An unselected group of patients seeking admission to a mental hospital were randomly assigned to experimental and control groups. The latter received hospital treatment linked with aftercare services. The experimental group received intensive services designed to provide them with the skills required to cope while residing in the community, thus avoiding rehospitalization. In succeeding years the Madison model underwent significant changes. Patients in the experimental program were taught such simple living skills as how to budget their money and how to use public transportation. They were provided with assistance with housing and jobs, and received a wide range of social support services. Provision was made for ongoing monitoring, including crisis intervention, and where possible family members were involved in the program. The model that evolved over time deemphasized traditional office psychiatry and the use of professional facilities. Its central concern was with the provision of care to patients in the community and at their place of residence.

Although subject to debate, the results of the Madison experiment seemed to suggest that it was possible for highly-impaired persons to be cared for in the community (thought not necessarily at less cost than in other settings). Clinical interventions appeared to have a more beneficial impact on those in the program, as compared with those in the control group. The former also tended to have better outcomes in terms of personal relationships, derived greater satisfaction, and had lower rates of hospitalization. Nevertheless, they remained marginalized and dependent—an indication that cure and recovery remained distant and remote possibilities.[36]

There were a number of attempts to replicate the Madison model both in the United States and abroad. Most had to make significant alterations if only because of the existence of important differences between Madison and the areas in which the model was duplicated. The most consistent finding was that assertive community care and treatment reduced hospitalization. The meaning of this finding however remained unclear. Were reductions in hospitalization, for example, accompanied by compensatory increases in other forms of supervision? Did such programs shift burdens to the families of patients? Until these and other questions would be answered, the relevance of the Madison experiment remained murky. Moreover, there were fundamental differences between Madison and much larger urban areas; what was effective in the former was not necessarily applicable to the latter.[37]

In an effort to improve services to the chronically mentally ill population, the Robert Wood Johnson Foundation—the nation's largest foundation concerned with health—created the Program on Chronic Mental Illness in 1985. Under this program nine cities were given resources to create a central mental health authority to deliver services to chronically mentally ill persons. Drawing upon the experiences of Madison as well as those of the Massachusetts Mental Health Center in Boston, the program grew out of the realization that individuals in urban areas fell under a variety of jurisdictions. Many urban governments, for example, had little or no responsibility for mental health services, but dealt with homelessness, welfare, and housing. The absence of linkages in most cities precluded continuity of care, thus vitiating efforts to assist the chronically mentally ill. The Robert Wood Johnson Foundation Program on Chronic Mental Illness was designed to demonstrate that community care could become a reality rather than a possibility if resources could be concentrated under a single mental health authority.

Preliminary findings suggested that in the nine cities selected services were being directed toward the care of the severely and persistently mentally ill; that a central authority was more likely to be concerned with the ways in which the system as a whole was serving client needs rather than being preoccupied with individual programs; that centralization improved levels of financial support; and perhaps most important, that change was possible. Whether or not the Robert Wood Johnson Program on Chronic

Mental Illness and others will succeed in redressing existing shortcomings remains an open question. "There is no quick fix for the problems that plague public mental health systems," David Mechanic conceded. "The problems are deeply entrenched and difficult to solve. Many public officials are concerned that investments in mental health will not yield significant visible benefits that justify taking political risks." Nevertheless, he insisted that the integration of different strategies—including the integration of assertive community treatment, approaches that unified diverse sources of funding and directed them toward meeting needs of disabled persons strong, local mental health authorities, and rational reimbursement structures—offered at least the potential for improvement.[38]

The persistence of problems, however, should not be permitted to conceal the more important fact that a large proportion of severely and persistently mentally ill persons have made a more or less successful transition to community life as a result of the expansion of federal disability and entitlement programs. To be sure, the media and the public are prone to focus on a subgroup of young adults who have a dual diagnosis of mental illness and substance abuse and who tend to be homeless. Their visibility on the streets often overshadows the inadvertent success of "deinstitutionalization." "In fact," two authorities have recently written, "the situation is indeed much better for many people, and overall it is much better than it might have been.... While many people still do not have adequate incomes or access to the services theoretically provided through Medicaid and Medicare, the fact that the structure exists within these federal programs to meet the needs of these individuals represents a major step forward."[39]

The history of mental health policy since World War II offers a sobering lesson to historians concerned with policy formulation, implementation, and outcomes. All too often we interpret policy within a rational model that emphasizes interest and pressure groups, voting behavior (both among the electorate and in legislative bodies), the availability of resources within a competitive environment, and data and knowledge. Admittedly all of these exercise some influence. Yet other seemingly extraneous factors often play an equally if not more compelling role. Indeed, serendipity may be a more accurate term to portray complex processes that often result in unanticipated policies and consequences.

The tangled web of deinstitutionalization is surely an example of a less than rational policy process. After World War II a faith in community care and treatment began to undermine the legitimacy in an older insti-

tutional policy. Success appeared to come in 1963 with the passage of the
Community Mental Health Centers Act. In reality, this legislation had a
relatively small impact upon the overwhelming majority of severely and
chronically mentally ill persons. Its major impact was on the expansion of
services to include new populations concerned with problems in living as
well as substance abuse. At about the same time the expansion of entitlement programs—few of which were initially directed toward the mentally
ill—played the most significant role in reducing the inpatient census at
public mental hospitals. Although the majority of severely mentally ill
persons clearly benefitted, the appearance of a new group of individuals
with a dual diagnosis of mental disorder and substance abuse posed new
challenges to the decentralized and fragmented system of the 1970s and
1980s. The fragmentation that occurred in the post–World War II decades was by no means limited to mental health policy but was characteristic of health and social policy generally. Perhaps Arthur Silverstein's
use of the term "impure science" is appropriate.[40] When uncertainty rather
than certainty prevails wider latitude is given to the play of external and
even seemingly extraneous or unconscious elements. The absence of
knowledge and/or data, moreover, rarely inhibits political discourse. Under such circumstances it is hardly surprising that the origins and outcomes of innovation often have little to do with initial claims and expectations. Nowhere is the accuracy of this generalization better illustrated
than in the evolution of mental health policy where fragmentation permitted the convergence of unrelated elements to create the illusion of a
clear and coherent policy.

*Rutgers University*

## Notes

1. See for example the data provided by Edward Jarvis in his *Report on Insanity and Idiocy in Massachusetts by the Commission on Lunacy Under Resolve of the Legislature of 1854* (Mass. House Document No. 144 [1855]) (Boston 1855), 18, 73.

2. For discussions of this theme, see Gerald N. Grob, *Mental Illness and American Society, 1875–1940* (Princeton, 1983), *From Asylum to Community: Mental Health Policy in Modern America* (Princeton, 1991), and "Government and Mental Health Policy: A Structural Analysis," *Milbank Quarterly* 72 (1994): 471–500.

3. Ellen Dwyer, *Homes for the Mad: Life Inside Two Nineteenth-Century Asylums* (New Brunswick, 1987), 150–51; U.S. Bureau of the Census, *Insane and Feeble-Minded in Hospitals and Institutions 1904* (Washington, D.C., 1906), 37; idem., *Insane and Feeble Minded in Institutions 1910* (Washington, D.C., 1915), 59; idem., *Patients in Hospitals for Mental Disease, 1923* (Washington, D.C., 1926), 36; Neil A. Dayton, *New Facts on Mental Disorders: Study of 89,190 Cases* (Springfield, Ill., 1940), 414–29.

4. Benjamin Malzberg, "A Statistical Analysis of the Ages of First Admissions to Hos-

pitals for Mental Disease in New York State," *Psychiatric Quarterly* 20 (1949): 344–66; idem., "A Comparison of First Admissions to the New York Civil State Hospitals During 1919–1921 and 1949–1951," *ibid.* 28 (1954): 312–19; New York State Department of Mental Hygiene, *Annual Report*, 42 (1939–1940): 174–75; Herbert Goldhamer and Andrew W. Marshall, *Psychosis and Civilization: Two Studies in the Frequency of Mental Disease* (Glencoe, Ill., 1953), 54, 91; American Psychiatric Association, *Report on Patients Over 65 in Public Mental Hospitals* (Washington, D.C., 1960), 5.

5. Statistics compiled from U.S. Bureau of the Census, *Patients in Hospitals for Mental Disease 1923*, and *Mental Patients in State Hospitals 1926 and 1927* (Washington, D.C., 1930), *Patients in Mental Hospitals 1940* (Washington, D.C., 1943), and Morton Kramer, *Psychiatric Services and the Changing Institutional Scene, 1950–1985* (DHEW Publication No. [ADM] 76–374: Washington, D.C.: Government Printing Office, 1977), 75.

6. Grob, *From Asylum to Community, passim.*

7. The most famous included Albert Q. Maisel, "Bedlam 1946," *Life* 20 (May 6, 1946): 103–18; Frank L. Wright, *Out of Sight Out of Mind* (Philadelphia, 1947); Mike Gorman, "Oklahoma Attacks Its Snakepits," *Reader's Digest* 53 (September 1948): 139–60; and Albert Deutsch, *The Shame of the States* (New York, 1948). Mary Jane Ward's novel *The Snake Pit* (New York, 1946), was subsequently made into a famous motion picture in 1948.

8. For a detailed discussion of the expanded role of the federal government, see Grob, *From Asylum to Community.*

9. Harold Sampson, David Ross, Bernice Engle, and Florine Livson, "Feasibility of Community Clinic Treatment for State Mental Hospital Patients," *Archives of Neurology and Psychiatry* 80 (1958): 77. A larger version of this study appeared under the title *A Study of Suitability for Outpatient Clinic Treatment of State Mental Hospital Admissions 1957*, California Department of Mental Hygiene Research Report No. 1 (1957).

10. See Morton Kramer, *Some Implications of Trends in the Usage of Psychiatric Facilities for Community Mental Health Programs and Related Research* (U.S. Public Health Service Publication 1434: Washington, D.C., 1967); idem., "Epidemiology, Biostatistics, and Mental Health Planning," in American Psychiatric Association *Psychiatric Research Reports* 22 (1967): 1–68; Kramer, C. Taube, and S. Starr, "Patterns of Use of Psychiatric Facilities by the Aged: Current Status, Trends, and Implications," in American Psychiatric Association *Psychiatric Research Reports* 23 (1968): 89–150.

11. Donald G. Langsley, "The Community Mental Health Center: Does It Treat Patients?," *Hospital & Community Psychiatry* 31 (1980): 815–19; Rosalyn D. Bass, *CMHC Staffing: Who Minds the Store?* (DHEW Publ. [ADM] 78–686: Washington, D.C., 1978); David A. Dowell and James A. Ciarlo, "An Evaluative Overview of the Community Mental Health Centers Program," in *Handbook on Mental Health Policy in the United States*, ed. David A. Rochefort (Westport, Conn., 1989), 206.

12. This paragraph is based upon an examination of the following sources: 92–2 Congress, *Extend Community Mental Health Centers Act: Hearing before the Subcommittee on Public Health and Environment of the Committee on Interstate and Foreign Commerce House of Representatives. . . 1972* (Washington, D.C., 1972); 93–1 Congress, *Public Health Service Act Extension 1973: Hearing before the Committee on Labor and Welfare United States Senate . . .1973* (Washington, D.C., 1973); 93–1 Congress, *Departments of Labor, and Health, Education and Welfare and Related Agencies Appropriations for Fiscal Year 1974: Hearings before a Subcommittee of the Committee on Appropriations United States Senate* (Washington, D.C., 1973); General Accounting Office, "Community Mental Health Centers Program— Improvements Needed in Management," July 8, 1971 (B-164031[2]) and "Need for More Effective Management of Community Mental Health Centers Program," August 27, 1974 (B-164031[5]); Public Law 94–63, *U.S. Statutes at Large*, 89:304–369 (July 29, 1975), Public Law 95–83, *ibid.*, 91:383–399 (August 1, 1977), and Public Law 95–622, *ibid.*, 92:3412–3442 (November 9, 1978). For analyses of the policy debates of the early 1970s see Henry A. Foley, *Community Mental Health Legislation: The Formative Process* (Lexington, 1975); Walter E. Barton and Charlotte J. Sanborn, eds., *An Assessment of the Commu-*

*nity Mental Health Movement* (Lexington, 1977); Henry A. Foley and Steven S. Sharfstein, *Madness and Government: Who Cares for the Mentally Ill?* (Washington, D.C., 1983); E. Fuller Torrey, *Nowhere to Go: The Tragic Odyssey of the Homeless Mentally Ill* (New York, 1988); and Lisa Reichenbach, "The Federal Community Mental Health Centers Program and the Policy of Deinstitutionalization," mss. prepared for the NIMH under Grant No. MH27738–02 (1980).

13. *Report to the President from The President's Commission on Mental Health 1978* (4 vols.: Washington, D.C., 1978); General Accounting Office, *Returning the Mentally Disabled to the Community: Government Needs to Do More* (Washington, D.C., 1977); *Mental Health Systems: Message from the President of the United States* (May 15, 1979) (Washington, D.C., 1979); 96–1 Congress, *Mental Health Systems Act, 1979: Hearings before the Subcommittee on Health and Scientific Research of the Committee on Labor and Human Resources United States Senate . . . 1979* (Washington, D.C., 1980); 96–1 Congress, *Mental Health Systems Act: Hearings before the Subcommittee on Health and the Environment of the Committee on Interstate and Foreign Commerce House of Representatives . . . 1979* (Washington, D.C., 1979); 96–2 Congress, *Community Mental Health Centers, Oversight: Hearing before the Subcommittee on Health and the Environment of the Committee on Interstate and Foreign Commerce House of Representatives . . . 1980* (Washington, D.C., 1980); Public Law 96-398, *U.S. Statutes at Large*, 94:1564–1613 (October 7, 1980). The best description of the history of the act is Foley and Sharfstein, *Madness and Government*, 118–34.

14. The literature dealing with mental health law since the 1960s is immense. For overviews see the following: Alexander D. Brooks, *Law, Psychiatry and the Mental Health System* (Boston, 1974), and the 1980 *Supplement* (Boston, 1980) to this volume; David Mechanic, *Mental Health and Social Policy* (3rd ed.: Englewood Cliffs, New Jersey, 1989), 213–34; Paul S. Appelbaum, "The Right to Refuse Treatment with Antipsychotic Medications: Retrospect and Prospect," *American Journal of Psychiatry* 145 (1988): 413–19; Gerald L. Klerman, "The Psychiatric Patient's Right to Effective Treatment: Implications of *Osheroff v. Chestnut Lodge*," ibid., 147 (1990): 409–18; Alan A. Stone, "Law, Science, and Psychiatric Malpractice: A Response to Klerman's Indictment of Psychoanalytic Psychiatry," ibid., 419–27.

15. See Alan Stone, "Overview: The Right to Treatment—Comments on the Law and Its Impact," *American Journal of Psychiatry* 132 (1975): 1125–34.

16. Group for the Advancement of Psychiatry, *Report No. 79* (November 1970): 662; Bruce C. Vladeck, *Unloving Care: The Nursing Home Tragedy* (New York, 1980).

17. General Accounting Office, *Returning the Mentally Disabled to the Community*, 81; Ann B. Johnson, *Out of Bedlam: The Truth About Deinstitutionalization* (New York, 1990), 94–5; Dorothy P. Rice, S. Kelman, L. S. Miller, and S. Dunmeyer, *The Economic Costs of Alcohol and Drug Abuse and Mental Illness: 1985* (San Francisco, 1990), 76, 108, 110.

18. Public Law 92–603, *U.S. Statutes at Large*, 86:1329–1492 (October 30, 1972); Johnson, *Out of Bedlam*, 96–9. See also Edward D. Berkowitz, *Disabled Policy: America's Programs for the Handicapped* (New York, 1987).

19. The claim that the massive decline in the number of inpatients at state mental hospitals began with the development of the psychotropic drugs in the 1950s in simply not substantiated by the data. See especially William Gronfein, "Incentives and Intentions in Mental Health Policy: A Comparison of the Medicaid and Community Mental Health Programs," *Journal of Health and Social Behavior* 26 (1985): 192–206.

20. NIMH, *Mental Health United States, 1990*, ed. Ronald W. Manderscheid and Mary A. Sonnenschein (Washington, D.C., 1990), 31, 158, 160; David Mechanic and D. A. Rochefort, "Deinstitutionalization: An Appraisal of Reform," *Annual Review of Sociology* 16 (1990): 308–13; Joseph P. Morrissey, "The Changing Role of the Public Mental Hospital," in *Handbook on Mental Health Policy*, ed. D.A. Rochefort, 311–38; Howard Goldman, C. A. Taube, D. A. Regier, and M. Witkin, "The Multiple Functions of the State Mental Hospital," *American Journal of Psychiatry* 140 (1983): 296–300.

21. See especially Henry Santiestevan, *Deinstitutionalization: Out of Their Beds and into*

*the Streets*, a pamphlet published by the American Federation of State, County and Municipal Employees in 1975 and reprinted in the *American Journal of Psychiatry* 132 (1975): 95–137.

22. Howard H. Goldman. N. H. Adams, and C. A. Taube, "Deinstitutionalization: The Data Demythologized," *Hospital & Community Psychiatry* 34 (1983): 129–34; Jon E. Guderman and Miles F. Shore, "Beyond Deinstitutionalization: A New Class of Facilities for the Mentally Ill," *New England Journal of Medicine* 311 (1984): 832–35.
The persistence of the state hospital, as a matter of fact, is mirrored in a variety of data. Between 1969 and 1983 expenditures for state hospital systems increased in current dollars from $1.8 to $5.5 billion (in constant dollars there was a slight decline from $1.8 to $1.7 billion). In 1986 there were 286 state and county hospitals, eleven more than in 1955 but down from the high of 334 in 1973. See NIMH, *Mental Health, United States, 1987*. ed. Ronald W. Manderscheid and S. A. Barrett (Washington, D.C., 1987), 56–57, and Mechanic and Rochefort, "Deinstitutionalization," 308ff.

23. Courtenay M. Harding, George W. Brooks, Takamaru Ashikaga, John S. Strauss, and Alan Breier, "The Vermont Longitudinal Study of Persons with Severe Mental Illness, I: Methodology, Study Sample, and Overall Status 32 Years Later," and "The Vermont Longitudinal Study of Persons with Severe Mental Illness, II: Long Term Outcome of subjects Who Retrospectively Met *DSM-III* Criteria for Schizophrenia," *American Journal of Psychiatry* 144 (1986): 718–35.

24. Esso Leete, "The Treatment of Schizophrenia: A Patient's Perspective," *Hospital & Community Psychiatry* 38 (1987): 486–91; Sarah Rosenfield, "Factors Contributing to the Subjective Quality of Life of the Chronic Mentally Ill," *Journal of Health and Social Behavior* 33 (1992):299–315.
In an as yet unpublished study, Allan Horwitz interviewed 142 individuals on the threshold of release from a mental hospital. Not a single individual expressed a preference for institutionalization; all looked forward to resuming their lives in the community. Allan Horwitz, personal communication, June, 1993.

25. U. S. Bureau of the Census, *Historical Statistics of the United States, Colonial Times to 1970* (2 vols.: Washington, D.C. 1975), I, 49; Kramer, *Psychiatric Services and the Changing Institutional Scene, 1950–1985*, 46; Leona L. Bachrach, "Young Adult Chronic Patients: An Analytical Review of the Literature," *Hospital & Community Psychiatry* 33 (1982): 189–97.

26. Bert Pepper, H. Ryglewicz, and M. C. Kirschner, "The Uninstitutionalized Generation: A New Breed of Psychiatric Patient," in *The Young Adult Chronic Patient*, ed. Pepper and Ryglewicz (San Francisco, 1982), 5. See also Bachrach, "The Homeless Mentally Ill and Mental Health Services: An Analytical Review of the Literature," in *The Homeless Mentally Ill: A Task Force Report of the American Psychiatric Association*, ed. H. Richard Lamb (Washington, D.C., 1984), 11–53.

27. Bachrach, "The Concept of Young Adult Chronic Psychiatric Patients: Questions from a Research Perspective," *Hospital & Community Psychiatry* 35 (1984): 574; Lamb, "Deinstitutionalization and the Homeless Mentally Ill," in *The Homeless Mentally Ill*, 65.

28. Pamela J. Fischer and W. R. Breakey, "The Epidemiology of Alcohol, Drug, and Mental Disorders Among Homeless Persons," *American Psychologist* 46 (1991): 1115–28; Deborah L. Dennis, J. C. Buckner, F. R. Lipton, and I. S. Levine, "A Decade of Research and Services for Homeless Mentally Ill Persons," *ibid.*, 1129–38; Dennis McCarty, M. Algeriou, R. B. Huebner, and B. Lubran, "Alcoholism, Drug Abuse, and the Homeless," *ibid.*, 1139–48; Robert E. Drake, F. C. Osher, and M. A. Wallach, "Homelessness and Dual Diagnosis," *ibid.*, 1149–58; Ron Jemelka, E. Trupin, and J. A. Chiles, "The Mentally Ill in Prisons: A Review," *Hospital & Community Psychiatry* 40 (1989): 481–91. See also *ibid.*, 43 (1992): 1253–54.

29. See Stuart R. Schwartz and S. M. Goldfinger, "The New Chronic Patient: Clinical Characteristics of an Emerging Subgroup," *Hospital & Community Psychiatry* 32 (1981): 473, and *Barriers to Treating the Chronic Mentally Ill*, ed. Arthur T. Meyerson (San Francisco, 1987).

30. Department of Health and Human Services, *Toward a National Plan for the Chronically Mentally Ill* (Washington, D.C., 1980).

31. Howard H. Goldman and A. A. Gattozzi, "Murder in the Cathedral Revisited: President Reagan and the Mentally Disabled," *Hospital & Community Psychiatry* 39 (1988): 505–09, and "Balance of Powers: Social Security and the Mentally Disabled, 1980–1985," *Milbank Quarterly* 66 (1988): 531–51.

32. In the late 1980s and early 1990s both television and the printed media highlighted two cases in New York of homeless mentally ill persons (Joyce Brown [more popularly known as Billy Boggs] and Larry Hogue). Descriptions of these cases can be found in Rael J. Isaac and V. A. Armat, *Madness in the Streets: How Psychiatry and the Law Abandoned the Mentally Ill* (New York, 1990), 256–60, 346–47

33. Pepper and Ryglewicz, *Young Adult Chronic Patient*, 121; John A. Talbott, "Deinstitutionalization: Avoiding the Disasters of the Past," *Hospital & Community Psychiatry* 30 (1979): 623; David Mechanic, "Correcting Misconceptions in Mental Health Policy: Strategies for Improved Care of the Seriously Mentally Ill," *Milbank Quarterly* 65 (1987): 203–30, and "Strategies for Integrating Public Mental Health Services," *Hospital & Community Psychiatry* 42 (1991): 797–801.

34. Richard C. Tessler and H. H. Goldman, *The Chronically Mentally Ill: Assessing Community Support Programs* (Cambridge, 1982); Chris Koyanagi and H. H. Goldman, "The Quiet Success of the National Plan for the Chronically Mentally Ill," *Hospital & Community Psychiatry* 42 (1991): 901; Koyanagi and Goldman, *Inching Forward: A Report on Progress Made in Federal Mental Health Policy in the 1980's* (Alexandria, Va., 1991), 55–6.

35. Richard C. Tessler, A. G. Bernstein, B. M. Rosen, and H. H. Goldman, "The Chronically Mentally Ill in Community Support Systems," *Hospital & Community Psychiatry* 33 (1982): 208–11; Koyanagi and Goldman, "The Quiet Success of the National Plan," 904.

36. For a review of the Madison model see Kenneth S. Thompson, E. E. H. Griffith, and P. J. Leaf, "A Historical Review of the Madison Model of Community Care," and Mark Olfson, "Assertive Community Treatment: An Evaluation of the Experimental Evidence," *Hospital & Community Psychiatry* 41 (1990): 625–41. See also Leonard I. Stein, ed., *Innovative Community Mental Health Programs* (San Francisco, 1992).

37. See Olfson, "Assertive Community Treatment," 640.

38. Miles F. Shore and M. D. Cohen, "The Robert Wood Johnson Foundation Program on Chronic Mental Illness: An Overview," Goldman, A. F. Lehman, J. P. Morrissey, S. J. Newman, R. G. Frank, and D. M. Steinwachs, "Design for the National Evaluation of the Robert Wood Johnson Program on Chronic Mental Illness," and Goldman, Morrissey, and M. S. Ridgely, "Form and Function of Mental Health Authorities at RWJ Foundation Program Sites: Preliminary Observations," all in *Hospital & Community Psychiatry* 41 (1990): 1212–30; David Mechanic, "Strategies for Integrating Public Mental Health Services," 797–801.

39. Koyanagi and Goldman, "The Quiet Success of the National Plan," 904.

40. The concept of "impure science" has been used by Arthur Silverstein in his *Pure Politics and Impure Science: The Swine Flu Affair* (Baltimore, 1981).

DAVID ROSNER AND GERALD MARKOWITZ

# Hospitals, Insurance, and the American Labor Movement: The Case of New York in the Postwar Decades

In the summer of 1989, an extended strike by the various "Baby Bell" telephone companies, including those of New York, Massachusetts, California, and thirteen other states in the Northeast, Midwest, and West Coast, brought to public attention the importance of health and hospital insurance to the nation's workers. In what the *Los Angeles Times* headline proclaimed was a "Phone Strike Centered on the Issue of Health Care," workers at NYNEX, Pacific Bell, and Bell Atlantic went out on strike over management's insistence that the unions pay a greater portion of their hospital insurance premiums.[1] In contrast to their willingness to grant wage concessions throughout most of the 1980s, the unions and their membership struck to protect what was once considered a "fringe" benefit of union membership. What had been a trivial cost to companies in the 1940s and 1950s had risen to 7.9 percent of payroll in 1984 and 13.6 percent by 1989.[2] Unable to control the industry that had formed around hospitals, doctors, drug companies, and insurance, portions of the labor movement redefined its central mission: the fringes of the previous forty years were now central concerns. In the words of one local president engaged in the bitter communication workers strike: " 'It took us 40 years of collective bargaining' to reach a contract in which the employer contributed [substantially to] the costs of health care, 'and now they want to go in one fell swoop backward.' "[3]

Historically, the role of labor in shaping the insurance and hospital industry in the half a century since World War II has barely been investigated. In large measure, historians who have studied this central institution and the critical changes in hospital finance that have shaped it have seen the institution as shaped primarily by policy and professional interests. The most sophisticated analyses of hospital evolution, for example, have detailed the growth of private and voluntary insurance in the postwar years and battles around national health insurance, but have rarely considered the underlying issues among the working communities that have framed the debate.

In this article we will briefly explore the evolution of labor interest in health and hospital care in the period before World War II and then trace the growing contention between management and labor and the labor and voluntary insurance agencies in the years following the war. While much of the analysis is applicable to other communities around the country and to a variety of other labor organizations, here we will focus specifically on New York City, and the contention that arose about the appropriate relationship among what has been until recently the dominant voluntary insurer, Blue Cross, the labor movement, and hospitals.

The history of the relationship of insurance and hospitals may be presented as the story of administrators, planners, and physicians. Yet the history of Blue Cross reveals an interaction between a rapidly changing social, political, intellectual, and medical environment of New York City and the labor movement. In the early years of this century, a wildly uneven patchwork of fraternal, union, and commercial health insurance plans was organized in the city to provide a small measure of protection to its immigrant and working-class populations. But even before the Depression, the instability and inadequacy of these self-administered and small-scale insurance systems had become evident. At the same time, dramatic shifts in prevailing popular assumptions about what constituted "good" health protection reinforced the authority and legitimacy of larger, bureaucratized systems. By the late 1940s, therefore, large segments of the working population of the city turned to Blue Cross, an insurance system that promised greater stability, uniformity, and order.

In the post-Depression era, other forces served further to undermine remnants of the older popular systems of health insurance, thereby enhancing the position of large-scale insurance enterprises. On the one hand, the growing importance of the hospital as the major locus of care for greater and greater numbers of New Yorkers made centralized financing systems appear more efficient. On the other hand, the waning centrality of ethnicity in defining America's communities, the growing antipathy toward labor, and the growing conservatism of the national and local labor movements made fraternal and union-controlled systems unappealing to large portions of the city's population. During the Cold War, Blue Cross membership grew enormously in the city as literally millions of union members were provided with health insurance coverage. By 1960, nearly the entire unionized workforce in the New York City area was covered by Blue Cross insurance.[4]

We suggest that the growth of Blue Cross was closely linked to the conservatism of New York's labor movement in the Cold War years. Throughout the first half of this century, workers' health and safety had been a major point of conflict between labor and management. In the years following World War II, health and safety was abandoned as a critical labor issue. During these years health insurance and hospital-care programs replaced safety and health in labor's health agenda. We propose that health insurance, administered through nonprofit "third parties," was adopted by labor unions during the 1950s as a means of avoiding conflicts with management. Bitter political disputes that raged during the Depression over union recognition, the speed of work, the safety of equipment, and the dangers of new chemicals were replaced by apolitical bargaining over wages and welfare benefits.

The growth of "third-party" insurance for New York's workers coincided with some of the most dramatic breakthroughs in the history of medical science. The development of a wide variety of antibiotic therapies, psychotropic drugs, and polio vaccines in the 1940s and 1950s was seen as proof of science's ability to conquer disease. During the 1950s, health propaganda and popular images of disease taught that disease was an objective condition, produced by germs or viruses, not by working conditions or management oppression. These "natural" agents appeared to strike arbitrarily and without cause outside one's own individual behavior. Institutions and professionals, outside the class-bound environment of work, now defined disease in scientific and objective terms. The different conceptions of workplace health and safety were manifested in the institutions that workers and organized labor developed to protect themselves from the ravages of disease. In the early twentieth century, when workers saw disease as a reflection of class and social conflict, it was essential for laborers themselves to organize and control fraternal and union health plans. By the 1950s, objective "third parties" were appropriate agents for insurance administration. The history of insurance can be understood as a reflection of a fundamental shift in labor's definition of health itself.

# The Early Twentieth-Century Worker and the Significance of Health Care

Labor historians have enriched our understanding of the effect of changing work processes on the lives of common and skilled laborers, organizing efforts of the American Federation of Labor and Congress of Industrial Organizations, and, most recently, the relationship between life on the job and life in the community. Yet there has been little effort to trace the impact of changing labor processes on the length of life or the degree of disability that has deeply affected the everyday experience of the American working class. Nor has there been much attention paid to the enormous political and organizational energy exerted by working-class groups to seek methods of protection. During the early years of the century, unsafe and poisonous conditions, unguarded machinery, and unregulated conditions created an environment that was often equated with the risks of warfare. As one observer noted in 1907, "To the unprecedented prosperity" of industrial production, "there is a seamy side of which little is said. Thousands of wage earners, men, women and children [are] caught in the machinery of our record breaking production and turned out cripples. Other thousands [are] killed outright." He went on to say that it was impossible to estimate the suffering caused by industrialism. "How many there [are] none can say exactly, for we [are] too busy making our record breaking production to count the dead."[5] Others editorialized on the "frightful increase in the number of casualties of all kinds in this country during the last two or three years. . . . A greater number of people are killed every year by so-called accidents than are killed in many wars of considerable magnitude." By the early years of this century, muckrakers and laborers alike were well aware of "how cheap human life has become under American conditions."[6] In addition, tuberculosis and silicosis, lung diseases that ravaged industrial populations in New York and elsewhere, were understood by laborers to be directly related to employment. Jewish clothing workers struck in 1910, before the famous Triangle Shirtwaist fire, demanding a "sanitary" commission to inspect garment shops. German bakers, suffering from "bakers' disease," demanded that every loaf of bread bear a bakers' union label so that consumers would know that it was baked under hygienic conditions.[7]

The very intensification of work led to a decline in the health status of specific groups of workers. There was a general improvement in health status for the American population as a whole. But the devastating experience of certain groups of workers forced the political system to respond with legislation, however conservative. The passage of workers' compensation legislation in the various states between 1911 and 1920 reflects the attention of labor and capital alike to the impact of unsafe working conditions on the larger society. It is essential to understand that the very life of working-class communities was shaped by the reality of long-term disease, disability and, death, and the history of labor-management relations can be understood in part as a struggle over the health and safety of the workforce. Increases in productivity were often paid for in shorter lives, greater physical suffering, and increased dependence and hardship for family members and communities:

> If employers thought of the pace of work in terms of the quantity and quality of their factories' output, workers thought of it in terms of their own health and longevity. . . . [A]ll [workers] knew that after the average man passed his mid thirties, the amount of working time he lost to sickness and injuries rose sharply. Employers could always find new workers, but each worker had only one body and one life.[8]

## Health Care Among the Laboring Class

Especially in New York City, immigrant workers and their dependents developed extensive, if inadequate, institutional infrastructures to insulate themselves from the ravages of industrial change in the early decades of the century. Sick and benevolent societies, fraternal lodges, and landsmanshaft groups were critical responses to capitalism's onslaught on labor's health and well-being. In New York City, literally thousands of "lodges" arose that, for a few pennies a month, provided medical services to its members.[9] In one study of fourteen fraternal societies and eleven trade unions, it was found that in these twenty-five organizations alone nearly 125,000 persons were provided with some form of health insurance.[10] In another study 22 percent of a sample had health insurance through one of these plans. Death-benefit societies were formed through a multitude of immigrant organizations. "It is probably true that a large proportion of the workers of the newer immigrant groups are insured in agencies and organizations providing health insurance than native and older immigrant workers," one observer noted. "This . . . appears to be due to the fact that immigrant fraternal and beneficial societies are closely connected with religious and racial organizations . . . which exercise a considerable influence for religious and racial solidarity."[11] In the coming years, political organizations such as the Socialist Party and, in the 1930s, the Communist Party as well would support death and sickness plans for their members.[12] By and large they were small plans that had uneven coverage, based on insufficient indemnity plans and inadequate financial reserves. However, they were significant in that, outside the systems developed for the destitute, they provided the only means of protection for the city's largely working-class population.[13] Similarly, union health and welfare plans were an outgrowth of the centrality of accidents, death, and disease in the life of working-class Americans. They reached a relatively small number of workers since only union members were eligible for coverage. Further, there were limitations on benefits, women were often excluded, and, for the great masses of low-wage workers, premiums even in the low-cost fraternal plans were prohibitive.[14]

In the absence of any government and with only a few proprietary alternatives to look toward, communities of immigrants were thrown on their own meager resources to provide themselves with protection. Even when reformers advocated for compulsory health insurance, however, organized labor rejected the notion out of hand. Their long-standing distrust of both management and government led the American Federation of Labor, especially, to reject reliance on the state and instead adopt a policy of self-reliance that would last through the Great Depression.[15] During the Wilson administration, when labor was first brought in to the governing Democratic coalition, Samuel Gompers, president of the AF of L, consistently attacked compulsory social and health insurance as a "paternalistic and repugnant" form of government involvement in the lives of workers. Gompers asserted that "workers had to rely on their own economic power rather than the state," and he worried "that a government insurance system would weaken unions by denying them the function of providing them social benefits."[16]

## The Original Two Parties to the Health and Welfare Debate

After wages and hours, the provision of health and welfare benefits was central to labor and management struggles over workplace control. Both management and organized labor sought to sponsor programs aimed at providing health and welfare benefits to workers. Beginning in the early nineteenth century, paternalist textile-mill owners in Lowell, Massachusetts, initiated what became known as the "Lowell Plan," in which young girls recruited from the countryside to work in the mills were provided with dormitory housing, religious training, and community services.[17] Later in the century, other corporations, most notably railroads and logging and mining companies, contracted with physicians to provide minimal health services to workers.

Management often portrayed its various health and welfare programs as a paternalist response to the felt needs of the workforce. But
most union representatives saw them as tools for undermining worker
and trade-union solidarity.[18] Management-initiated programs were seen
as attempts to make workers dependent upon the goodwill of the company, thereby creating a nonmilitant, acquiescent labor force. At best,
workers saw the programs as inadequate and temporary. At worst, they
were perceived as tools in management's attempts to cover up the dangers of the workplace and to hide deaths or disability caused by unsafe
and unclean working environments. Because of the distrust of
management's motivations, workers and unions themselves organized
health and benefit societies, self-insurance programs, disability compensation, old-age pensions, and even clinics and hospitals.[19]

By the mid-twentieth century, there were well over two hundred group health plans in the country. Of these, two-thirds were
organized through specific industries either by employers, employees, or joint action.[20] Among the more important employee-spon-
sored plans were the Hospital and Medical Care Program of the
United Mine Workers of America Welfare and Retirement Fund;
the Labor Health Institute of Saint Louis (Local 688, International
Brotherhood of Teamsters, AFL); the Health Institute of the United
Auto Workers, CIO, Detroit; the Union Health Center, International Ladies' Garment Workers' Union, AFL, Boston; the AFL
Medical Service Plan of Philadelphia, and the Sidney Hillman
Medical Center of the Male Apparel Industry of Philadelphia
(Amalgamated Clothing Workers, CIO).[21] All these programs, especially those affiliated with the United Mine Workers, the Amalgamated, and the ILGWU, grew out of labor's interest in providing their members with alternatives to management-sponsored
health programs. Many would become focal points of controversy
in the mid-1950s.

In New York City, unions followed a similar pattern of health-
center organization. The ILGWU, a union organized and led by
skilled immigrant workers, and born out of early twentieth-century struggles over workplace safety and health, organized its own
health clinic as early as 1913. But other unions, most notably the
Hotel Trades Council and the Amalgamated Clothing Workers, a
union with a long socialist tradition, organized their clinic and
health plans in the early 1950s.

## The Abandonment of the Ideology of Self-Reliance

The 1930s are a critical period for understanding labor's changing attitude toward what labor leaders considered their long support for "voluntary"—that is, union controlled—health and welfare programs. During this time, under the financial pressures of the Depression and a growing accord with the New Deal administration in Washington, labor considered new models for the provision of health and welfare services to its members.

During the Depression, organized labor faced innumerable problems as millions of its workers found themselves unemployed and dependent. Also during the Depression, the long-standing supremacy of the American Federation of Labor was challenged by the organizing drives in heavy industry spurred by the Congress of Industrial Organizations. With the development of the CIO in the second half of the decade, organized labor faced an internal split in its ranks. It also found itself divided over the long-held position concerning self-reliance. For the first time in labor history, significant sectors of organized labor looked to the national government for support and protection and sometimes even for advice. In the context of the Depression, as the new CIO became deeply involved in organizing millions of workers, significant portions of the labor movement supported governmental programs in the area of social welfare, protective legislation, and even hours and wages. Walter Reuther and the UAW, along with other leaders of the CIO, even went so far as to endorse various calls for national health insurance.[22]

This was a dramatic break with the traditions of the AF of L regarding self-reliance in the development of critical labor programs. Here, labor for the first time accepted the notion of outside or "third-party" intervention. This would prove important in the more conservative postwar years as Blue Cross emerged as a viable, nongovernmental, and nonmanagement insurance alternative.

## The Birth of Blue Cross

It was during this period of labor unrest and economic depression that Blue Cross was first organized by the hospitals of New York City. During the Depression, the inability of patients to pay for their hospital care had forced many institutions to shut down and curtail services. In response to this crisis, the United Hospital Fund, an organization that represented the city's nongovernment hospitals, organized this nonprofit insurance plan as a means of providing hospitals with needed funds and providing patients with the security of knowing that, in case of sickness, their hospital costs would be covered. Its early advertising boasted that for "pennies a day" New Yorkers could be protected from the insecurity caused by the costs associated with illness. Originally called the "3-cents a day plan," Blue Cross began signing up members individually. But within a few months it began to sign up "groups" of workers through a payroll-deduction plan: management automatically deduced Blue Cross charges from a worker's check.

A number of factors account for labor's growing interest in Blue Cross in the 1930s and 1940s. First, the plan was nonprofit and not associated with private insurance companies. As such, Blue Cross was untainted by long-standing objections to private insurance. Second, Blue Cross was closely associated with a hospital system that still wore a mantle of charity and social service. Third, Blue Cross sought to portray itself as a "community" plan that was to be directed by community needs. Fourth, Blue Cross was not connected either to management or to government, the two shibboleths of the more conservative American Federation of Labor leaders.[23] Another important factor affecting labor was the passage in 1935 of the National Labor Relations Act and specifically its mandate for management and labor to engage in collective bargaining. While collective bargaining had always existed in industrial and labor relations, the passage of the act greatly expanded the number of industries that reached agreements on any number of management-labor issues. The development of "nonpartisan" or "third-party" insurance schemes at the same time that collective bargaining was made the law of the land gave tremendous impetus to both labor's and management's interest in this new approach. Finally, during World War II, wage raises were restricted and many unions turned to expanding fringe benefits. For income tax purposes, "legitimate insurance plans for employees could be deducted from gross income as a proper business expense," which "stimulated the growth of union health and welfare programs under collective bargaining."[24]

Despite the apparent congruence of interest between labor and Blue Cross nationally, locally, at least, the relationship was problematic. In part, this arose from the complexity of medical-labor politics in New York during the 1930s. During the Depression the medical community was deeply involved in organizing the profession around a set of national and local issues that sometimes put them in conflict with organized labor. The national issues that aroused heated interest among physicians was the threat of compulsory health insurance. The local issue was the reorganization of the Workmen's Compensation system in New York State and the desire of the local medical community to gain some measure of control over its administration and, therefore, over its fee schedule.[25] But it was over the issue of compulsory health insurance where the tentative alliance reached between labor and management disintegrated. Medicine was unalterably opposed to any form of compulsory coverage, while labor representatives were divided. Fearing that a plank for national health insurance might be included in the Social Security Act, organized medicine sought to join with labor "in opposition to compulsory health insurance."[26] One leading American Federation of Labor representative from New York State broke with organized medicine specifically on the issue of self-reliance:

> I am confident there is no serious disagreement between organized labor and organized medicine on the desirability . . . of workers' receiving "sufficient compensation for their labor to enable them to provide themselves with the necessities of life, including reasonable compensation for needed medical care. . . . But pray, what will the workers do pending this ideal state of affairs? What of our millions of unemployed, our millions of partially employed, our millions of underpaid employees? I can understand well the apprehensions of organized medicine in the proposal for compulsory health insurance, but what has organized medicine done . . . to enhance the enrichment and prevention of impoverishment of the masses? I have yet to hear of any important group or outstanding individual in the medical profession to align itself or himself with the cause of organized labor and publicly plead for that which you so eloquently term as essential to prevent the regimentation of the medical profession.[27]

In the depths of the Depression, even the most conservative elements of organized labor, the AFL leadership, questioned the ability of labor to provide for itself. While still opposed to compulsory health insurance, conservative labor leaders were open to new possibilities. Blue Cross, as a nonmanagement and nongovernmental health insurance alternative, met the traditional AF of L objection to government or management control while appeasing the more radical elements of the CIO, who wanted governmental provision of health insurance.[28] Within a decade, labor began to seek an accommodation with Blue Cross and within two decades workers become the backbone of Blue Cross membership.

Throughout the Depression and World War II, many unions held to the belief that self-reliance and self-protection were their ultimate goals in health and welfare programs. Some leftist unions such as District 65 of the UAW developed their own clinic and insurance plans.[29] Yet most attempted to work within the social and political realities that existed during the Depression and the war. The United Auto Workers laid out the fundamental problem faced even by progressive unions. While a "union-owned-and-operated hospital or medical center" was clearly preferable to Blue Cross, this was unattainable at the time. The union maintained that "until such a time [as] the union is in a position to realistically contemplate construction of its own hospital and medical service institutions," it was necessary to work with Blue Cross. "In short, the union is simply using the best available institutions dealing in hospital and medical care, to obtain immediate benefits for our people, and to prepare our union for the anticipated day when it will be able to organize its own plan for health protection."[30]

In New York, several unions joined Blue Cross in the mid-1940s. Among the unions were the Pocketbook Workers, the Furniture Workers, the Painters, the Optical Workers, the Retail Drug Store Employees (soon to emerge as representatives of the hospital workers), the Chefs, Cooks, and Pastrycooks, waiters and waitresses, taxi workers, cigar workers, fur and leather workers, office and professional workers, cemetery workers, meat choppers, and others.[31] But very quickly tensions between Blue Cross and labor began to rise as their agendas came into conflict. In March 1943, the Greater New York Industrial Union Council, which represented most of the leftist unions in the city, wrote to Louis Pink, president of Blue Cross of New York, complaining about the lack of progress "in meeting some of the apparent shortcomings of the [Blue Cross] plan."[32] Three major issues emerged that initially led the city's unions to say that "they could not now recommend adoption of Blue Cross plan" to their membership. The first major issues was the lack of accountability of Blue Cross to the unions. The board of directors of Blue Cross was "composed predominantly of hospital and medical" people and lacked labor representation. They contended that labor could not endorse a plan when it had no voice in the management or control of the plan. Second, they objected to Blue Cross's apparent collusion with management. Blue Cross, seeking to increase membership, had appealed to employers suggesting that adoption of the Blue Cross contract "cost them nothing" because of the payroll-deduction plan. Labor complained that while management got credit for providing a health plan for its members, labor, not management, was footing the bill. Blue Cross, in contrast, was wary of allowing too much power to slip into the hands of labor. Louis Pink responded to the union demand for board membership by stating that "there were no vacancies on the Board at present." He proposed instead a labor advisory committee.[33]

## The Growing Dependency of Labor and Blue Cross

Despite the larger policy issues that separated Blue Cross and the unions, there were significant gains in union participation in the years following World War II. One example of the developing interrelationship is the case of the Pocketbook Workers Union and its negotiations with Blue Cross regarding the collection of members' fees. In 1946, shortly after the end of the war, the executive director of the union wrote Louis Pink a detailed memo explaining the problems that his workers would face in subscribing to Blue Cross through a payroll-deduction scheme. He specifically noted that his membership, like the membership of many of New York's unions, was not highly concentrated in one or a few large plants. Rather, his union represented workers who were scattered throughout the city. The members worked in plants, warehouses, sweatshops, and lofts often "employing less than [ten] workers in many shops." Only a limited number of shops employed more than one hundred workers. The problems for his workforce were numerous, especially when the protection under the Blue Cross plan depended upon unreliable small businessmen who failed to pay premiums necessary to maintain employees' benefits. Few of these shops, he held, had the capabilities to maintain up-to-date records of employment and coverage. He suggested that any success was really a product of the degree of union control over administration and that such control should be increased.[34] From labor's point of view, the central administration of benefits should come through the union itself in order to protect workers from inefficient, uncaring, and sometimes dishonest businessmen. Unlike many other communities throughout the nation that were dominated by one or two big companies, the New York labor force was employed in thousands of small shops, factories, and service industries. The centralized, bureaucratic nature of Blue Cross had a special appeal to the city's labor union leaders.

In New York City the event that cemented the bond between Blue Cross and the unions was the decision in 1946 by the municipal government to pay for half "the total cost of . . . [medical and] hospital care for municipal employees who elect to enroll in [HIP and] . . . Blue Cross."[35] Nationally, the settlement of the steel strike of 1950 spurred the development of Blue Cross as well.

This expansion of Blue Cross occurred within the context of massive political upheavals within New York's labor and liberal establishments. During the last years of the Depression and World War II, the American Labor Party emerged as a powerful force in New York City. Originally organized in 1936 "by leaders of New York's heavily Jewish garment trades to provide a mechanism for supporting Franklin Roosevelt and Fiorello LaGuardia," the party was a coalition of left-wing and liberal politicians and unions. The party's importance in local politics can be measured by LaGuardia's margin of victory in 1937 and 1941 by votes cast on the ALP line. After World War II, the Cold War accelerated and the New Deal coalition between liberals and the left dissolved. Within the ALP, liberal labor leaders such as David Dubinsky, president of the International Ladies Garment Workers Union, and Alex Rose, president of the Hat, Cap, and Milliners Union, bolted from the party, charging that it was dominated and controlled by the American Communist Party. In its stead, these important New York labor leaders organized the Liberal party, which had a major political impact on city politics and became tied to the anticommunist labor movement in the city. In contrast to the ALP, which had been organized around Italian, Jewish, and black political clubs in the city, the Liberals were much more centrally controlled and appealed primarily to the Jewish trade unions and the middle class.[36] With these political challenges to the city's left-wing labor leaders and the passage of the Taft-Hartley Act in 1947, the mainstream of the union movement in New York moved farther to the right. Incipient critiques of Blue Cross that had been developed by the left-wing union leaders associated with the Greater New York Industrial Union Council were muted. Thus, by the early 1950s, some long-standing concerns of unions regarding the role of third parties in managing welfare and health benefits were submerged under the weight of more pressing and practical matters. Especially in the antilabor environment of the postwar years, labor did not seek to press its traditional goal of self-reliance and independence. Furthermore, by taking the administration of health benefits out of the traditional arena of labor-management disputes and placing them in the hands of ostensibly neutral and voluntaristic associations, a source of friction between labor and management was avoided. The impact on Blue Cross was immense. In the words of one observer, "In place of precedents, we are now watching a parade . . . a mass migration," of unions into Blue Cross.[37]

## Growing Tensions and the Reaffirmation of Self-Reliance

For a time, this accord among labor, management, hospitals, and the Blue Cross flourished. But in the late 1950s, long-term underlying questions regarding the control of Blue Cross began to undermine the tentative relationship that was being built. The tension over self-reliance reemerged within the labor movement as hospitals themselves actively worked to shed the remnants of their older, paternalistic practices by raising hospital charges, decreasing the length of stays for patients, and altering hiring and management practices. As hospitals changed, they became the focus of union organizing drives as it became apparent to union leaders in the city that the hospital workforce was among the poorest paid and least protected. Led by Leon Davis, a left-unionist who headed Local 1199 of the Pharmacy Union, an active organizing campaign began in the mid-1950s. Because of its close association with the city's hospitals and its role as the hospitals' financing agent, Blue Cross was perceived by some left-wing union leaders as a tool of hospital management. Blue Cross lost its image as a "third party" above the fray of labor-management discord.[38] Now it was directly involved in labor-management conflicts on the side of management. The growing demands for rate increases from Blue Cross in the late 1950s highlighted by unions' awareness of the enormous financial burden on their membership undercut Blue Cross's neutrality. By the end of the decade, a growing number of New York's labor leaders viewed Blue Cross, the hospitals, and industry as co-conspirators in the exploitation of workers.

The early warning of the coming breakdown in union-Blue Cross relations came in 1956 at a meeting sponsored by the Central Trades and Labor Council and the Greater New York Fund. At this time, one lone voice, the left-wing leaders of District 65 of the UAW, called on unions to pay greater attention to what they considered the huge reserves held by Blue Cross.[39] But the fight was really joined in the fall of 1957, when Blue Cross asked the Insurance Commissioner of New York State to approve a 40 percent raise in the rates charged its members. Even the accord reached in the early 1950s between liberal labor leaders, Blue Cross, and the hospitals broke down. In the words of the *New York Times* headline, "City and Labor are Against It, Hospitals in Favor."[40] In this early skirmish between labor and hospitals, two major themes emerged in the arguments against a rate increase. First, union representatives argued that the "crisis" in Blue Cross's financing was a technical accounting problem that could be simply addressed by reorganizing the books. Harold Faggen, an accountant for District 65, argued that "by slightly altered bookkeeping Blue Cross should show a net profit of more than two million rather than a loss for the last year."[41] Second, it was argued that "commercial thinking and standards were creeping into Blue Cross policy making" and that Blue Cross was little more than a representative of the hospital industry's interests. Liberal representatives of the labor movement such as Walter Eisenberg, economic consultant to the Central Trades and Labor Council of Greater New York and the New York City CIO Council, suggested that "the fundamental idea underlying Blue Cross has been and should be that of a joint user and supplier vehicle for the provision of pre-paid hospital service, rather than a non-profit producer's cooperative run for the primary purpose of stabilizing an ever-larger portion of the income of the suppliers, that is, the hospitals." Echoing the historic interest of organized labor in controlling the administration of health benefits, Eisenberg went on to demand that Blue Cross reorganize its board so that fifty percent of its members would be drawn from labor.[42] This union analysis struck a responsive chord among the liberal establishment throughout the city. Michael M. Davis, a renowned elder statesman of health-care policy and then chairman of the executive committee of the Committee of the Nation's Health, warned that "such policies may cause organized labor . . . to turn away from Blue Cross and seek other forms of hospitalization insurance."[43]

The *New York Times* expanded on this theme that Blue Cross specifically in New York was violating the public trust.[44] A few months later Blue Cross, citing increased costs and the fact that their rates had not been increased since May 1, 1952, applied for an increase of about 40 percent.[45] Shortly thereafter, the State Superintendent of Insurance tried to resolve the differences between labor and Blue Cross by granting a rate increase of 22.3 percent.[46]

For nearly a year Blue Cross avoided requests for new rate increases, and for nearly a year labor avoided directly challenging the Blue Cross organization. But it is clear that tensions between important elements in the labor movement and Blue Cross were great and on the verge of emerging again. In an attempt to forestall such conflict, Blue Cross decided to appoint four new directors, three of whom were drawn from the ranks of organized labor.[47] But this attempt to give labor a greater voice was largely offset by other changes on the board. Recognizing that a major fight with labor was brewing over both Blue Cross and the role of organized labor within the hospitals themselves, the United Hospital Fund, representing sixty-six voluntary hospitals throughout the city, decided in May 1959 to exercise its statutory right to appoint twenty-one of the thirty members of the Blue Cross board. At the board of directors meeting in June 1959, the United Hospital Fund "placed seven new members who subscribed to its views on the Blue Cross Board of Directors and obtained reelection for 10 backers already on the Board." As the *New York Times* reported, the effect was that "the United Hospital Fund exercised its long-unused voting control power yesterday to assert its right of parentage over the [Blue Cross]."[48] Simultaneous with these changes in board membership, Blue

Cross decided to ask for another increase in its rates of 34.2 percent.[49]

In order to understand the coming storm of protest from labor and the rapidly unfolding events of the coming year, we need to take a step back and look at labor's relationship to the broader hospital industry during the late 1950s and specifically at the labor organizing drives that occurred. At the same time that the controversy over Blue Cross rate requests was unfolding, labor was engaged in a bitter and prolonged conflict with the voluntary hospitals as Leon Davis and Local 1199 sought to organize hospital workers for the first time. In 1957, Davis began the campaign to gain recognition for his union from Montefiore Hospital. Between December 1957 and August 1958, Local 1199 signed up a majority of Montefiore's workers, and in March 1959 the union negotiated its first contract with Martin Cherkasky, the head of that hospital. Shortly thereafter, 3,500 workers struck for forty-six days at the city's major voluntary hospitals. This was a bitter and prolonged strike that created deep animosities not only between Local 1199 and the Voluntary hospitals but also between organized labor and the hospital community.[50]

The significance of these two events for the future of labor-Blue Cross relations cannot be overestimated.[51] Bernard Greenberg, speaking for the New York State AFL-CIO, denounced the proposed increases as "excessive and unjustified." He linked the hearing over Blue Cross directly to the ongoing labor struggles when he said that the "increased rates given to hospitals in past years had not been reflected in higher wages for hospital workers."[52] The pressure from organized labor was so great that Mayor Robert Wagner publicly opposed the rate increase. In a page-one story, the New York Times reported that Wagner, citing the hospital strike, "has come out in opposition to Blue Cross application for rate increases." The Times continued that the mayor was upset that "only a small part of the proposed 34.2 percent increase would go to improving the distressingly low wage level of non-professional hospital workers."[53] While the results of these hearings were generally favorable to Blue Cross and the hospital industry, the rift this created between labor and Blue Cross was profound. Blue Cross became identified with a hospital industry that was rapidly losing legitimacy among important elements of the city's radical and liberal community.[54] The prevailing opinion of labor leaders was that "there was a startling identity between the hospitals and Blue Cross."[55] In the words of another observer, Blue Cross was emerging as "little more than a collection agency for the hospitals."[56]

The schism had become so severe that in the fall of 1959 the labor movement in New York set up a committee to study the feasibility of "using pension and welfare trust funds to build and operate hospitals and insurance programs for hospital and medical care."[57] Harry Van Arsdale Jr., president of the New York City Central Labor Council, "reported that 26 major New York unions were represented in a special committee on health and hospitals authorized by the council." He directly connected the formation of this committee to the bitter struggle to form the hospital union and the displeasure with Blue Cross administration and programs. Van Arsdale said, "We have sweat shop health standards in our hospitals. They underpay their staffs and underserve their patients. Yet, we are confronted with sky-rocketing costs that must be paid out of our Welfare Funds. . . . The program is under the control of big business and the hospital administrators. We intend to develop the program that will benefit all the people of the city."[58]

Despite the fact that the labor movement itself was divided and this proposal had little chance of being acted upon in the highly contentious and competitive New York labor scene, it is important to remember that Van Arsdale was voicing a long-standing belief that unions must be self-reliant if they are truly to protect their workers. From the very earliest days, unions have sought to develop their own health and welfare programs, sometimes organizing services for themselves as well. They had accepted Blue Cross in the postwar period as a temporary expedient but had come to rely on it as they became mutually dependent. By the late 1950s, it was probably wishful thinking on labor's part to believe that they could go outside the existing hospital and insurance system to establish their own institutions and payment mechanisms. But their desire to do so was not simply the result of a temporary pique. Union leaders rejected calls from the hospital and Blue Cross representatives that "we all work together on this."[59]

In the midst of this controversy, the "Trussell Report," a study conducted by members of Columbia University's School of Public Health to assess health planning in the state, was released. The report spoke to a number of issues that over the years had been causing friction between labor and Blue Cross. It recommended, for example, that the commission and regional councils be broadly representative and should include hospital and medical organizations, labor, industry, and local health and welfare departments. It acknowledged that more rate increases were inevitable not only because of constantly increasing hospital costs, but because the public had been receiving care "subsidized by underpaid hospital personnel." The report went on to urge Blue Cross to "overhaul their own Board of Directors to make them more representative." It specifically suggested that "not more than half the Board members be hospital trustees, physicians, hospital administrators or other professional personnel."[60] Ray Trussell, a professor at the university, recognized the significance of the ongoing struggle between labor and the hospital industry of New York as a significant factor in shaping the health-care system. Both in the report and in subsequent comments, he sought to link the crisis in the health system to the crisis in labor-industry relations. In calling for a restructuring of New York's health system, he and his staff sought to provide an alternative to what was then emerging as a severe Blue Cross-labor confrontation. He sought to create the conditions that would reestablish the credibility of Blue Cross as a reasonable "third party" in providing health insurance to the workforce. "The survival of Blue Cross is 'entirely up to labor and industry,' according to Dr. Ray E. Trussell," reported the *Times* in 1960. " 'They are the major decision-makers—they could pull the rug right out and then decide what other way to provide care,' he declared."[61]

By the 1950s, health care in New York had indeed become a major industry and this further eroded the power of organized labor. Federal support for medical school research, the development of health planning agencies, the provision of federal and state monies for the construction of hospitals, and a host of other changes had solidified the control that professionals, physicians, and insurance companies exerted over the system. Furthermore, the apparent successes of medical science had led many in the liberal labor community to believe that health issues were truly amenable to scientific intervention. In this context, labor had little chance to build an alternative set of institutions or develop a system of care that could bypass the more modern institutions.

Between 1900 and 1960, health services slowly moved out of the control of working-class or ethnic communities and became the province of the "third party," apparently objective institutions and professionals who not only provided different kinds of services but essentially defined health in a very different way. The story of labor's movement toward third-party insurance is part of a larger story in which health and health care was fundamentally redefined within the labor movement in New York and the United States. What was once a deeply political and class-based understanding became, by the late 1950s, an understanding rooted in the ideology of seemingly objective, neutral science and antilabor business.

*Baruch College and City University Graduate Center*
*John Jay College and City University Graduate Center*

Notes

This essay was adopted from Gerald Markowitz and David Rosner, "Seeking Common Ground: A History of Labor and Blue Cross," *Journal of Health Politics, Policy, and Law* 16 (Winter 1991): 695–718.

1. See "Phone Strike Centered on Issue of Health Care," *Los Angeles Times*, August 9, 1989, 1.

2. "Facing Off over Health Care Benefits," *Wall Street Journal*, August 11, 1989, B1.

3. "Phone Strike Centered on Issue of Health Care," *Los Angeles Times*, August 9, 1989, 1. See also "NYNEX Reaches Accord with Striking Unions," *Wall Street Journal*, November 14, 1989, A3.

4. The system of insurance coverage is even more complex than we have described here. For example, Blue Cross is a *hospital* insurance system paying solely for the "hotel" costs of a patient's hospital stay: bed, nursing, operating room, and other expenses. It does not pay for doctors' services and an entirely different insurance system covers most of the physicians' charges in the hospital. There are a host of other insurance companies, such as Blue Shield, Group Health Insurance, Aetna, and others.

5. Arthur B. Reeve, "The Death Roll of Industry," *Charities and the Commons* 17 (1907): 791.

6. Editorial, "Slaughter by Accident," *The Outlook* 78 (October 8, 1904): 359.

7. "A Strike for Clean Bread," *The Survey* 24 (June 18, 1910): 483–88; "Investigations have disclosed the Fact that Unhealthy and Poisonous Bread is Made in Non-Union Bake Shops," *The Woman's Label League Journal*, June 1913, 13; See also David Rosner and Gerald Markowitz, "The Early Movement for Occupational Safety and Health," in Judith Leavitt and Ronald Numbers, eds., *Sickness and Health in America*, 2d ed. (Madison, Wis., 1985), 507–21. See also David Rosner and Gerald Markowitz, eds., *Dying for Work: Workers' Safety and Health in Twentieth-Century America* (Bloomington, Ind., 1987), and Gerald Markowitz and David Rosner, eds., "*Slaves of the Depression: Workers' Letters about Life on the Job* (Ithaca, N.Y., 1987) for other work detailing the concerns of workers in safety and health in the twentieth century.

8. David Montgomery, *The Fall of the House of Labor* (New York, 1987), 192.

9. Anna Kalet, "Voluntary Health Insurance in New York City," *American Labor Legislation Review*, June 1916, 142, quoted in Edgar Sydenstricker, "Existing Agencies for Health Insurance in the United States," *Bulletin No. 212*, United States Department of Labor, Bureau of Labor Statistics, June 1917 (Washington, D.C., 1917), 430.

10. Anna Kalet, "Voluntary Health Insurance in New York City," *American Labor Legislation Review*, June 1916, 143. See also H. C. Chapin, *The Standard of Living in New York City* (New York, 1914), 192. In other studies of other communities, it was found during the early decades of the century that upward of 60 percent of workers had health insurance plans either through unions or lodges. See Sydenstricker, "Existing Agencies for Health Insurance," 433.

11. Sydenstricker, "Existing Agencies for Health Insurance," 434.

12. Some of these groups, such as the Workmen's Circle, closely affiliated with the Socialists, are still around today. The Communist party supported the International Workers' Order, which broke off from the Workmen's Circle in 1931. It was forced out of existence by the New York State Insurance Department in the early 1950s because of its affiliation with the Communist party. We are now tracing its history.

13. See Joan B. Trauner, "From Benevolence to Negotiation: Prepaid Health Care in San Francisco, 1850–1950," Ph.D. diss., University of California, San Francisco, 1977, for a detailed discussion of the centrality of the fraternal societies in the development of prepaid care in that city. See also Sydenstricker, "Existing Agencies for Health Insur-

ance," 469. Sydenstricker pointed out the difficulty of establishing accurate data on the overall importance of the fraternal and union plans and that few studies had been conducted to determine their adequacy. But he believed that existing data suggested that the percentage of workers who had some form of health insurance was large (432–34).

14. Sydenstricker, "Existing Agencies for Health Insurance," 471.

15. Arguments abound among historians as to the reasons that such organizations as the Knights of Labor or the American Federation of Labor opposed government involvement in social protection for workers and their dependents. Some maintain that American labor came to maturity well before the development of an effective central state, thereby creating a philosophy of independence. Others see American beliefs in laissez-faire and individualism as being the major influence; still others explain the opposition to government arising from the pluralistic nature of the membership in the American labor movement. See Michael Rogin, "Voluntarism: The Political Functions of an Anti-Political Doctrine," *Industrial and Labor Relations Review* 15 (July 1962): 521-35, cited in Gwendolyn Mink, *Old Labor and New Immigrants in American Political Development* (Ithaca, N.Y., 1986), chap. 1.

16. Paul Starr, "Transformation in Defeat: The Changing Objectives of National Health Insurance, 1915–1980," in Ronald L. Numbers, ed., *Compulsory Insurance: The Continuing Debate* (Westwood, Conn., 1982), 120.

17. Thomas Dublin, *Women at Work: The Transformation of Work and Community in Lowell, Massachusetts, 1826–1860* (New York, 1979).

18. Robert Asher, in Rosner and Markowitz, eds., *Dying for Work.*

19. Alan Derickson, *Workers' Health, Workers' Democracy: The Western Miners' Struggle, 1891-1925* (Ithaca,N.Y., 1988).

20. Margaret C. Klem, *Prepayment Medical Care Organizations*, Federal Security Agency, Social Security Board, Bureau of Research and Statistics, Bureau Memorandum Number 55, Washington, D.C., June 1944, 117.

21. Margaret C. Klem and Margaret F. McKiever, *Management and Union Health and Medical Programs*, U.S. Department of Health, Education, and Welfare, Public Health Service Publication no. 329, Washington, D.C., 1953.

22. We do not see it as our mandate to detail the history of medical practice and hospital care during the 1930s. Suffice it to say, the hospitals and physicians themselves were undergoing their own internal struggles over a range of economic and political issues. During the 1930s, the long-standing opposition of the American Medical Association to group practice, national and compulsory health insurance, and "contract" practice intensified and those advocating such programs were often accused of sponsoring "socialized" medicine. In all of its actions, the AMA sought to protect the autonomy of the practicing physician. The hospital community at this time was struggling through its own financial crisis as demand increased and income dwindled. Within this context, the first Blue Cross and Blue Shield plans were organized and they incorporated the concerns of the professionals who backed them. BC/BS promised a way out of the hospitals' and doctors' dilemma for, while providing a stable source of income to their members, they neither depended on government nor, in the words of the medical community of the 1930s, "sacrificed the autonomy" of the doctors.

On the local level, the medical community was involved in a number of parallel efforts to counter the growth of group practice and calls for national health insurance. But it was also involved in gaining a greater say in a program of direct interest to labor: the administration of workmen's compensation. It was here that labor and medicine had its most intense and involved relationship and where the first overtures from the medical community to labor first developed.

23. Before the development of Blue Cross programs, there was no insurance alternative for labor other than commercial insurance and unions were wary of commercial insurance because of their antagonistic encounters with insurance carriers in Workmen's Compensation proceedings.

24. Klem and McKiever, *Management and Union Health and Medical Programs*, 7.

25. Dan Fox notes the developing relationship between labor and organized medicine in the 1950s. It appears from this correspondence that, in New York at least, the relationship can be traced to the 1930s and the debates around Workmen's Compensation. See Daniel Fox, *Health Policies, Health Politics: The British and American Experience, 1911–1985* (Princeton, 1986), 195–97. See Woll to Elliott, May 1, 1934 (Elliott Papers, Blue Cross Archives; hereafter referred to as Elliott Papers). Also, Anon. to Arthur Bedell, May 3, 1934, Elliott Papers.

26. Elliott to Woll, January 31, 1935, Elliott Papers. "I am sure that it is the opinion of the men in medicine that the workman should receive sufficient compensation for their labors to enable them to provide themselves with the necessities of life, including the reasonable compensation for needed medical care," Elliott concluded.

27. Woll to Elliott, February 5, 1935, Elliott Papers.

28. Empire Blue Cross Archives, New York City.

29. See, for example, Murray Sargent, director of New York Hospital, to Louis Pink, November 22, 1947, complaining to the president of Blue Cross that Local 65 has organized its own "Security Plan" covering 15,000 workers and 30,000 more dependents. Pink replied that Sargent should not worry too much about the extension of this plan to more members because of the poor experience such union-sponsored plans had after the first year. "I do not think this sort of thing is too serious unless it should grow, and I do not think it will." See Pink to Sargent, November 25, 1947, in Pink Papers.

30. *Report of UAW-CIO Health Committee*, 7th Annual Convention, UAW-CIO, Chicago, August 1942.

31. Louis H. Pink, "New York Blue Cross Sets Pace for Employer-Union Cooperation," address before Hospital Association of New York State, June 11, 1946, Pink Papers, Blue Cross Archives.

32. Saul Mills to Louis Pink, March 16, 1943, Pink Papers.

33. See Conference Notes, "April 12, 1943- Saul Mills and Martin Segal representing CIO Council. Mr. Pink, Van Dyk, Sesan, Thomson, Keller, deSocarras, Breed," in Pink Papers.

34. Ossip Walinsky to Louis Pink, June 17, 1946, Pink Papers. He noted that "the hospitalization service is represented right in our office" and "the records of all shop employees are constantly being checked as against the union membership on our records."

35. *New York Times*, April 2, 1947, 16. See also ibid., April 8, 1947, 36. Here Blue Cross acknowledged the importance of this agreement and went on to note the "inclusion of hospitalization plans in the welfare programs of many unions."

36. See Martin Shefter, "Political Incorporation and the Extrusion of the Left: The Insertion of Social Forces into American Politics," (manuscript) to be published in *Studies in American Political Development*, vol. 1, for a fascinating and detailed account of the politics of New York City in the postwar period.

37. Robert Tilove, "Recent Trends in Health and Welfare Plans," *Proceedings of New York University Third Annual Conference on Labor*, [c. 1950], 145.

38. See Leon Fink and Brian Greenberg, "Organizing Montefiore," in Susan Reverby and David Rosner, eds., *Health Care in America: Essays in Social History* (Philadelphia, 1979).

39. *New York Times*, May 20, 1956, 88.

40. Ibid., November 19, 1957, 35.

41. Ibid., October 1, 1957, 35.

42. Ibid., November 19, 1957, 35.

43. Ibid., January 6, 1958, 58.

44. Ibid., December 27, 1957, 18. Given this kind of opposition, it is not surprising that the New York State Insurance Commissioner rejected Blue Cross's rate-increase request at the end of January 1958.

45. Ibid., June 3, 1958, 33; see also ibid., June 8, 1958, E9. Bernard Greenberg, an

economist for the United Steel Workers of America, spoke on behalf of the State CIO Council and the State Federation of Labor: "Labor in New York insists that Blue Cross policies must be directed away from the single-minded concern with meeting unquestionably every demand of the hospitals and toward a balanced view which impartially gives equal weight to the needs of hospitals, subscribers and the public interest."

46. Ibid., June 18, 1958, 1.

47. The new members of the Blue Cross board were Thomas Carey, district business manager of the International Association of Machinists; Louis Hollander, vice president of the Amalgamated Clothing Workers' Union; and Charles Zimmerman, a vice president of the International Ladies' Garment Workers Union. The existing member was Harold J. Garno, secretary-treasurer of the AFL-CIO.

48. *New York Times*, May 10, 1959, 69; ibid., June 10, 1959, 38.

49. Ibid., May 6, 1959, 43.

50. Fink and Greenberg, "Organizing Montefiore," 226–44.

51. *New York Times*, May 22, 1959, 14. One of the first labor spokesmen to give testimony at the hearings over Blue Cross rate increases in May 1959 was Leon Davis, whose hospital workers were then in the midst of a vicious and prolonged struggle with the voluntaries. He demanded that the hearing be adjourned until the strike was settled.

52. *New York Times*, May 23, 1959, 50.

53. Ibid., June 21, 1959, 1. In the end, Blue Cross substantially prevailed against this opposition and the State Insurance Commissioner granted an increase of 26.5 percent.

54. In the late 1960s hospitals and Blue Cross would become the focus of academic and activist critiques. See, e.g., Sylvia Law, *Blue Cross: What Went Wrong?* (New Haven, 1974); various publications and pamphlets of the Health Policy Advisory Center (*Health PAC*), especially *The American Health Empire* (New York, 1971).

55. *New York Times*, May 23, 1959, 50.

56. Selig Greenberg, "Crisis in the Hospitals," *The Progressive*, May 1961, 33.

57. *New York Times*, September 27, 1959, IV:9.

58. Ibid., September 21, 1959, 1, 22.

59. Ibid., December 31, 1959, 19.

60. Ibid., April 30, 1960, 1, 10.

61. Ibid., August 3, 1960, 31.

DIANE PAUL

# From Eugenics to Medical Genetics

Sheldon Reed coined the expression "genetic counseling" in 1947, the same year he succeeded Clarence P. Oliver as Director of the University of Minnesota's Dight Institute for Human Genetics. In reflections written more than a quarter-century later, Reed noted that the term had occurred to him "as a kind of genetic social work without eugenic connotations." Sharply distinguishing the aims of eugenics and counseling, he explained that whereas the former promotes the interests of the larger society, the latter serves the interests of individual families—as families perceive them. Reed never denied that he or other postwar medical geneticists were concerned with population improvement. But he maintained that counseling served a different purpose. Commenting on the history of the Dight Institute, Reed asserted: "There were certainly no attempts to benefit society as a whole in dealing with these families. This was not thought of as a program of eugenics."[1]

The historical record suggests a rather more complex story. In the 1950s and 1960s, genetic counseling was characterized by most of its practitioners as an extension of eugenics. Thus in a 1950 application to the Rockefeller Foundation, Reed himself stated: "Counseling in human genetics is the modern way of carrying on a program in Eugenics . . . the term 'Eugenics' has fallen by the wayside and 'Counseling in Human Genetics' is taking its place."[2] And two years later, he wrote that, "it could be stated as a principle that the mentally sound will voluntarily carry out an eugenics program which is acceptable to society *if* counseling in genetics is available to them."[3]

Given the protean meanings of "eugenics," a plausible case can be made for each of his claims. In some respects, Reed seems decidedly antieugenicist. Long before neutrality became fashionable, Reed argued that counselors ought not to impose their own values on their clients. The role of the counselor, he consistently argued, was "to explain thoroughly what the genetic situation is but the decision must be a personal one between the husband and wife, and theirs alone."[4] Moreover, he wrote that the net effect of counseling might well be dysgenic. Reed often noted that the desire to compensate for the birth of an affected child was usually strong, while the recurrence risk was typically lower than the family had feared. Hence on balance, the effect of genetic counseling would be to encourage people to have more children than they otherwise would—thereby spreading the defective gene through offspring who were normal carriers.[5] Reed's views on the appropriate stance for counselors and probable impact of their work hardly seem consistent with his characterization of counseling as the modern form of eugenics.

But Reed also believed that normal people could be relied on to make "rational" decisions—that is, to avoid bearing children at high risk for seriously abnormal conditions. Thus the *impact* of counseling could be described as eugenic even if its aim were relief of individual suffering rather than changes in the distribution of births and its means—provision of information to those who asked for it—were wholly voluntary. Second, while counseling might increase the incidence of particular disease genes, Reed and most of his peers assumed both that mental traits were more important than physical ones and that individuals who availed themselves of counseling services were generally impressive in intelligence and character. Therefore, counseling could be considered dysgenic in respect to disease and eugenic in respect to behavior. Third, any impact on the incidence of disease genes would be felt only in the distant future, with the immediate consequence being a reduction in the birth of affected children. Whether counseling appears to be dysgenic or eugenic is thus also a function of whether concern focuses primarily on long- or short-term effects. Depending on which factors are emphasized and how they are interpreted, counseling could be equated with eugenics—or with its antithesis.

That is why Reed could plausibly claim in the 1950s that counseling was a form of eugenics and with equal plausibility in the 1970s claim that it was not. But the question remains: Why would anyone *want* to identify counseling with such an ostensibly discredited enterprise? As we will see, "eugenics" in the 1950s still retained positive connotations for many scientists and their sponsors. Indeed, following Watson and Crick's 1953 discovery of the double-helical structure of DNA, it enjoyed a temporary resurgence in popularity. In the years immediately following the end of

World War II, the word "eugenics" virtually vanished from scientific journals. While arguments for selective breeding did not disappear, they were
now mostly relegated to the conclusions of more general articles on eugenics or birth control.[6] But publication of the Watson and Crick paper
seems to have emboldened some geneticists. "Eugenics" began to reap-
pear in the titles of articles in scientific journals. And as we will see, their
arguments became more forceful and direct.

   Thus there was little reason to avoid the association of eugenics with
counseling. By the mid-1970s, however, "eugenics" had once again become a term of abuse. The shift in emotional resonance was accompanied by a contraction in the meaning of the word. Now that the association was damning, "eugenics" was typically restricted to compulsory programs. On the narrow definition, it was made unambiguously distinct
from counseling.

   This essay explores the ethos of medical genetics and genetic counseling as these fields developed in America and Britain in the two decades
following World War II. In prior decades, some individual geneticists,
such as Charles Davenport at Cold Spring Harbor and Lawrence Snyder
and Madge Macklin at Ohio State University, had provided "marriage
advice" to those who sought their help. Formal clinics had been established in Germany and Denmark during the 1930s. But in the Anglo-
American world, genetic counseling was first institutionalized in the 1940s,
when clinics were opened in Britain at the Hospital for Sick Children
and in the United States at the Universities of Michigan and Minnesota.
This essay asks: What were the aims of the field in the two decades following the end of World War II? How were sometimes disparate goals
reconciled? How were these goals reflected in clinical practice? Are
some of the tensions that once marked the field still manifest and, if so, in
what ways?

## Establishing Medical Genetics: Scientists and Their Sponsors

The Dight Institute was founded in 1941 with the explicit aim of promoting eugenics.[7] A passage from the second annual Dight lecture exempli-
fies its ethos in the institute's early years:

> In a commendable exhibition of sympathy and generosity, the nonpro-
> ductive classes of society are being cared for on a plane of living which
> our productive members cannot afford for themselves. Very little is
> being done to protect our social system by our procedure in respect to

these dysgenic classes. The burden has already become so great that a surprising amount of our public expenditures in so-called normal times goes for the care of these nonproductive classes.[8]

The eugenic orientation reflected the aims of Charles Fremont Dight, a Minneapolis physician who left his estate to the University of Minnesota "to promote biological race betterment." Dight's many causes included birth control, socialism, and eugenics. A president of the Minnesota Eugenics Society, member of the Minnesota Birth-Control League, unsuccessful congressional candidate of the Public Ownership Party (1906), and socialist alderman for Minneapolis's 12th ward (1914 to 1918), Dight lobbied for a state sterilization law and, after its passage in 1925, for its extension to the noninstitutionalized.[9] The equally eccentric Charles M. Goethe, a bank president and founder of the playground movement, also left much of his estate to what was by then the Dight Institute for its eugenic work, while the reactionary textile magnate "Colonel" Wycliffe C. Draper supported the Department of Medical Genetics at the Bowman-Gray School of Medicine in Winston-Salem, North Carolina (the first Department of medical genetics at an American university) and its director, C. Nash Herndon.[10]

With the exception of the U.S. Public Health Service, which funded cancer-related projects, virtually all institutional patrons of work in medical genetics and genetic counseling also had eugenic motivations. These included the Rockefeller, Carnegie, Wenner-Grenn, McGregor, and Rackham foundations, the Commonwealth and Pioneer Funds (the last founded by Draper in 1937), and the American Eugenics Society.[11]

Across a wide political spectrum, scientists with an interest in medical genetics agreed that the field should serve to improve the race. To many scientists, it seemed self-evident that reproduction was properly a social and not just a private matter. Thus Ashley Montagu asserted in 1959 that, "there can be no question that infantile amaurotic family idiocy is a disorder that no one has a right to visit upon a small infant. Persons carrying this gene, if they marry, should never have children, and should, if they desire children, adopt them."[12] Linus Pauling, who believed that genetic defects were a primary source of human misery, proposed in 1968 that all young people be tested for the presence of the sickle-cell and other deleterious genes and a symbol be tattooed on the foreheads of those found to be carriers.[13] In his 1970 presidential address to the American Association for the Advancement of Science, Bentley Glass speculated on the changes that would be prompted by exponential population growth. He wrote: "In a world where each pair must be limited, on the average, to two offspring and no more, the right that must become paramount is not the right to procreate, but rather the right of each child to be born with a sound physical and mental constitution, based on a sound geno-type. No parents will in that future time have a right to burden soci-ety with a malformed or a mentally incompetent child."[14]

Through the 1960s, most of the leading figures in medical genet-ics—including Oliver, Curt Stern, Lee R. Dice, Herluf Strandskov, Gordon Allen, William Allen, C. Nash Herndon, Franz Kallmann, Harold Falls, Madge Macklin and C. Clarke Fraser in the United States and Canada, Eliot Slater and Cedric Carter in Britain, and Tage Kemp in Denmark—bluntly described their work as a form of "eugenics." The links between medical genetics and eugenics are nicely illustrated by the early history of the American Society of Human Genetics (ASHG), which was founded in 1948. Four of the first five Presi-dents—Dice, Snyder, Oliver, and Kallmann—were members of the Board of the American Eugenics Society. (Herndon also served as President of the ASHG in 1955, Reed in 1956, Stern in 1957, and Macklin in 1958.)

The exception was H. J. Muller. An ardent critic of "mainline" eugenics, Muller argued that eugenics in capitalist societies was hope-lessly distorted by class and racial bias. But he was not opposed to eugenics per se. His 1949 presidential address to the American Soci-ety of Human Genetics, published as "Our Load of Mutations," argued that identifying individuals carrying more than their share of the ge-netic load and convincing them not to reproduce was a matter of ur-gent necessity. But he consciously avoided using the word "eugenics" to describe his scheme. In Muller's view, eugenic goals were best pur-sued under another rubric.[15] Thus Muller differed from his peers in his view of appropriate tactics, not ultimate goals. He would certainly have agreed with Lee R. Dice, the first director of the University of Michigan's Heredity Clinic, that "the heredity of the population should be of at least as much concern to each commonwealth as infectious diseases."[16] Summarizing a 1952 panel discussion on genetic counsel-ing, Dice asserted: "We must give due concern to the possibility of eliminating, or, perhaps, of perpetuating, undesirable or desirable genes. We must not only be concerned with the particular family concerned, but also with whether or not harmful heredity may be continued or spread in our population."[17] That this was the prevailing view explains why the practice of genetic counseling was usually directive, and some-times strongly so.

In the 1950s, genetic services came to be centered in major medi-cal centers and physicians, who are trained to be directive, assumed a greater role. A common view—that the attitude of neutrality "origi-nated with counselors who were not engaged in patient care and who may have felt some reluctance, therefore, to enter into the lives of their counselees in the way a practicing doctor frequently does"—may thus seem plausible.[18] But most of the research-oriented Ph.D. geneti-cists felt a similar responsibility to guide their clients. The views of Reed's predecessor, C. P. Oliver, were typical: "A geneticist should prevail upon some persons to have at least their share of children as well as show a black picture to those with the potentiality of produc-ing children with undesirable traits."[19]

While the early postwar literature on counseling is replete with as-sertions that reproductive decisions belong to parents, they do not necessarily imply support for a neutral stance. Thus Oliver declared that parents should make their own decisions after they have been given all the facts. But physicians would also "make the picture as dark as possible" to help particular parents reach the conclusion that it would be best not to have more children.[20]

Some clinicians expressed optimism that, advised of their heredi-tary defect, clients would generally follow their doctor's advice. But most thought they needed at least a gentle push. Thus C. Nash Herndon, one of the two original staff members of the Heredity Clinic and first director of the Department of Medical Genetics at Bowman-Gray School of Medicine, thought that "the counselor should attempt to encourage the marriage of persons of average or superior physical or mental capabilities, and should encourage such persons to have fami-lies. On the other hand, those with obvious hereditary defects . . . should be discouraged."[21] Franz Kallmann similarly believed that "per-sons requesting genetic advice cannot always be presumed to be ca-pable of making a realistic decision as to the choice of a mate, or the advisability of parenthood, without support in the form of directive guidance and encouragement."[22] In his popular textbook, Curt Stern even anticipated the day when:

Natural selection will be superseded by socially decreed selection. In the course of time . . . the control by man of his own biological evolution will become imperative, since the power which knowl-edge of human genetics will place in man's hands cannot but lead to action. Such evolutionary controls will be world wide in scope, since, by its nature, the evolution of man transcends the concept of unrestricted national sovereignty.[23]

## Distinguishing Good Eugenics from Bad

On conventional accounts, eugenics was wounded by the Depression and died with revelations of Nazi atrocities following World War II. Word and concept are said to have fallen into disrepute. But this generalization is much too broad. It is true that much of the public soon came to equate eugenics with the policies of the Third Reich. It is also true that the 1950s witnessed developments in medical genetics—broadly defined—that had little if any connection to eugenics. Research on the "inborn errors of metabolism" first identified by Sir Archibald Garrod at the turn of the century is particularly important, for it showed that some genetic diseases could be treated—a crucial step in the expansion of genetic services in the 1960s.[24]

The idea that a genetic disease might be treatable was first suggested to a broad audience by Lionel Penrose in his 1946 inaugural lecture as professor of eugenics and head of the Galton Laboratory at University College, London. In "Phenylketonuria: A Problem in Eugenics," Penrose stressed the complex causes of mental deficiency and argued that eugenical measures could have only a slight impact on its incidence. He also suggested that phenylketonuria (or PKU), although a genetic disease, might one day be ameliorated through an environmental intervention.[25]

That day was in fact not far off. The severe mental retardation and other symptoms associated with PKU result from an excess of blood phenylalanine. (Due to a defective liver enzyme, phenylketonuric individuals are unable to catalyze the conversion of the essential amino acid phenylalanine to another amino acid, tyrosine.) In the mid-1950s, a number of groups began experimental treatment of phenylketonuric infants and children with low-phenylalanine diets. While their efforts initially met with only mixed success, the prospect of treating a genetic disease generated great excitement among public health officials, parents' groups, and the press.[26] In an influential 1958 report commissioned by the National Association of Retarded Children, the neurologist Richard Masland wrote: "The fact that a disease is hereditary does not indicate that there is no form of therapy conceivable or that sterilization or other eugenic practices are the only hopes for modification of the problem. The modification of the stressful features of our environment, in the broadest sense of the word, may be an entirely proper and effective means of dealing with many genetic disorders."[27]

Two years later, a cheap and simple blood test, suitable for mass screening, became available. Within a decade, newborn screening for PKU and other inborn errors had become routine in the United States, Britain, and much of Europe. These programs were defended in cost-benefit terms. Although all the metabolic disorders were rare, screening advocates successfully argued that the cost to the state of lifetime institutionalization for untreated individuals greatly exceeded the cost of the screening programs and diet required by affected infants and children.

Thus a competing model for medical genetics had already emerged in late 1950s. While preserving the orientation toward public health, and its associated cost-benefit language, newborn screening problems focused on treatment, not on selective breeding. (Most researchers in the area of human metabolic disorders were physicians and biochemists rather than geneticists.) At the same time, work in human cytogenetics was rapidly expanding. Joe-Hin Tjio, Albert Levan, Charles Ford, Paul Polani, Murray Barr, and Jerome Lejune, among others, greatly refined the analysis of chromosomes and thus laid the scientific groundwork for prenatal diagnosis.[28] Like the metabolic researchers, the cytogeneticists were generally uninterested in eugenics. Thus medical genetics had already begun to fragment as younger scientists with different interests entered the field.

At the same time, many geneticists whose professional careers began before World War II worried that eugenics' rational core would be abandoned in the reaction to past abuses. Some even thought that a program of artificial selection was made more urgent by postwar military and medical uses of radiation, which they assumed were increasing the human mutation rate. Throughout the 1940s, 1950s, and even the 1960s, few geneticists objected to the characterization of applied medical genetics as "eugenics." (Lionel Penrose, who insisted that his position as Professor of Eugenics be retitled Professor of Human Genetics, is a major exception.) For example, Lawrence Snyder noted that the practical applications of a knowledge of genetics include "the setting up of eugenic programs for the protection and improvement of society."[29] In an article on X-linked mental retardation, William Allan, C. Nash Herndon, and Florence Dudley wrote that "when a sufficient body of data has been assembled to permit us to predict with accuracy the probably occurrence of mentally deficient children, we believe that a program of negative eugenics will do much to reduce the supply of disastrous children from these causes."[30] In the 1950s and early 1960s, leading figures in the field routinely defined medical genetics as a worthy form of eugenics.[31]

Thus older geneticists generally continued to speak the language of eugenics, condemning past abuses but also taking for granted that reproduction was an act with social consequences and was thus legitimately a matter of social concern. The eugenics of the past, they conceded, was distorted by racial and class prejudice and simplistic scientific assumptions. But they insisted that eugenics has a rational core, which should be preserved. Some genes are unreservedly bad. Those that produce Tay-Sachs disease, muscular dystrophy, Huntington's Chorea, and other serious conditions bring only misery to their bearers and unnecessary expense to society. The struggle to eliminate disease genes must be sharply demarcated from past policies that targeted ethnic and religious minorities and the poor.[32]

That was also the position adopted by the American Eugenics Society. Under the leadership of Frederick Osborn, distinguished scientists such as Theodosius Dobzhansky and Tracy Sonneborn were recruited to its board of directors. Osborn also increasingly turned the society's efforts toward the apparently neutral fields of birth control and human genetics. In 1954, the first issue of its new journal announced a series on "heredity counseling." During the next four years, an article on this theme appeared in almost every issue. In fact, between 1954 and 1958, the journal published more articles on counseling than on any other topic. The contributors constituted a virtual "who's who" in the field, most stressing its eugenic potential.

Public aversion to anything labeled eugenics ultimately swamped the "reform eugenics" movement. The society's general membership declined steeply. In a concession to public sentiment, its journal *The Eugenics Quarterly* was renamed *Social Biology* in 1968. Although some geneticists continued to employ the label into the 1970s, it was by then generally recognized that a successful eugenics program must be called something else. Commenting on the new title, Osborn remarked that "birth control and abortion are turning out to be great eugenic advances of our time. If they had been advanced for eugenic reasons it would have retarded or stopped their acceptance."[33] Or as he wrote in a popular 1968 book: "Eugenic goals are most likely to be attained under a name other than eugenics."[34]

The commitment to birth control is not surprising. In the 1910s and 1920s eugenicists had divided on the question of its value. Some feared that the widespread practice of contraception "would prejudice the production of sufficient babies by the competent and far-seeing section of the community."[35] Others argued that the fittest members of society already limited their births and that the extension of contraception would therefore improve the race. Over time, as the futility of preventing its spread among middle- and upper-class women became increasingly evident, many eugenicists converted to the birth-control cause.

Furthermore, changing public opinion had left eugenicists with few other options. Coercive programs were no longer in vogue. Birth-control advocates argued that, at least in respect to the normal population, there was no need for compulsion. The race would be improved by the voluntary actions of poor women who wanted to limit their births. The American Eugenics Society began aggressively to promote contraception. In 1952, Osborn was appointed the first director of the Population Council, an organization funded by John D. Rockefeller III to promote what was now often called "family planning."

But what could genetic counseling actually offer eugenicists? The answer is: very little. Those who turned to geneticists for advice (typically parents who already had a child affected with a genetic disorder or who were anxious about transmitting a trait that ran in the family) were confronted with a stark choice based on often vague estimates of risk. Until abortion was legalized in the United States by the 1973 Supreme Court decision in *Roe v. Wade* and in Britain by a 1967 Act of Parliament, the only legal way to avoid genetic risk was not to reproduce. But the right to terminate a pregnancy would have had little impact in the absence of practical methods for detecting genetic disorders during pregnancy. In the 1960s the first such method—amniocentesis—was developed, and by the mid-1970s it had become a routine part of clinical practice. The convergence of prenatal diagnosis and legalized abortion produced explosive growth in the field of genetic counseling. But in the three decades following World War II, it was practiced on too small a scale to make an appreciable difference in the population frequencies of the diseases in question. Thus from a eugenical standpoint, counseling was insignificant. Moreover, its impact was as likely to increase as reduce the incidence of particular disease genes (which is why Reed thought that genetic counseling might well be dysgenic).

The society's embrace of genetic counseling in part reflects its limited options in the postwar period. It also reflects the fact that eugenicists have in fact rarely focused on long-term effects. With few exceptions, such as Muller, the "gene pool" has been a distant abstraction. Eugenicists' have typically emphasized immediate impacts. Whether motivated by a desire to prevent suffering or to diminish the financial burden on society—or both—the focus has been on reducing the supply of "disastrous children" in the near term.

That eugenicists have always been more concerned with mental than physical traits also helps explain the indifference to potential dysgenic effects of counseling. Much early work on the heredity of clinical diseases was pursued by eugenicists who were at least as interested in behavior as health. Charles Davenport, for example, worked simultaneously on the inheritance of Huntington's Chorea, epilepsy, a cheerful tempera-

ment, and "nomadism." The 1931 edition of the influential textbook
*Human Heredity* by Erwin Baur, Eugen Fischer, and Fritz Lenz describes
hundreds of anomalies and normal traits, some of which are today considered hereditary and some not. Like all human genetics textbooks in the
1930s and 1940s, it discussed diseases, socially aberrant behaviors, and a
host of mental and temperamental characteristics. Its catalogue of traits
included glaucoma, various cancers, Parkinson's disease, susceptibilities
to rickets, hypertension, and gallstones, as well as schizophrenia, manic-
depressive insanity, homosexuality, idiocy, genius, power of imagination,
and talents for painting, technical invention, and science.

Most geneticists would have agreed with Lenz that "the mental differences among men are not only much greater than the physical, but also
far more meaningful."[36] In Germany, the physically handicapped were
subjected to sterilization and, later, murder. But even there, eugenicists
emphasized mentality and behavior. Most sterilizations carried out under
the 1933 Law for the Prevention of Progeny with Hereditary Diseases law
were for feeblemindedness, schizophrenia, and alcoholism. Only about
one-tenth were for physical disorders.[37]

The interest in behavior carried over into the postwar period. For
example, the principal projects of the Dight Institute in 1952 included
mental deficiency and "normal intelligence and differential fertility" along
with more obviously medical studies. Even after the American Eugenics
Society began to support work in medical genetics, mentality remained
its primary concern. Osborn thought that the eugenics movement should
not emphasize physical health. What really matters is a change in reproductive behavior by the intellectual elite.[38] Physical improvement will
follow from any program concerned with mental qualities, which are in
any case much more important. "Eugenics is particularly interested in
the psychological traits of intelligence and personality, because these traits
are of major importance to civilization," he explained. "If there is justification for a broad eugenics movement, it is chiefly because of the part
played by heredity in providing the necessary potentials for the development of high qualities of intelligence and personality."[39]

The trait valued above all others was intelligence. In Muller's view,
"For man, it is world of mental life which counts by far the most, the rest
being pretty much subsidiary," while Neel claimed that, "given that the
most important and precious asset of any human being is his intelligence,
the impact of a convincing demonstration of this on national priorities
would surely exceed the conquest of a dozen rare genetic diseases."[40]

Most clinicians believed that it was the total genotype, not the single
gene, that mattered. Thus Herndon argued that "one must not only con-

sider the obvious abnormality which prompts the patient to seek genetic advice; one must also take into account all evidence that may be obtainable concerning the total genetic potential of the parties concerned."[41] Concerning a case where the wife had surgery for a harelip and cleft palate, he concluded that the couple's intellect and general genetic endowment were "sufficiently above normal that their reproduction might be advantageous to society as a whole, offsetting the disadvantage of the possible continuation of the defective gene."[42] Dice likewise believed that "the obligations of a heredity clinic will not be fully discharged . . . if it confines itself entirely to the heredity of medical pathologies." Thus in giving advice, the geneticist should take into account "mental ability, and social worth in addition to hereditary defects."[43] According to Madge Macklin, "In dealing with these patients who ask advice, one must consider not only the fact that they have inherited diseases which they may transmit, but also whether they have highly desirable characters which they may pass on."[44]

The belief that those who availed themselves of counseling were superior in mentality and character to the general population illuminates some objections to directive counseling. Reed believed that "the counselor has never suffered the particular circumstances which the parents of the affected child suffered and therefore cannot completely understand their feelings."[45] He also assumed that individuals motivated to consult a counselor were usually well above average in character and intellect. Thus behavior that is dysgenic with respect to a particular defective gene might still be desirable since, "those people who are sufficiently concerned about their future children to come to the Dight Institute for counseling have commendable concepts of their obligations as parents and these laudable characteristics should be transmitted to the next generation."[46] Harold Falls argued that the fact that they seek genetic advice indicates that the prospective parents are more intelligent and socially and morally responsible than most and reasoned that they "should actually be encouraged to have children (anticipating transmission of superior qualities) providing the gene to be transmitted does not impose too serious a handicap on the affected child."[47]

Clinicians who opposed directiveness also assumed that their clients did not need guidance to make the right choice. "From my experience in giving advice about heredity to families in all walks of life I can affirm that every parent desires his children to be free from serious handicap," wrote Dice. "If there is known to be a high probability of transmitting a serious defect, it would be an abnormal person indeed who would not refrain from having children."[48] Thus counseling would automatically serve

the interests of both individuals and society. Given adequate information, the type of middle-class people who availed themselves of genetic
services would act rationally. Neel consistently condemned eugenics and
opposed directive counseling; he also argued that we should use all ethical means to limit the number of those unfortunates incapable of fully
participating in our complex society. In his view, genetic counseling represented one such means, "since once the principle of parental choice of
a normal child is established, it seems probable that in large measure the
parental desire for normal children can be relied on to result in the purely
voluntary elimination of affected fetuses."[49] Cedric Carter likewise noted
that most parents and patients act sensibly on the basis of the counselor's
advice.[50] Or as Reed remarked, "People of normal mentality, who thoroughly understand the genetics of their problems, will behave in the way
that seems correct to society as a whole ."[51]

   Irrational individuals were a different matter. Writing of problems in
counseling individuals with phenylketonuria, Reed argued that "no couple
has the right to produce a child with a 100 per cent chance of having
P.K.U., and it is doubtful whether a couple has the right deliberately to
take a 50 per cent chance of producing such a serious defect."[52] (Since
the fitness of the recessive homozygote is nearly zero, there would be no
effect on the "gene pool.") Thus the case against directive counseling
was based on the assumption that most families would act responsibly,
not on a principle of procreative liberty.

## The New Ethos of Genetic Services

Two decades later, counseling services in the United States and Canada
began a rapid expansion. The first master's level program for professional
counselors, at Sarah Lawrence College, was established only in 1969. At
that time, about eighty percent of counselors were physicians, while another eleven percent were Ph.D. geneticists.[53] While few of these counselors admitted to giving outright advice, most thought that it appropriate to inform their clients in such as way as to guide them to an appropriate decision. In 1973, F. Clarke Fraser noted that, over time, he had
"evolved in a more rather than less directive approach in giving genetic
advice."[54] But forces were quickly building in the opposite direction.

   Primary among these was the transformation in public attitudes toward reproductive responsibility that took place in the 1960s and 1970s.
No longer was it assumed that society had a legitimate interest in who
reproduced. Within genetic counseling, concern for the future of the

population was replaced by concern for the welfare of individual families, as defined by the families themselves. That change reflected events specific to the field as well as general trends in the culture. Master's-level genetic counseling developed largely outside the field of medical genetics. Thus none of the founders of the first program at Sarah Lawrence were geneticists.[55] In other ways as well, the new counselors were different from their predecessors. All but a handful were women, who generally value reproductive autonomy more than do men.[56] They were also trained in "client-centered" therapy, which stresses the counselor's role in clarifying the client's own feelings.

In a classic 1972 article, Claire Leonard, Gary Chase, and Barton Childs asserted that "genetic counseling is preventive medicine and should be so regarded."[57] By the end of the decade, few counselors would agree. They had rejected not just eugenics but also the public-health orientation that informed the world of researchers on human metabolic disorders. These counselors rarely spoke the language of cost-benefit analysis, much less of selective breeding. They did not aim either to spare future generations' suffering or to save the state money. Instead, they hoped to empower their clients to make their own decisions according to their own values.[58] "Individual choice" and "personal autonomy" became the new catchwords. Of course theory and practice may sometimes—or even often—diverge. But at least in North America, the shift in ethos was dramatic.

Genetic services are now everywhere justified as increasing the choices available to women. In its 1983 report, the President's Commission for the Study of Ethical Problems in Medicine and Biomedical Research identified the primary value of screening for cystic fibrosis (CF), the most common recessive genetic disease among Caucasians of European descent, as providing people with the information they would consider helpful in autonomous decision-making—an aim reiterated in a 1992 report of the Office of Technology Assessment (OTA).[59] On the new view, counselors aim to serve only their clients, never society. The Professional Code of Ethics of the National Society of Genetic Counselors defines the counselor-client relationship as "based on values of care and respect for the client's autonomy, individuality, welfare, and freedom."[60] This view is likewise reflected in the 1994 recommendations of the Institute of Medicine's Committee on Assessing Genetic Risks. "The standard of care should be to support the client in making voluntary informed decisions" to the committee. *The goal of reducing the incidence of genetic conditions is not acceptable, since this aim is explicitly eugenics; professionals should not present any reproductive decision as 'correct' or advantageous for a person or society.*"[61]

But at the level at which public policy is made, genetic services were and are still funded in hopes of reducing the incidence of genetic disease and thus saving the state money. In the 1970s, the U.S. government played a major role in promoting amniocentesis. Theodore Cooper, then assistant secretary of the Department of Health, Education, and Welfare, wrote at the time: "By focusing on prevention we increase the resources available for other programs. Few advances compare with amniocentesis in their capability for prevention of disability."[62]

Given the current bitter debate over abortion, it is unlikely that he would speak so openly today. A recent government report on health-care objectives illustrates how reticient officials have become. It proposes the goal of increasing to at least ninety percent the proportion of women enrolled in prenatal care who are offered prenatal screening and counseling for fetal abnormalities. The authors explain that "in the event of a fetal abnormality, testing and counseling early in the pregnancy provides an opportunity for families to prepare for a disabled infant, and increasingly, for medical interventions to correct some problem in utero." Abortion is never mentioned. Indeed, cross-pressures from the anti-abortion movement have produced schizophrenic policies in some states. For example, Tennessee forbids the use of public funds for prenatal diagnosis of conditions for which there is no effective therapy on the grounds that abortion is against public policy—while also legislating that public funds may be used for abortion in the case of fetuses with "severe physical deformities or abnormalities, or severe mental retardation."[63] But while cost-saving is often at war with other motivations, and today is rarely made explicit, it remains an important aim of genetic services programs. As the philosopher Arthur Caplan has noted, "When the state of California offers [a test] to all pregnant women it does so in the hope that some of those who are found to have children with neural tube defects will choose not to bring them to term; thereby, preventing the state from having to bear the burden of their care."[64] Economic appraisals of prenatal screening programs generally assume that benefits arise only from abortion of an affected fetus.[65]

As in the past, many presume that these individual and social interests are congruent—that families will act "rationally." Thus policy analyses of screening programs typically presume that all identified fetuses will be aborted.[66] Today, everyone favors increasing the choices available to women. But fostering reproductive autonomy is rarely, if ever, the primary goal of governments when they choose to fund genetic services.[67] That states expect to save money is evident in the arguments actually made to legislatures, which are typically framed in cost-benefit terms.

Thus it seems that the new consensus on reproductive autonomy rests on the old assumption that families will ordinarily make the "right" decisions.

That assumption is questionable. As Rayna Rapp has noted, "There is no inevitable bridge between a positive diagnosis and an abortion."[68] The women she interviewed did not necessarily, or even generally, equate testing with abortion. Under hypothetical circumstances, most people are receptive to the idea of being screened. But many of those who express positive attitudes toward prenatal testing indicate that they would not abort even if the test identified a serious genetic condition.[69]

That finding is confirmed by studies of attitudes toward pregnancy termination for specific disorders. In general, they show a reluctance to abort for medical conditions except where certain early death or severe mental retardation is involved. For example, while most women are interested in knowing their CF carrier status, they are hesitant to use that information to prevent the birth of an affected child.[70] Thus only twenty percent of parents of children with CF say they would abort an affected fetus—a higher percentage than for many other conditions, such as an incurable, severe, painful disorder that strikes at age forty.[71] Of three hundred women participating in a program of MSAFP screening for neural tube defects, seventy-one said they would refuse abortion "even if the fetus had multiple, severe handicaps such as hemiplaga and bowel and bladder incontinence."[72] Although ninety-seven percent of individuals at high risk for autosomal dominant polycystic kidney disease (a late-onset disorder that results in renal failure), and fifty percent would use prenatal testing, only eight percent would terminate a pregnancy for that reason.[73] Of course people may behave differently when facing an actual choice than they say they would when presented with a hypothetical scenario. But the proportion of women choosing abortion is often much lower than predicted on the basis of attitude surveys.[74] The actual reluctance of women to terminate pregnancies for fetal conditions helps explain the low utilization rates for some DNA-based tests.

Many eugenicists thought that the job of ridding the world of the "unfit" could be as easily—or even better—carried out by individuals themselves. They only needed to be educated and given the tools for the job. But even women who are not opposed to abortion per se are often uneasy with *selective* abortion. Willingness to abort for fetal conditions is associated with class and ethnicity; nonwhites, and the less wealthy and educated, are more tolerant of handicaps.[75] Their resistance to selective abortion has exposed stresses that were muted when genetic counseling was a small-scale enterprise, clients were overwhelmingly white, educated, and middle class, and prenatal diagnosis was unavailable. With the expansion and increasing diversity of the client population, it is becoming evident that reproductive choice and "public health" models of genetic services do not easily cohere.

As genetic tests become cheaper and more reliable, and as they become increasingly applicable to common diseases (representing large markets), incentives will mount to screen more women for more disorders at an earlier age. The 1992 OTA report on the implications of CF carrier screening noted: "Without offering judgment on its appropriateness or inappropriateness, OTA finds that the matter of CF carrier screening in the United States is one of when, not if."[76] As screening programs expand, counseling is increasingly provided by obstetricians who do not fully share the professional counselors' commitment to principles of autonomous decision-making and informed consent and fear becoming targets of malpractice or wrongful-birth suits if they fail to test.[77] Thus screening tests are increasingly framed as a routine part of medical care.[78] Indeed, the strongest variable in determining uptake of screening is not the attitudes of consumers but the approach taken by the health-care provider; high usage is achieved by active recruitment.[79] The contradictions between autonomy and public health models is thus intensifying. How they are resolved—or suppressed—will reveal whether the contemporary consensus on reproductive autonomy is apparent or real.

*University of Massachusetts at Boston*

## Notes

1. Sheldon Reed, "A Short History of Genetic Counseling," *Dight Institute Bulletin*, no. 14 (1974), 4–5.

2. "Proposal," *Rockefeller Archive Center*, North Tarrytown, N.Y.; Record Group 1.1, Series 200, Box 154, Folder 1393. I am grateful for the Division of Research Programs of the National Endowment for the Humanities for its research support. Special thanks are due Sheldon Reed for allowing me access to his papers and to Peter Coventry, Sharon Durfy, and Robert Resta for insightful comments on earlier drafts of this essay.

3. Sheldon Reed, "Heredity Counseling and Research," *Eugenical News* 37 (1952): 43.

4. Sheldon Reed, *Counseling in Medical Genetics* (Philadelphia, 1955), 14.

5. Ibid., 4–15.

6. Susan Johnson, "Eugenics in the Aftermath of WWII: A Study of Articles in *Science, Nature,* and the *Scientific Monthly.*" paper, History of Eugenics seminar, University of Massachusetts/Boston, 1995.

7. Clarence P. Oliver, "A Report on the Organization and Aims of the Dight Institute," *Dight Institute Bulletin*, no. 1 (1943), 2.

8. Elmer Roberts, "Biology and Social Problems," *Dight Institute Bulletin*, no. 4, 18.

9. Phelps, "The Eugenics Crusade of Charles Fremont Dight," *Minnesota History* 49

(1984): 99–108: Sheldon Reed, "A Short History," 1–3; E. Swanson, "Biographical Sketch of Charles Fremont Dight," *Dight Institute Bulletin*, no. 1 (1943), 9–22.

10. For standard accounts of the founding of Bowman-Gray, see Ian Porter, "Evolution of Genetic Counseling in America," in H. A. Lubs and F. de la Cruz, eds., *Genetic Counseling* (New York, 1977), 26, and Marston Meads, *The Miracle at Hawthorne* (Winston-Salem: Medical Center of Bowman-Gray School of Medicine and North Carolina Baptist Hospital, 1988), 51, where Draper is characterized as "a New York philanthropist with a deep interest in population genetics." Draper wished to fund individuals and institutions with the proper attitudes toward "(a) miscegenation, (b) immigration quotas, (c) improving population quality by (1) positive, (2) negative measures." Ruggles Gates to Sheldon Reed, August 13, 1954.

11. On the Pioneer Fund, see Barry Mehler, "The New Eugenics: Academic Racism in the U.S. Today," *Science for the People* 15 (May/June 1983): 18–23, and essays by Adam Miller, "Professors of Hate," and J. Sedgwick, "Inside the Pioneer Fund," in R. Jacoby and N. Glauberman, eds., *The Bell Curve Debate: History, Documents, Opinions* (New York, 1994), 162–78, 144–61. On the Rockefeller Foundation, see Diane B. Paul, "The Rockefeller Foundation and the Origins of Behavior Genetics," in K. Benson et al., eds., *The Expansion of American Biology* (New Brunswick, N.J., 1991), 262–83.

12. Ashley Montagu, *Human Heredity* (New York, 1959), 305–6.

13. Linus Pauling, "Reflections on the New Biology," *UCLA Law Review* 15 (1968): 267–72.

14. Bentley Glass, "Science: Endless Horizons or Golden Age?" *Science* 17 (1971): 28.

15. H. J. Muller, "Our Load of Mutations," *American Journal of Human Genetics* 2 (1950): 111–76; see also Diane B. Paul, "'Our Load of Mutations' Revisited," *Journal of the History of Biology* 20 (1987): 321–35.

16. Lee R. Dice, "The Structure of Heredity Counseling Services," *Eugenics Quarterly* 5 (1958): 40.

17. Lee R. Dice, "Concluding Remarks," in "A Panel Discussion: Genetic Counseling," *American Journal of Human Genetics* 4 (1952): 346.

18. Barton Childs, "Genetic Counseling: A Critical Review of the Published Literature," in B. Cohen, ed., *Genetic Issues in Public Health and Medicine* (Springfield, Ill., 1978), 347. This is also the view of James R. Sorenson, "Genetic Counseling: Values That Have Mattered," in D. M. Bartels et al., eds., *Prescribing Our Future: Ethical Challenges in Genetic Counseling* (New York, 1993), 3–14.

19. Clarence P. Oliver, "Human Genetics Program at the University of Texas," *Eugenical News* 37 (1952): 25–31.

20. Clarence P. Oliver, "Statement," in "A Panel Discussion: Genetic Counseling," *American Journal of Human Genetics* 4 (1953): 343.

21. Nash Herndon, "Human Resources from the Viewpoint of Medical Genetics," *Eugenical News* 35 (1950): 8.

22. Franz Kallmann, "Types of Advice Given by Heredity Counselors," *Eugenics Quarterly* 5 (1958): 48–50.

23. Curt Stern, *Principles of Human Genetics* (San Francisco, 1949), 603.

24. I say "broadly defined" because genetics has been largely irrelevant both to the diagnosis and treatment of metabolic disorders. Thus PKU is a genetic disease, but it is identified through a blood test and treated through diet and social support.

25. Lionel S. Penrose, "Phenylketonuria: A Problem in Eugenics," *The Lancet* (June 29, 1946): 949–51. For a discussion of Penrose's contributions to human genetics, see Daniel J. Kevles, *In the Name of Genetics: Genetics and the Uses of Human Heredity* (New York, 1985), 148–63, 176–78, 213–15, 220–22.

26. Diane B. Paul and Paul J. Edelson, "The Struggle over Screening," in D. de Chadarevian and H. Kamminga, eds., *Molecularising Biology and Medicine: New Practices and Alliances, 1930s–1970s* (Reading, England, forthcoming).

27. Richard L. Masland, "The Prevention of Mental Subnormality," in R. L. Masland

et al., *Mental Subnormality: Biological, Psychological, and Cultural Factors* (New York, 1958), 15.

28. On developments in human cytogenetics, see Kevles, *In the Name of Eugenics*, 238–68.

29. Lawrence Snyder, "Heredity and Modern Life," in R. G. Gates et al. eds., *Medical Genetics and Eugenics*, vol. 2 (Philadelphia, 1943), 24.

30. William Allan et al., "Some Examples of the Inheritance of Mental Deficiency: Apparently Sex-Linked Idiocy and Micro-encephaly," *American Journal of Mental Deficiency* 48 (1944): 28.

31. For example, see Gordon Allen, "Perspectives in Population Genetics," *Eugenics Quarterly* 2 (1955): 91; James V. Neel and William Schull, *Human Heredity* (Chicago, 1954), 256; Tage Kemp, "Genetic Hygiene and Genetic Counseling," *Acta Genetica et Statistica Medica* 4 (1953): 297, and Gardner Murphy, "A Research Program for Qualitative Eugenics," *Eugenics Quarterly* 1 (1954): 209–12.

32. For example, see L. L. Cavalli-Sforza and W. F. Bodmer, *The Genetics of Human Populations* (San Francisco, 1971), 757–58.

33. Frederick Osborn, Transcript, Oral History Interview (July 10, 1974), Columbia University, New York, 7.

34. Frederick Osborn, *The Future of Human Heredity* (New York, 1968), 25.

35. E. W. MacBride, "British Eugenists and Birth Control," *Birth Control Review* 6 (1922): 247.

36. Fritz Lenz, "Die Erblichkeit der Geistigen Eigenschaften," in E. Baur et al., *Menschliche Erblichkeitslehre und Rassenhygiene, Band I: Menschliche Erblehre* (Munich, 1936), 661.

37. Robert Proctor, *Racial Hygiene: Medicine Under the Nazis* (Cambridge, Mass., 1988), 107–8.

38. Frederick Osborn, "Editorial," *Eugenics Quarterly* 1 (1954): 2.

39. Frederick Osborn, *Preface to Eugenics*, 2d ed. (New York, 1951), 82.

40. Muller, "Our Load of Mutations," 165; James V. Neel, "On Emphases in Human Genetics," *Genetics* 78 (1974): 39.

41. C. Nash Herndon, "Heredity Counseling," *Eugenics Quarterly* 1 (1954): 66.

42. C. Nash Herndon, "Statement," in "A Panel Discussion: Genetic Counseling," *American Journal of Human Genetics* 4 (1952): 335.

43. Lee R. Dice, "Heredity Clinics: Their Value for Public Service and Research," *American Journal of Human Genetics* 4 (1952): 6.

44. Madge T. Macklin, "The Value of Medical Genetics to the Clinician," in C. B. Davenport et al., *Medical Genetics and Eugenics* (Philadelphia, 1940), 138.

45. Reed, *Counseling in Medical Genetics*, 339.

46. Sheldon Reed, "Heredity Counseling," *Eugenics Quarterly* 1 (1954): 48–49.

47. Harold Falls, "Consideration of the Whole Person," in H. Hammons, ed., *Heredity Counseling* (New York, 1959), 99; see also V. Cowie, "Genetic Counseling and the Changing Impact of Medical Genetics," and A. Barnes, "Prevention of Congenital Anomalies from the Point of View of the Obstetrician," in *Second International Conference on Congential Malformations* (New York, 1964), 375, 378–79.

48. Lee R. Dice, "Heredity Clinics: Their Value for Public Service and Research," *American Journal of Human Genetics* 4 (1952): 2.

49. James V. Neel, "Lessons from a Primitive People," *Science* 170: 820–21; see also his *Physician to the Gene Pool* (New York, 1994), 361.

50. C. O. Carter, "Prospects in Genetic Counseling," in A. Emery, ed., *Modern Trends in Human Genetics I* (New York, 1970), 340–41.

51. Sheldon Reed, "Heredity Counseling and Research," *Eugenical News* 37 (1952): 43.

52. Sheldon Reed, *Parenthood and Heredity* (New York, 1964), 85.

53. J. R. Sorenson and A. J. Culbert, "Genetic Counselors and Counseling Orientation—Unexamined Topics in Evaluation," in H. A. Lubs and F. de la Cruz, eds., *Genetic*

*Counseling* (New York, 1974).

54. F. Clarke Fraser, "Genetic Counseling," in V. McKusick and R. Claiborne, eds., *Medical Genetics* (New York, 1973), 225.

55. Melissa Richter, who first suggested the program, was a physiologist and Dean for the Center of Continuing Education at Sarah Lawrence; Joan Marks, the program's director, was trained as a psychiatric social worker, and Virginia Apgar, developer of the Apgar system for scoring newborns, was a teratologist. I am grateful to Robert Resta for pointing out the disjunction between the program's founders and the major players in human genetics.

56. Dorothy Wertz and John Fletcher, "Ethical Decision Making in Medical Genetics: Women as Patients and Practitioners in Eighteen Nations," in K. Ratcliff et al., *Healing Technology: Feminist Perspectives* (Ann Arbor, 1989), 221–41.

57. C. O. Leonard et al., "Genetic Counseling: A Consumers' View," *New England Journal of Medicine* 287 (1972): 437.

58. See Seymour Twiss, "The Genetic Counselor as Moral Advisor," *Birth Defects*, Original Articles Series 15 (1979), 201.

59. U.S. Congress, Office of Technology Assessment, *Cystic Fibrosis and DNA Tests: Implications of Carrier Screening*, OTA-BA-532 (Washington, D.C., August 1992), 213.

60. D. Bartels et al., eds., "Code of Ethics: National Society of Genetic Counselors," in *Prescribing Our Future: Ethical Challenges in Genetic Counseling* (New York, 1993), 170.

61. Lori B. Andrews et al. eds., *Assessing Genetic Risks: Implications for Health and Social Policy* (Washington, D.C., 1994), 14–15. Italics in original.

62. Theodore Cooper, "Implications of the Amniocentesis Registry Findings," unpublished report (October 1975), 2.

63. Ellen Wright Clayton, "Reproductive Genetic Testing: Regulatory and Liability Issues," in E. Thomson et al., eds. *Reproductive Genetic Testing: Impact upon Women. Supplement to Fetal Diagnosis and Therapy* 8 (Basel, 1993), 54–55; and *Health Children 2000. DHHS Publication No. HRSA-M. CH 91-92. U.S. Department of Health and Human Services, Public Health Service, Health Resources and Services Administration, Maternal and Child Health Bureau* (Washington, D.C., 1991), 153.

64. Arthur Caplan, "Neutrality Is Not Morality: The Ethics of Genetic Counseling," in D. Bartels et al., eds., *Prescribing Our Future: Ethical Challenges in Genetic Counseling* (New York, 1993), 159.

65. Gavin Mooney and Mette Lange, *Social Science and Medicine* 37 (1993): 873.

66. Ruth Faden et al., "Prenatal Screening and Pregnant Women's Attitude Toward the Abortion of Defective Fetuses," *American Journal of Public Health* 77 (1987): 3.

67. Ruth Chadwick, "What Counts as Success in Genetic Counselling?" *Journal of Medical Ethics* 19 (1993): 43–46.

68. Rayna Rapp, "Chromosomes and Communication: The Discourse of Genetic Counseling," *Medical Anthropology Quarterly* 2 (1988): 152.

69. Eleanor Singer, "Public Attitudes Toward Genetic Testing," *Population Research and Policy Review* 10 (1991): 235–55.

70. J. Botkin and S. Alemagno, "Carrier Screening for Cystic Fibrosis: A Pilot Study of the Attitudes of Pregnant Women," *American Journal of Public Health* 82 (1992): 723–25.

71. Dorothy Wertz et al., "Attitudes Toward Abortion Among Parents of Children with Cystic Fibrosis," *American Journal of Public Health* 81 (1991): 992–96.

72. Faden et al., "Prenatal Screening," 3.

73. Eva Sujansky et al., "Attitudes of At-Risk and Affected Individuals Regarding Presymptomatic Testing for Autosomal Dominant Polycystic Kidney Disease," *American Journal of Medical Genetics* 35 (1990): 510–15.

74. For example, see A. M. Manicol et al., "Implications of a Genetic Screening Programme for Polycystic Kidney Disease," *Aspects of Renal Care* 1 (1986): 219–22; Watson et al., "Adult Polycystic Kidney Disease," *British Medical Journal* 300 (1990): 62–63, S.

Adam et al., "Five Year Study of Prenatal Testing for Huntington's Disease: Demand, Attitudes, and Psychological Assessment," *Journal of Medical Genetics* 30 (1993): 549–56; Sabine Eggers et al., "Facioscapulohumeral Muscular Dystrophy: Aspects of Genetic Counseling, Acceptance of Preclinical Diagnosis, and Fitness," *Journal of Medical Genetics* 30 (1993): 589–92; Mooney and Lange, "Ante-Natal Screening," 875.

75. Wertz, "Attitudes Toward Abortion," 992–96.

76. U.S. Congress, Cystic Fibrosis and DNA Tests, 18.

77. Ibid., 151–52. There are currently only about one thousand Master's-level counselors in the United States.

78. See Nancy A. Press and Carol H. Browner, "Collective Silences, Collective Fictions: How Prenatal Testing Became Part of Routine Prenatal Care," in K. H. Rothenberg and E. J. Thomson, *Women and Prenatal Testing: Facing the Challenge of Genetic Technology* (Columbus, Ohio, 1994), 201–18.

79. Hilary Bekker et al., "Uptake of Cystic Fibrosis Testing in Primary Care: Supply Push or Demand Pull?" *British Medical Journal* 306 (June 1993): 1584–86. See also Ellen Wright Clayton et al., "Lack of Interest by Nonpregnant Couples in Population-Based Cystic Fibrosis Carrier Screening," *American Journal of Human Genetics* 58 (1996): 617–27.

JAMES HARVEY YOUNG

# Health Fraud:  A Hardy Perennial

Quackery forms a gaudy thread in the fabric of health care through the course of American history.  In the colonial years, the American market for commercial self-dosage was dominated by "patent medicines"—some of them actually patented—shipped overseas from the mother country.[1] Packed in containers of distinctive shape, sealed in wrappers printed with boastful therapeutic claims, advertised in the slender newborn press, these British nostrums far overshadowed occasional American imitators.

The Revolution ended this monopoly, and cultural nationalism generated an outpouring of made-in-America nostrums promoted in advertising that flaunted the flag and the eagle.  The nascent industry kept expanding aided by cultural democracy linked to the political democracy associated with Andrew Jackson's name.  Common schooling made the nation's citizens literate enough to read the lurid advertising in the county weeklies of the west and the penny press of eastern cities.  Nostrum makers, pushed by competition, became brash and braggart, pioneering the ingenious ramifications of the psychology of advertising.

In the post–Civil War Gilded Age, the nostrum boom soared to new heights.  Wood-pulp paper expanded the press enormously, and magazine advertising truly took hold.  As of 1900, patent medicines led all product categories in the amount of money spent for national advertising.  Chromolithography created colored trade cards.  "The advertising quack," observed a physician in the 1880s, "is the black wolf, aye, the Bengal tiger of the profession. . . .  He is full of shrewdness and cunning, and knows poor, weak human nature like a book."[2]

The charlatan's ads often sought to induce sickness in the healthy reader by translating mild transitory conditions such as low spirits, mild insomnia, or spots before the eyes into harbingers of insanity and syphilis.  Scaring the would-be customer was preliminary to offering hope, the promise of certain cure for the most dreaded diseases. This message was offered both directly and symbolically. Ben Hur fought for kidney vigor; Ponce de León promised renewal of youth. The American Indian, pictured in printed media or appearing live in touring medicine shows, offered white Americans the protection of curative products from the red man's forests.

Religion was appropriated to sanctify nostrums. The Bible was quoted in advertising. The Good Samaritan passed not by but stopped to recommend a packaged remedy. Praise from clergymen became profuse, and even popes gave testimonials. Patriotism continued to boost nostrums. Military heroes presented civilians with therapeutic secrets, and Uncle Sam signed a testimonial certifying that he was using one hundred thousand boxes of Ex-Lax every month.[3] The makers of a proprietary tonic acquired so many testimonials from members of the Congress that a skeptical congressman jibed on the House floor: "Peruna seems to be the favorite Congressional drink."[4]

Most testimonials came from humble citizens, and that very fact made them persuasive to other average men and women. Some such words of praise were faked, but there was scant need of this. Nostrum proprietors knew they could get, gratis or for a modest fee, sincere assertions of cure. Most ailments were self-limiting, but a nostrum rather than nature's healing power received enthusiastic credit. Or, feeling better because of the placebo effect, a nostrum taker would testify to a cure before that effect wore off. "If your brains won't get you into the papers," counseled a newspaper editor, "sign a 'patent medicine' testimonial. Maybe your kidneys will."[5]

Physicians, pharmacists, and other shrewd observers had criticized the quack's methods from the start. In the late nineteenth century, as patent medicine promotion burgeoned and as the science of medicine, represented most notably by demonstration of the germ theory, established firmer roots, the condemnation of pseudoscience grew keener. With the new century, the atmosphere for critics of society's many evils became more hospitable as journalists launched in popular magazines a muckraking crusade.

The most forthright critic of quackery was a former premedical student and crime reporter, Samuel Hopkins Adams, who published a blistering exposure in the pages of *Collier's* during 1905 and 1906. "Gullible America," Adams charged, "will spend this year some seventy-five millions of dollars in the purchase of patent medicines. In consideration of this sum it will swallow huge quantities of alcohol, an appalling amount of opiates and narcotics, a wide assortment of varied drugs ranging from powerful and dangerous heart depressants to insidious liver stimulants; and, far in excess of all other ingredients, undiluted fraud. For fraud, exploited by the skilfulest of advertising bunco men, is the basis of the trade."[6]

Adams followed this general charge with specific case examples. Inert ingredients were claimed as cures for the most threatening ailments, such as consumption, epilepsy, and heart disease. Virtually pure water was vended as a universal microbe killer. Soothing syrups for the very young contained unacknowledged opium, and catarrh powders contained unlabeled cocaine. It was a "shameful trade," Adams observed, "that stupefies helpless babies, and makes criminals of our young men and harlots of our young women."

"The Great American Fraud" series was quickly transformed into a book, published by the American Medical Association, an organization of the nation's mainline physicians that, under Dr. Arthur Cramp's direction, itself had launched a campaign to expose the menace of patent-medicine quackery.[7]

This forthright attack came at a crucial time, the final phase of a quarter-century campaign to get the Congress to enact a law to control a congeries of deceptions and hazards afflicting the nation's food and drug supply. Adams's articles and AMA lobbying proved indispensable in placing modest control provisions concerning proprietary medicines in the law that Congress passed and President Theodore Roosevelt signed in 1906.[8]

Nearly three centuries earlier, in 1630, in the Massachusetts Bay Colony, Nicholas Knopp had been either whipped or fined five pounds for selling as a cure for scurvy "a water of no worth nor value."[9] Such cases of quackery suppression had been extremely rare in local and state courts during subsequent years. Late in the nineteenth century, the Post Office Department began to use its fraud statutes to halt an occasional nostrum promotion, especially in the "lost manhood" category. Mormon Bishop Pills had come in three colors: red, white, and blue.

During early enforcement of the 1906 Food and Drugs Act, the Supreme Court decided that the law's taboo against "false and misleading" labeling statements did not apply to therapeutic claims. In plugging this loophole in 1912, Congress banned only those labeled claims that were both false and fraudulent. Proving fraud in court vastly increased a prosecutor's burden.

Most major marketers of proprietary remedies accepted the restraints of the 1906 law, which, after all, were squelching their more unscrupulous competitors. At first the large firms moved their excessive claims from labeling to advertising, still uncontrolled. When the Federal Trade Commission, established in 1914, began to view exaggerated therapeutic claims as an unfair trade practice, major firms softened their advertised promises and even changed them radically. In the slick magazines of the 1920s, dread diseases appeared hardly at all. Instead, in advertising expanded in scope and transformed in allure by the new psychology, proprietary makers promised relief from acid indigestion, athlete's foot, body odor, calendar fear, halitosis, intestinal fatigue, paralyzed pores, sandpaper hands, scalp crust, sneaker smell, and underarm offense. Major proprietors, pushed by law and the desire to be considered law-abiding, sensing economic advantage in such a stance, responding also to factors like the stage of scientific knowledge and the state of public opinion, modified their ingredients and their claims and preened themselves on their enhanced respectability. The pattern of this impact after 1906 has been repeated in subsequent decades, especially when new laws were passed as a result of sagging standards in industry, rising ethical concerns in society, new discoveries in science, and frightening episodes of health disaster.

For five years during the New Deal, Food and Drug Administration officials and their allies, especially women's organizations, sought legislation to strengthen the law's overall authority. Medicine proprietors fought vigorously to block this effort. The Food, Drug, and Cosmetic Act finally made it through Congress, signed by President Franklin D. Roosevelt in 1938.[10] This statute expanded FDA's weapons against quackery. All false and misleading statements in the labeling of a proprietary remedy were banned; fraudulent intent with respect to label claims need no longer be proved. False labeling included not only incorrect positive statements but also failure to reveal germane facts, especially warnings when medicines might have harmful side effects. Formula disclosure must be more complete: the common names of all active ingredients were required on labels, and for narcotic, hypnotic, and other potent drugs quantity and proportion had to be given. New drugs, both prescription and over-the-counter, could not be marketed until FDA officials had been persuaded by their manufacturers of their safety. This clause had resulted from the marketing of the new wonder drug, sulfanilamide, in a liquid dosage form with a poisonous solvent, diethylene glycol, leading to more than a hundred deaths. The new law also took account of medical devices and articles affecting the body's structure, like nose straighteners and breast developers. Penalties for violation were increased, and the FDA secured a new weapon to seek in court—the injunction. The agency had striven to gain control over nostrum advertising, but Congress denied it this authority, instead strengthening the FTC's power in this regard.

The 1938 law lofted controls in both a preventive and a policing way, ensuring greater safety of both prescription and over-the-counter medications. The next important watershed came in 1962 with the enactment of the Kefauver-Harris Amendments to the Food, Drug, and Cosmetics Act.[11] This new legislation was preceded by Senator Estes Kefauver's investigations of prescription drugs and was sped unanimously through Congress by the thalidomide scare, the revelation that this new European sedative caused dreadful deformities in babies whose mothers had taken it during pregnancy. For a decade the Food and Drug Administration focused its energies on the law's provisions applying to prescription drugs. But the law's stipulation that new drugs must be effective as well as safe applied also to self-medication products. In 1972 the FDA set in motion machinery for achieving this result.[12] To reconsider individually each of the thousands of proprietary products would be an impossible task. So the FDA determined on evaluation by product categories. Panels composed of leading specialists, with representatives from industry and consumer organizations sitting in, would determine which ingredients were safe and effective at what dosage levels, which were not, and which needed more testing before a determination could be made. The panels also would determine what legitimate therapeutic claims might be made in labeling. A proposed monograph containing each panel's judgment would be published to elicit public comments. With these comments and its own expertise, the FDA would revise the monograph and issue a tentative final monograph. More comments and further revision would lead to a final monograph that would govern all individual OTC medicines offered for sale in that product category. Panels were responsible for such categories as antacids, antimicrobials, antiperspirants, nonprescription contraceptives, hemorrhoidals, and internal analgesics.

The task has moved along steadily but slowly. After nearly a decade, an evaluator indicated that panels had decreed over a quarter of the ingredients examined either unsafe or ineffective, about a third safe and effective, and well over a third requiring more testing.[13] The ingredients condemned had been discarded by manufacturers, in some cases even before the end of the judgmental process. Labeling claims had been modified. A recent appraisal suggests that some seventy percent of FDA's review task has been completed, advancing toward the assurance of an over-the-counter supply of medications for minor ailments easily self-diagnosed that are safe, effective, and accurately labeled.[14]

During the same decades, FDA admitted new prescription drugs to the marketplace. The line between prescription and nonprescription medications was more sharply drawn by Congress in 1951. After 1962 the agency restudied for efficacy all new drugs admitted under the merely safe standard since 1938. Henceforth, all new drugs approved for marketing must be both safe and effective. The burden of proof placed on pharmaceutical companies kept enlarging, and the time taken by the FDA review kept lengthening. But, as the chemotherapeutic revolution proceeded, many classes of vitally important new drugs stocked the physicians' arsenal. In time, especially with the arrival of AIDS, speeding up the review process became an urgent priority. In December 1995, FDA Commissioner David Kessler could announce major accomplishment in this respect.[15]

Thus the obligations of regulators, during the nine decades after 1906, to ensure sound and useful medications for physicians to prescribe and for consumers to buy on their own for approved self-medication have steadily and enormously expanded. The same may be said as to responsibility for assuring a safe food supply. Successive laws also provided regulators with better weapons with which to combat quackery.

With such stronger regulatory capabilities, bolstered by the tide of more effective legitimate medicines, added to societal factors such as the expansion of compulsory education creating a presumably more knowledgeable population, it might be assumed that the quackery so keenly exposed and sharply condemned by Samuel Hopkins Adams at the start of the twentieth century would have shrunk into insignificance by the end of it. But that has not been the case. Instead, in a distressing paradox, as scientific medicine advanced and regulatory law gained greater power, pseudoscience also grew, so that in our own day larger sums are expended on quackery than ever before in our nation's experience.

How may such a paradox be explained? In part the reason lay in the fact that regulatory agencies had heavy obligations assigned to them by Congress, and in their setting of priorities they often could pursue only the most blatant and hazardous examples of quackery. In due course, indeed, Congress itself, heavily pressured by lobbies, placed some restraints on the FDA's control of abuses in the promotion of nutritional supplements and took other steps that favored unorthodox medical approaches. Another major factor in the expansion of health fraud was the boundless ingenuity of its promoters. All the clever techniques developed over the centuries lay close at hand for reuse and refashioning, and new modes of attracting a victim's attention and convincing him or her to trust in the quack's wares were borrowed from the nation's changing business and technological culture. A further fundamental feature of expanding quackery rested on continuing credulity. Anxiety about chronic ailments such as cancer and heart disease, for which, during the therapeutic revolution, no absolute cures appeared, and, in due course, panic about new diseases such as AIDS and reviving plagues like tuberculosis, led many people to fall prey to clever new lures promising sure prevention and certain cure. Factors in the broader intellectual environment seemed to crush caution about exaggerated health claims.

The 1906 law did not cover medical devices, so much quackish energy flowed in that direction. Dr. Albert Abrams of San Francisco developed a series of complex but inert gadgets that, trafficking on the public fascination with radio, allegedly diagnosed and treated disease over vast distances. Abrams's disciples kept variants of his machines at work for decades.[16]

In the wake of the 1938 law, while the FDA tested out its provisions by clamping down on the worst offenders with drugs, promoters turned to what they deemed a greener pasture, the pitching of nutritional products.[17] Lecturers toured the country praising their own supplements and both selling them after their lectures and placing them in the expanding ranks of health-food stores. Equally popular was the door-to-door approach, with pyramidal teams of salespersons bringing their pulverized alfalfa and complex mixes of vitamins and minerals into the parlors of America. The products might be innocuously labeled as far as the law was concerned, but that did not hinder some clerks in health-food stores and doorbell ringers from making false claims of the most extreme nature.

Another boom enterprise for skirting the law's demands was the unorthodox clinic, a means of evading interstate commerce at which unscrupulous physicians, sectarian practitioners, and untrained laymen treated patients with impressive machines and drugs or pseudodrug products.

The FDA won impressive victories in some hard-fought cases, as did the Federal Trade Commission and the Post Office Department, but agency officials realized that quackery had not been vanquished. Still, it came as a surprise to regulators themselves, in the mid-1950s, to sense quackery's immensity and truculence. When the separate segments of pseudomedical deception were added together by a new wave of muckraking journalists, the total annual cost to the American people came to a billion dollars.[18] Not only was the size staggering, so too was the belligerence with which major promoters fought back against regulatory attack. Nor were these engagements isolated battles. Foes of regulation seemed intent on welding their forces together. Harry Hoxsey, an untrained layman who ran a cancer clinic in Dallas, persuaded and purchased allies from among the naturopaths and chiropractors, from the radical right of religion and politics, and from the National Health Federation, organized by leading gadget and food-fad promoters.[19]

A period of revived regulatory vigor followed, with the FDA receiving an expanded budget for enforcement. As the agency's foes had sought to league together, so now opponents of quackery did likewise, the regulatory agencies with the American Medical Association, the American Cancer Society, the Arthritis Foundation, the National Better Business Bureau, and other organizations.[20] The common effort aimed at increasing public awareness of the deceptions and hazards posed by quackery. Major events in this campaign were a series of National Congresses on Quackery, the first held in Washington, D.C., in 1961, sponsored by the AMA and the FDA. To an assembled cross section of American society, the regulators told of their triumphs and defeats, and physician-experts elucidated patterns. The Congress received widespread publicity, and a second Congress two years later, again in the nation's capital, explored in greater detail quackery's continuing appeal. At a third Congress in Chicago in 1966, the only prosecutor in the nation specializing in medicolegal crimes, John W. Miner of California, gave an informed estimate of quackery's annual financial toll.[21] His figure, two or more billion dollars, doubled the estimate of a decade earlier. Quackery constituted "a criminal activity as harmful as any in society," Miner believed, "but against which the law has done the least."

In the 1970s, the coordinated campaign against quackery sagged while the ingenuity, vigor, and collaboration of those promoting unproven theories intensified. And currents in the broader environment enhanced vulnerability to the quack's appeals. The optimistic way in which Americans had viewed the future began to reverse itself. Many people "shifted their gaze from utopias to dystopias."[22] Occult beliefs became "a pervasive part of our culture."[23] The disenchanted young came to distrust reason and to treasure extreme examples of unreason. Astrology became a fixture of firm belief, a theme of rich reward to publishers. Numerology, palmology, and tarot cards flourished. Paperbacks on these themes topped bestseller lists in university bookstores across the country.[24] A popular magazine proclaimed: "Witches are rising everywhere."[25]

Vietnam and Watergate left a legacy of disillusion with big government, including its regulatory function, that grew ever stronger as the century neared its end. Environmental alarms, especially relating to nuclear energy, increased skepticism of government's scientific role. An ironic expression of this sentiment came in a commencement address by Kurt Vonnegut. "We would be a lot safer," the novelist told the graduates, "if the Government would take its money out of science and put it into astrology and reading palms."[26]

Consumer literacy concerning science and medicine, and with it popular trust in scientific professionals, tumbled downward. Carl Sagan considered the level of science education in school abysmal.[27] John C. Burnham, tracing the subject of popular science and health through American history, compressed his conclusion into his title, *How Superstition Won and Science Lost*.[28] The interpretation of medical unorthodoxy in the popular media, print and electronic, shifted away from the muckraking exposure that had dominated the 1960s toward uncritical acceptance and often drum-beating support. One rare critic described the vast majority of self-help health books on the market as an "R for Disaster."[29] Another skeptic assessed the science in the checkout-counter tabloids as a "new medieval fantasy world of magic, mystery and miracle."[30] Television and radio talk shows often gave promoters of unscientific health products a welcome warm enough to constitute endorsement. Indeed, some programs were truly infomercials pitching "cures" for baldness, obesity, and impotency.

Direct contact with vulnerable consumers became possible through the availability of increasingly detailed private records about age, location, income, and medical condition. The pitch was made over banks of WATS-line telephones, the sales by credit card, delivery by private systems to avoid postal inspectors. "This is the new electronic midway," the attorney general of Maine informed a House subcommittee. "Two-headed cows are easily ignored compared to the late night phone call to your home by an out-of-state caller who uncannily knows that you are an elderly person suffering from a medical ailment and who can convince you to invest large amounts of money for relief and magic lures."[31] Now, in the 1990s, health deception is keeping up with the communications revolution.[32] "Snakeoil . . . [is] oozing between the pixels of your computer screen." Quackery has invaded the Internet.

An increasing number of Americans, losing faith in established institutions, began to take health and well-being into their own hands.[33] Aging baby boomers, concerned with staying young, vigorous, slender, and free of disease, strayed beyond orthodox boundaries in their health choices. If ignorance played into the hands of dubious promoters, education did not guarantee protection against quackery. Investigation of cancer and AIDS quackery revealed that the better educated and more affluent seemed to be *most* susceptible to the deceiver's lures.[34] In 1984 a close student of quackery had estimated the nation's annual toll for health deception at $26 billion.[35] Less than a decade later, the National Research Council raised the sum to $40 billion.[36]

The major cancer quackery campaign from the 1960s into the 1980s, precipitating "one of the most politicized medical disputes in American history," concerned Laetrile.[37] Marketed by Ernst Krebs, a physician, and his son, Ernst Krebs Jr., Laetrile was chemically almost identical with amygdalin, a cyanide-containing compound found in the kernels of some nuts, especially almonds. Through its course of notoriety, the Krebs gave several differing explanations for its alleged therapeutic action. Its fame depended on the vigorous propagandizing and lobbying of organized groups, especially the John Birch Society and the International Association of Cancer Victims and Friends. Flying the "freedom of choice" banner, these groups won some legal decisions in lower courts, got pro-Laetrile laws enacted in half the states, and came close to removing the effectiveness provision from federal drug law. The Food and Drug Administration staunchly fought the tactics of Laetrile promoters, and eventually the National Cancer Institute sponsored clinical trials that proved Laetrile ineffective for treating cancer and, in its own right, hazardous. Laetrile treatment retreated to Mexico, and cancer quackery in the United States adopted a multifaceted regimen that included diet patterns, detoxification, and mind-control, guided in part by New Age philosophies and religions from the Orient.[38]

When the tragedy of AIDS, a brand-new disease, came to the public's attention in 1981, both those who acquired the causative virus and members of the broader public fearful of contagion from such instruments as public telephones fell prey to victimization by quacks.[39] Scientifically established therapy for combating the virus and the opportunistic afflictions that preyed on the body's weakening immunity developed slowly and did not reach the stage of certain cures. So deceptive cure had a field day. No single promotion came to dominate the AIDS scene in the way that Laetrile had done for cancer. "Practically every piece of snake oil that's ever been used for anything," said William Jarvis, a close observer of quackery's trends, was "being adapted for use in AIDS."[40] Purported AIDS cures by means of injections alone encompassed a long list, including amino acids, cells from fetal animals, Easter lily bulbs, hydrogen peroxide, ozone, polio vaccine, pond scum, snake venom, and the sufferer's own filtered urine. Nor has the ingenuity of promoters hunting a market among the growing AIDS population ceased.[41] In 1995 a device was being sold with the claim that, if a person's picture was inserted in the machine, it would diagnose and cure AIDS by means of healing power conveyed direct to the individual's brain through a subliminal tape.[42]

In recent decades, the largest monetary segment of quackery, and the trickiest to regulate, has concerned nutrition.[43] A *Study of Health Prac-*

*tices and Opinions,* sponsored by seven federal agencies, found that susceptibility to most kinds of quackery was guided by no coherent body of theory, but self-treatment with food supplements bore a distinct resemblance to a nutrition myth that had been deliberately concocted by manufacturers of nutritional wares, health-food-store proprietors, door-to-door salesmen, popular lecturers, television pitchmen, and authors of pamphlets and books.[44] The myth's main tenets held that most disease resulted from improper diet, that food grown on the nation's fields had lost its value because of worn-out soil, that fertilizers had poisoned almost all crops, that food processing destroyed natural nutrients and added more poisons. Salvation lay, the myth held, in certain "wonder" foods and herbs and in supplementing the diet with megadoses of vitamins, minerals, and other exotic items, most often sold in complex mixtures.

On a case-by-case basis, the Food and Drug Administration had used the 1938 act to attack the most outrageous pseudonutritional promotions.[45] In 1962 the agency sought to bolster this approach by revising its regulations, two decades old and seriously outmoded, so as to introduce scientific rationality into marketing of food supplements, and held marathon hearings that accumulated a record of 32,000 pages.[46] In 1973 FDA issued revised proposals. The health-food industry counterattacked, getting their customers to deluge Congress with mail, its volume exceeding that prompted by Watergate. The result was an amendment to the 1938 law enacted in 1976, the first retrogressive legislative step with regard to self-treatment since 1906. The amendment, as the FDA viewed it, would bar the agency from "limiting the potency of vitamins and minerals in dietary supplements to nutritionally useful levels, classifying a vitamin or mineral preparation as a 'drug' because it exceeds a nutritionally rational and useful potency; requiring the presence in dietary supplements of nutritionally essential vitamins and minerals; [and] prohibiting the inclusion in dietary supplements of useless ingredients with no nutritional value."[47] Commissioner Alexander Schmidt judged the result "a charlatan's dream."

The terms of the 1976 law and the shock of its enactment reduced nutritional supplements to a low priority at the Food and Drug Administration for more than a decade, while public eagerness to assume more responsibility for health decisions led to a boom in supplement sales. Two events ended the uneasy truce between regulators, on one side, and supplement promoters and their committed customers, on the other, leading to renewed battles. Again industry, aided by the Congress, rendered the FDA and unwitting consumers a defeat.

Ironically, the first event was the enactment of a law in 1990, the Nutritional Labeling and Education Act, that benefited the public by mak-

ing the labeling of foods more explicit so as to permit the careful consumer to buy wisely in the interest of a healthy diet. At the last minute,
however, Senator Orrin Hatch of Utah arranged an amendment calling
for special consideration for dietary supplements and similar subtances,
such as amino acids, enzymes, and herbal tinctures.[48]

The other event was the arrival in 1991 at the Food and Drug Administration of David Kessler as commissioner. Dr. Kessler held the firm conviction that food and drug laws must be obeyed. The regulations proposed for enforcing the new labeling law revealed this rigor, as did the
rejection of a proposal from the American Herbal Products Association
for a review committee to make decisions for FDA on the approval of
herbs.[49] The commissioner also appointed a Diet Supplement Task Force
to study the vexed question and propose policy solutions. Its report in
May 1992 insisted on safety of supplements as the "overriding concern"
and made precise recommendations about stringent standards, good manufacturing practices, properly supported claims, and accurately informa-
tive labeling.[50]

By this time the supplement manufacturers had become alarmed.[51]
Besides the imminent threatening report, there were two bills in Congress to strengthen the power of both the FDA and the Federal Trade
Commission to combat fraud. In February, industry leaders met and formed
the National Health Alliance to let all segments of the supplement industry coordinate a massive letter-writing and telephoning campaign directed to members of the Congress protesting the FDA's policies. One
Democratic representative alone received ten thousand phone calls.[52]
Sellers of nutritional wares were warned that if they didn't complain loudly
they'd go broke. Customers were frightened by being told that the FDA
intended to deprive them of their vitamins. Some health-food stores gave
discounts to buyers who came in bringing a letter of protest. The pressure
got a Hatch bill through Congress approving a year's moratorium on the
implementation of the FDA's supplement regulations. More important,
the next April, Hatch in the Senate and Bill Richardson in the House
introduced companion bills entitled the Dietary Supplement and Health
Education Act of 1993 that would severely shrink FDA's power to police
supplements most broadly defined. In an editorial the *New York Times*
denigrated the proposed statute as "The 1993 Snake Oil Protection Act."[53]
Kessler, testifying before a congressional committee, denied his agency's
evil intentions as charged in the producers' propaganda, warned how the
pending bill would eviscerate consumer protection, and  described the
grave evils in the existing supplement marketplace.[54] The commissioner
drew his evidence from a just-released document prepared by his agency,

*Unsubstantiated Claims and Documented Health Hazards in the Dietary Supplement Marketplace.*[55] This cited promotional literature containing unsubstantiated claims relating to half a dozen dread diseases. It gave examples of recent regulatory actions. It listed illnesses and injuries linked to the use of specific supplements. And it reported the false advice given by employees in health-food stores to agency inspectors who asked about their products' efficacy for treating high blood pressure, weakened immunity, and cancer.

As 1993 ended, the FDA announced its regulations for supplements that would go into effect in mid-June, and these did not retreat from the demanding standards Dr. Kessler had forecast.[56] But Congress was to have, if somewhat delayed, the last word. Meanwhile, the tempo of the propaganda campaign against the FDA heightened. A videotaped public-service announcement dramatized governmental interference with the public's right to take vitamins. The video showed a SWAT team with guns drawn invading a private home to arrest its owner (acted by Mel Gibson), who is found in the kitchen holding a bottle of vitamin C. As Gibson is handcuffed, he complains: "It's only vitamins; vitamin C, you know, like in oranges."[57]

In 1994 a majority of the members in both Houses had signed on as co-sponsors of the somewhat revised Hatch-Richardson bill, and in October the bill was passed and signed into law by President Bill Clinton.[58] The law creates a new category, separate from foods or drugs, that is almost impossible to reach by the rules the FDA formerly used to challenge questionable supplements. Supplements are defined very broadly to encompass almost everything promoters would seek to sell. Products require no efficacy test before marketing. The burden of proof for determining safety has changed from the marketer to the FDA. The maker must merely furnish "reasonable assurance" that no ingredient provides "a significant or unreasonable risk of illness or injury." No manufacturing standards could be set by the FDA for at least two years. Claims may be made on labels, not assurances of prevention or cure of disease, but as to the way a supplement affects the body's "structure or function," so long as the claim is true and not misleading. The evidence to support claims may be minimal. The label is not required to state that claims have not been approved or reviewed by the FDA. Ingredient and nutrition labeling is mandatory. Retailers may make available books and articles to help customers learn about health-related benefits of dietary supplements, so long as the material is true and does not promote a particular product. A Commission on Dietary Supplements is mandated by the law to study and make recommendations on regulation of label claims and on procedures for evaluation of claims. An Office of Dietary Supplements is ordered to be set up in the National Institutes of Health. Most of the provisions of the law were to become effective on the first day of 1997. The President decided whom he would appoint to the commission; the National Institutes of Health opened what it named the Office of Dietary Supplement Research in November 1995; the Food and Drug Administration began to propose for comment the rules it must make to guide regulation under the law, a law more precise with respect to supplements but less demanding upon their manufacturers and distributors. How consumers will fare is yet to be seen.

In the year of the Dietary Supplement law's enactment, the preface was signed to a thick volume that addressed herbal medicines, along with a wide range of other unorthodox medical themes.[59] Despite the FDA's skepticism, the authors stated, an increasing number of Americans were resorting to herbal preparations, especially people afflicted with chronic diseases such as AIDS, arthritis, cancer, and diabetes. "Pharmaceutical drugs are seen increasingly as overprescribed, expensive, and dangerous. Herbal remedies are seen as less expensive and less toxic."

The book in which these words appeared, *Alternative Medicine: Expanding Medical Horizons*, summarized presentations at a Workshop on Alternative Medicine held in Chantilly, Virginia, in September 1992, a gathering characterized by a complete open-door policy, welcoming spokespersons of every variety of therapeutic persuasion. Sponsor for the meeting was the Office of Alternative Medicine in the National Institutes of Health. The report's foreword warned that the NIH did not endorse the therapies mentioned in the book and cautioned readers "not to seek the therapies described . . . for serious health problems without consultation with a learned physician," because many of the treatments had "not been subjected to rigorous scientific investigation to prove safety or efficacy."[60] Nonetheless, some presenters at Chantilly did make their presence there seem as if that meant their unorthodox therapies had won NIH endorsement.[61]

The Office of Alternative Medicine—briefly called the Office of Unconventional Medical Practices—had been established in 1992 at the direction of Congress in the bill appropriating funds for the National Institutes of Health.[62] Alternative medicines of possibly marvelous merit, Iowa Senator Tom Harkin had been persuaded to believe, were being neglected by governmental health agencies. Chief persuaders included two other Iowans, former Representative Berkley Bedell and Frank Wiewel.[63] Bedell, engaged in fishing-tackle manufacturing, held that an unconventional remedy processed from cow's milk had cured him of Lyme disease and that another unorthodox treatment, 714-X, made in Canada by Gaston Naessens, had prevented recurrence of his prostate cancer after surgery for that ailment. Wiewel had been a vigorous champion of immunoaugmentative therapy for cancer, scorned by orthodox specialists, and then began operating People Against Cancer, a referral agency for questionable cancer treatments. After Harkin had sponsored the law that secured OAM's creation, he himself became a true believer in an unorthodox "cure."[64] On Capitol Hill, Bedell introduced the Senator to Royden Brown of Arizona, maker of High Desert bee-pollen capsules. Harkin took 250 capsules over five days and rejoiced that his allergies had been cured. He did not know at the time that, several months previously, Brown had paid a $200,000 settlement under a consent agreement with the Federal Trade Commission, in which he promised to stop making dozens of false therapeutic claims for his capsules in his television infomercials. These ads had also averred that Ronald Reagan and "the risen Jesus Christ, when he came back to Earth" had consumed bee pollen.

National Institutes of Health officials launched the new office with an acting director and an ad hoc advisory panel of twenty members that included Bedell and Wiewel and leading advocates of major elements of alternative medicine.[65] A few qualified researchers represented the medical establishment, including Barrie Cassileth, an expert scholar of the sociology and psychology of quackery. Some severe critics of quackery were consulted and considered but not, in the end, selected.

After a deliberate search, the NIH, in October 1992, a month after the Chantilly conference, appointed a director for the Office of Alternative Medicine, Joseph Jacobs. His background, a journalist noted, seemed "custom-tailored for the job."[66] Son of a Mohawk mother and a part-Cherokee father, Jacobs had been treated by his mother with herbs and healing ceremonies, as well as with orthodox medicine, as he was growing up. He attended college at Columbia, then medical school at Yale, followed by further medical training at Dartmouth. To repay the expense of his medical education, Jacobs went with his wife, a student of Chinese calligraphy who he met at Yale, to serve as a pediatrician for three years in the Indian Health Service near Gallup, New Mexico. There he gained respect for the Navajo medicine men who worked in collaboration with the doctors of Western medicine in a way he deemed helpful. Jacobs returned east, secured an M.B.A. in health-care administration from the Wharton School of the University of Pennsylvania, worked for the Public Health Service in Rockville, Maryland, then for the Aetna Life Insurance Company in Hartford, Connecticut, as medical director of research and program development, before being hired to assume the challenging new position in Bethesda.

Jacobs had faith that the broad realm of alternative medicine would yield products and practices of great benefit to humanity. "Traditional methods of healing in other cultures," he observed, "do represent several thousand years of trial and error, and they are being used by a majority of the world's population. It's technological arrogance on our part to fail to recognize this."[67] Moreover, there were many contemporary clues, such as the dedication to massage in the sports field and the satisfaction many people suffering with back pain receive from chiropractors.[68] Even crystal therapy, Jacobs "wouldn't rule . . . out completely." Current medical practice had become too technological, and specialists had a skewed view of the world because of their narrow focus.[69] Jacobs had high hopes for the OAM's mission: "We may help promote a revolution in thinking among practitioners and researchers. It's a bold new venture, sort of like being on the starship *Enterprise*. We're going where no one has gone before."[70]

The route to discovery, however, required the use of the most capable science: "I'm not going to be able to wave a magic wand over a particular alternative practice and declare it valid or invalid. I think my job is clear; to support research. And once we get results we will publish them for other people to see."[71]

Jacobs planned to place his main trust in the prevailing research methods of orthodox science, grants awarded after careful peer review, and research centers to be established at prestigious medical schools.[72] This approach was not that most favored by members of the advisory committee who had sold the OAM concept to Senator Harkin. At an early panel meeting, Frank Wiewel had stated: "People from the alternative community aren't on N[ational] C[ancer] I[nstitute] review boards. . . . Let's get real—this is an ingrained bureaucracy. We've got to break the bureaucracy of the past and establish a new order."[73] What Bedell, Wiewel, and their like-minded colleagues favored were quick field studies that would validate alternative treatments.[74] Jacobs accepted the concept of such studies, even though they were less sophisticated than sound clinical trials, so long as they were carefully carried out and checked for accuracy of data. His deliberation and safeguards seemed excessive to Harkin's allies, who protested to the Senator, who conveyed the message to NIH. Jacobs stood his ground, arguing that politics should not replace the scientific method. One of the first field trials scheduled would investigate bee-pollen capsules. Jacobs himself went to Arizona to discuss plans for the tests with Royden Brown.[75] It was agreed that a professor at the University of Texas Medical Center at Tyler would prepare the protocal governing the double-blind placebo controlled study using patients with pollen-sensitive asthma and hay fever. Later, when Senator Harkin called a hearing before his subcommittee to inquire why research in the Office was not proceeding more rapidly, especially studies in the field, Jacobs explained the demands of sophisticated science. And he provided a countertestimonial to Harkin's praise of Brown's product. "When I was there," Jacobs told the Senator, "I was suffering really badly from allergies. . . . I took his therapy and became nauseous and almost vomited. . . . I tried the bee pollen. It did not work for me."

Critics worried that the OAM would turn into a haven for quacks. "It could be true," Jacobs replied, "if we didn't apply rigorous scientific evaluation to the various therapies. Yes, there are plenty of charlatans out there. Some may test us. Some may even engage us and try to enhance their marketability just by their association with NIH, no matter what we conclude. But 'casting call for quacks' definitely gives us something to work away from."[76] He trusted that his office would at least take away from quacks "the Galileo ploy," the assertion that, in time, their castigators would have to acknowledge that their nostrums were indeed miracle medicines.[77]

Amid such tensions, the work of the OAM got gradually under way. The publication of an article in the *New England Journal of Medicine* in January 1993 focused national attention on the object of the Office's concern.[78] The Harvard authors, the leading one, David Eisenberg, a member of the OAM's policy committee, surprised the nation's medical community by reporting how prominent a role alternative medicine played in Americans' health-care choices. One out of three Americans in 1990 had resorted to unconventional therapies when sick. The total bill came to $14 billion. A third of such users saw alternative practitioners, averaging nineteen visits during the year. Indeed, the total visits to alternative therapists outnumbered visits to primary-care physicians by 425 million to 388 million. The survey considered therapies not being considered by the OAM, especially commercial weight-loss programs. It included therapies that most analysts would deem properly part of regular medicine, such as exercise, relaxation methods, and self-help groups. So the survey was criticized for overstating the case.[79] Alternative medicine, indeed, a "buzzword" to one critic, encompassed a long amorphous spectrum, ranging from procedures already tested and respectable, through sects of the nineteenth century regaining energy, such as homeopathy and naturopathy, through imports of ancient Oriental systems from China and India, to indubitable domestic quackery whose promoters sought to crowd under a canopy that seemed to be rising in notoriety, if not in respect.[80]

With a budget of $2 million—which Jacobs joked was "a homeopathic level of funding"[81] —the OAM announced its first competition for grants to investigate and validate alternative medicine practices.[82]   Standard NIH peer-review procedures were carefully followed in evaluating the 425 proposals received, and thirty grants of $30,000 to last for a year were awarded.[83]   Recipients represented major universities across the country. Diseases involved included AIDS, asthma, cancer, cystic fibrosis, depression, and Parkinson's disease.  Modalities also ran a broad gamut, including acupuncture, antidepressants, Ayurveda, electrochemical current, guided imagery, homeopathy, hypnosis, macrobiotic diet, massage, music therapy, t'ai chi, and even the influence of intercessory prayer.

Jacobs's plan for a series of university centers to perform sophisticated research on alternative medicine, an idea strongly supported by David Eisenberg, met firm opposition from an entrenched segment of his advisory committee.  Only two such centers were authorized: at Bastyr University in Seattle, to assess unconventional therapies for AIDS, and at Minneapolis Medical Research, to focus on alternative therapies for addiction.[84]

Jacobs, in turn, was cautious about proceeding with field investigations, sometimes referred to as outcomes research. Senator Harkin at his hearing threatened to use "the power of the purse" unless the planned studies were speeded up.[85]   These included Brown's bee-pollen capsules, as well as three cancer studies, involving shark cartilage and the unorthodox and much criticized therapies of Stanislaw Burzynski of Houston and Emanuel Revici of New York City.[86]

The bitterness of controversy and the sense of hopelessness about the outcome finally broke Jacobs's will to fight. Senator Harkin's four cronies on the advisory council blocked his scientific plans, and he would not yield to the travesty of certain field investigations.  The director had wanted a member of the American Cancer Society's Committee on Questionable Methods of Cancer Management to be appointed to the permanent council, a plan vetoed by Harkin's allies, who retained their own seats in the shift from the ad hoc to the regular body.[87]  So, full of frustration, Jacobs resigned, leaving office at the end of September 1994 after a tenure of less than two years.[88]  He spoke freely of how Harkin and his staff and allies on the council had pressed him repeatedly to fund their pet projects. Jacobs charged that the Harkin cronies represented neither the alternative community nor the patient community, but only their own agenda. Wiewel had been sent a warning letter about exploiting the NIH name to promote his business.[89]

In departing to move back to his former home, Jacobs said: "I prefer the ticks of Connecticut to the politics of Washington."[90] "We had a senator who chairs the appropriations committee telling us: 'This is what you've got to do.' "[91] The *Los Angeles Times* editorialized, anticipating that valuable results would still come from scientific evaluation of alternative medicine, but regretting the pressures that had forced Jacobs to resign.[92] "However, there are dangers," the editorialist opined. "Alternative medicine has provided fertile ground for all manner of snake-oil salesmen and other scam artists who prey on the desperate and gullible. . . . There is a crying need for an agency like the NIH to separate the wheat from the chaff."

In July 1995, ten months after Dr. Jacobs's departure, Dr. Wayne B. Jonas became director of the Office of Alternative Medicine.[93] He came from his post as director of the Medical Research Fellowship at Walter Reed Army Institute of Research, where he taught research methodology and performed laboratory research in immunology and toxicology.[94] Dr. Jonas's training had included experience in several alternative subfields. He had become involved with the OAM at its first formal meeting, having spoken on the theme of research techniques. Later he chaired a conference on research methodology in alternative medicine and contributed on the topic to the volume *Alternative Medicine*.

Upon arrival, Dr. Jonas reorganized the office into six functional sections and set forth guiding principles for research, including that it be "scientifically rigorous and contextually sensitive."[95] NIH deputy director Ruth Kirchstein asserted: "The OAM has a sense of activity and stability for the first time."[96] Its staff had doubled, and so had its budget, Congress having raised its appropriation to $6 million.[97]

The controversial Field Investigations Program received a new name: the Research Development and Investigation Program.[98] Its projects, all "stalled for various reasons," were "essentially starting over and . . . [would] have to undergo screening and evaluation." Dr. Jacobs's cherished goal of research groups at major universities to focus on alternative treatments for chronic health conditions took a major step forward in October 1995, when eight such centers were funded at universities across the nation from Harvard to Stanford.[99]

Not many decisive judgments have yet been rendered. In October 1995, the OAM co-sponsored a conference on "Integration of Behavioral and Relaxation Approaches Into the Treatment of Chronic Pain and Insomnia."[100] The independent panel endorsed meditation, hypnosis, and biofeedback for these purposes. And Dr. Jonas was optimistic about valuable results to be achieved in the future.[101]

Some skeptics of the OAM's mission had hoped it might find and pub-licize negative results, expose quackery, and debunk superstition.[102] That hasn't been happening, and Dr. Jonas has defined this role essentially out of his mission.[103] His office does not test "every unlikely claim." Prob-ably over ninety percent are "screened out as low priority and are not evaluated." This leaves unexposed a quantity of devious deviltry to keep the quackery quotient soaring.

*Emory University*

## Notes

1. The historical section that launches this essay has been adapted from my publica-tions: *The Toadstool Millionaires: A Social History of Patent Medicines in America before Federal Regulation* (Princeton, 1961); *The Medical Messiahs: A Social History of Health Quackery in Twentieth-Century America* (updated edition: Princeton, 1992); "From Hooper to Hohensee," *Journal of the American Medical Association* 204 (April 1, 1968): 100–104; "American Health Quackery: An Historical View," *Georgia Journal of Science* 38 (1980): 33–40; "The Foolmaster Who Fooled Them," *Yale Journal of Biology and Medicine* 53 (1980): 555–66.

2. Willis P. King, *Quacks and Quackery in Missouri* (St. Louis, 1882), 6.

3. Bella C. Landauer Collection, The New York Historical Society.

4. James Luther Slayden of Texas, *Congressional Record*, 59th Cong., 1st sess., June 22, 1906, 8987; James Harvey Young, "Pe-Ru-Na: A Catarrh Cure from Columbus," *Timeline* 12 (November-December 1995): 2–17.

5. *Toronto Star* cited in Arthur J. Cramp, *Nostrums and Quackery and Pseudo-Medicine* (Chicago, 1936), 197.

6. Adams's series appeared in *Collier's* between October 7, 1905, and February 17, 1906. It was published in book form as *The Great American Fraud* (Chicago, 1906).

7. James Harvey Young, "Arthur Cramp: Quackery Foe," *Pharmacy in History* 37 (1995): 176–82.

8. Food and Drugs Act, June 30, 1906, 34 Stat. 768, and Sherley Amendment, August 23, 1912, 37 Stat. 416.

9. *Records of the Governor and Company of the Massachusetts Bay in New England* (Bos-ton, 1853), I, 83.

10. Federal Food, Drug, and Cosmetic Act, June 25, 1938, 52 Stat. 1040. The best study of the securing of this legislation is Charles O. Jackson, *Food and Drug Legislation in the New Deal* (Princeton, 1970).

11. The Kefauver-Harris Amendments, 76 Stat. 78. Studies of the enactment of this law are Richard Harris, *The Real Voice* (New York, 1964), and Richard McFadyen, "Estes Kefauver and the Drug Industry," Ph.D. diss., Emory University, 1973). The FTC statute was the Wheeler-Lea Act, 52 Stat. 111.

12. *Food and Drug Administration Annual Report, 1971*, p. 26; *1972*, 181–82; James Harvey Young, *American Self-Dosage Medicines: An Historical Perspective* (Lawrence, Kan., 1974), 51–52.

13. Jean S. Welch, "Legislation Affecting Manpower," *American Pharmacy* 20 (Sep-tember 1980): 22.

14. Doug Podolsky, "Questionable Medicine," *U.S. News & World Report*, May 15, 1995, 101–5.

15. David Kessler, Remarks to the Food and Drug Law Institute, December 12, 1995.

16. Young, *The Medical Messiahs*, 137–42, 260–81.

17. Ibid., 333-59; Stephen Barrett and Victor Herbert, *The Vitamin Pushers* (Amherst N.Y., 1994).

18. James Cook, *New York Post* series, May 20-June 2, 1957.

19. Young, *The Medical Messiahs*, 360–89.

20. Ibid., 390–407.

21. Ibid., 421–22.

22. Harry Levin, "The Great Good Place," *New York Review of Books*, March 6, 1980, 47–49.

23. Barry Singer and Victor A. Benassi, "Occult Beliefs," *American Scientist* 69 (January-February 1981): 49–55.

24. Bennett Kremen and Peter Collier, "Unrequired Reading: East and West," *New York Times Book Review*, February 15, 1970, 5, 24, 26.

25. Brian Vachon, "Witches Are Rising," *Look*, August 24, 1971, 40–44.

26. Cited in James Wolcott, "Mod Apostle," *New York Review of Books*, November 22, 1979, 11–12.

27. Sagan on MacNeil/Lehrer News Hour, PBS, February 9, 1983; William Celis 3d, "Science I.Q. of Americans Is Not O.K., Survey Shows," *New York Times*, April 21, 1994.

28. John C. Burnham, *How Superstition Won and Science Lost* (New Brunswick, N.J., 1987).

29. "Self-Health Books: R for Disaster?" *American Council on Science and Health News & Views* 1 (1979), 1.

30. David Leff, "Four Wondrous Weeks of Science and Medicine in the Amazing, Incredible Supermarket Press," *National Association of Science Writers Newsletter* 2 (1980), 3.

31. James E. Tierney testimony, *Quackery: A $10 Billion Scandal, Hearings before the Subcommittee on Health and Long-Term Care of the Select Committee on Aging*, House of Representatives (98th Cong., 2d sess., 1984), 178; Anthony Ramirez, "A Crackdown on Phone Marketing," *New York Times*, February 10, 1995; NBC Today Show, February 26, 1996.

32. Tony Cappasso, "Cyber Cures?" *The State Journal-Register*, Springfield, Ill., February 4, 1996; Edward Baig, "The Medical Hot Line in Your PC," *Business Week*, February 20, 1995, 101–2.

33. Suzanne Hamlin, "Diverse and Pricey Newsletters Flooding Mailboxes," *New York Times*, August 9, 1995; Marian Burros, "A New Goal Beyond Organic: Clean Food," ibid., February 7, 1996.

34. Barrie R. Cassileth et al., "Contemporary Unorthodox Treatments in Cancer Medicine," *Annals of Internal Medicine* 101 (1984): 105–12; William Robins, "Doctors Urge Campaign Against AIDS Quackery," *New York Times*, March 16, 1988.

35. Victor Herbert testimony, *Quackery: A $10 Billion Scandal*, 1984 House Hearings.

36. William Barnhill, "Panacea or Poison? Unproven Remedies under Surveillance," *Arthritis Today* 6 (January-February): 30–31.

37. James C. Petersen and Gerald E. Markle, "Expansion of Conflict in Cancer Controversies," *Research in Social Movements: Conflicts and Change* 4 (1981): 151–69; James Harvey Young, "Laetrile in Historical Perspective," in Young, *American Health Quackery: Collected Essays* (Princeton, 1992), 205–85.

38. Barrie R. Cassileth, "After Laetrile, What?" *New England Journal of Medicine* 306 (1982): 1482–84.

39. James Harvey Young, "AIDS and Deceptive Therapies," in Young, *American Health Quackery*, 256–85.

40. Janny Scott and Lynn Simross, "AIDS: Underground Options—The Search for Hope," *Los Angeles Times*, August 16, 1987.

41. "Statement of Representative Charles E. Schumer, D-NY[,] Chairman, House

Subcommittee on Crime and Criminal Justice[,] Oversight Hearing on Health Care Fraud: AIDS Fraud—Deceit, Dollars and Despair[,] May 27, 1993."

42. Don Aird to John Swann, July 5, 1995, History Office, Food and Drug Administration, Rockville, Md.

43. Victor Herbert testimony, *Quackery: A $10 Million Scandal*, 1984 House Hearing; Barrett and Herbert, *The Vitamin Pushers*.

44. Young, *The Medical Messiahs*, 350–54.

45. Ibid., 205–8, 338–59.

46. Ibid., 446–49; James Harvey Young, "The Agile Role of Food: Some Historical Reflections," in John A. Hathcock and Julius Coon, eds., *Nutrition and Drug Interrelations* (New York, 1978), 1–18.

47. Harold Hopkins, "Regulating Vitamins and Minerals," *FDA Consumer* 10 (July-August 1976): 10–11; FDA Talk Paper, 1976

48. Stephen Barrett, "Assault on FDA Continues," *Nutrition Forum* 16 (May/June 1993): 26.

49. Mark Blumenthal, "The FDA Rejection," *HerbalGram*, no. 26 (Winter 1992): 23, 41.

50. Food and Drug Administration, *Dietary Supplements Task Force Final Report*, May 1992.

51. Barrett and Herbert, *The Vitamin Pushers*, 430-35.

52. Stephen Barrett, "Supplement Bill Passes," *Nutrition Forum*, 12 (January-February 1995): 9–11.

53. "The Snake Oil Protection Act," *New York Times*, October 5, 1993.

54. Statement by David A. Kessler . . . before the Subcommittee on Health and the Environment, Committee on Energy and Commerce, United States House of Representatives, July 29, 1993.

55. Food and Drug Administration, *Unsubstantiated Claims and Documented Health Hazards in the Dietary Marketplace*, July 1993.

56. FDA News Release, December 29, 1993; Marian Burros, "Eating Well," *New York Times*, December 15, 1993.

57. Barrett and Herbert, *The Vitamin Pushers*, 433.

58. Dietary Supplement Health and Education Act of 1994, An Act to amend the Federal Food, Drug, and Cosmetic Act to establish standards with respect to dietary supplements, October 25, 1994 108 Stat. 4325; Dietary Supplement Health and Education Act of 1994, [FDA summary], December 1, 1995; "Herbal Roulette," *Consumer Reports* 60 (1995): 698–705; "NIH Office of Dietary Supplements Research," October 27, 1995; "FDA Published Dietary Supplement Rules," January 2, 1996.

59. *Alternative Medicine: Expanding Medical Horizons* (Washington, D.C., [1995]), 185–86.

60. Ibid., vii.

61. Paul Trachtman, "NIH Looks at the Implausible and the Inexplicable," *Smithsonian* 25 (September 1994): 110–23; Stephen Budiansky, "Cures or 'Quackery'?" *U.S. News & World Report*, July 17, 1995, 48–51.

62. *Alternative Medicine, Hearing before a Subcommittee of the Committee on Appropriations*, United States Senate (103d Cong., 1st sess.), June 24, 1993 (Washington, D.C., 1993), 1–2; "Office of Science Policy and Legislation, Unconventional Medical Practices, FY 1992, Activities and Plans."

63. Ibid., 95–107; Margaret Mason, "Health Quest," *Washington Post*, June 26, 1992; Stephen Budiansky, "Cures or 'quackery'?" *U.S. News & World Report*, July 17, 1995, 48–51.

64. Ibid; *Alternative Medicine* (Hearing), 2–4.

65. Jim Bryant, "NIH Panel Reviews 'Unconventional' Medical Practices," *The NIH Record* 44 (July 7, 1992): 1, 6; Stephen Barrett, "'Alternative' Therapy Buzzword for the '90s," *Nutrition Forum* 10 (January-February 1993): 1–2; Barrett and Herbert, *The Vitamin*

*Pushers*, 371.

66. Natalie Angier, "Where the Unorthodox Gets a Hearing at N.I.H.," *New York Times*, March 16, 1993. Jacobs's career is also sketched in Marilyn Achirov and Linda Kramer, "Medicine Man," *People* 39 (April 12, 1993): 95–97, and in Diana McLellan, "Medicine Man," *Washingtonian* 23 (May 1993): 46–47, 124–25.

67. Trachtman, "NIH Looks at the Implausible and the Inexplicable," 121.

68. McLellan, "Medicine Man," 46–47, 124–25.

69. Trachtman, "NIH Looks at the Implausible and the Inexplicable," 115.

70. Anastasia Toufexis, "Dr. Jacobs' Alternative Mission," *Time*, March 1, 1993, 43–44.

71. Trachtman, "NIH Looks at the Implausible and the Inexplicable," 117.

72. Ibid., 117–19.

73. Bryant, "NIH Panel Reviews 'Unconventional' Medical Practices," 8.

74. *Alternative Medicine* (Hearing), 105–6; Trachtman, "NIH Looks at the Implausible and the Inexplicable," 117; Kenneth Silber, "Alternative Medicine Agency Can't Bridge Gap," *Washington Times*, December 8, 1994.

75. *Alternative Medicine* (Hearing), 116–17, 134.

76. McLellan, "Medicine Man," 125.

77. Silber, "Alternative Medicine Agency Can't Bridge Gap."

78. David M. Eisenberg et al., "Unconventional Medicines in the United States—Prevalence, Cost, and Patterns of Use," *New England Journal of Medicine* 328 (1993): 246–52.

79. Barrett, "'Alternative' Therapy Buzzword for the '90s," 2.

80. Ibid.; Norman Gevitz, ed., *Other Healers: Unorthodox Medicine in America* (Baltimore, 1988); Andrew Stanway, *Alternative Medicine* (London, 1980); Jack Rasso, "*Alternative*" *Health Care: A Comprehensive Guide* (Amherst, N.Y., 1994); Kurt Butler, *A Consumer's Guide to Alternative Medicine* (Amherst N.Y., 1992).

81. Trachtman, "NIH Looks at the Implausible and the Inexplicable," 121.

82. Ibid., 117–18.

83. NIH OAM Grant Recipients, October 6, 1993.

84. *Alternative Medicine* (Hearing), 7–12; Eliot Marshall, "The Politics of Alternative Medicine," *Science* 265 (September 30, 1994), 2000–2002; Silber, "Alternative Medicine Agency Can't Bridge Gap."

85. *Alternative Medicine* (Hearing), 110; Mary Beth Regan, "Will a Cup of Cow's Whey Keep the Doctor Away?" *Business Week*, December 12, 1994, 96.

86. Editorial, "Offbeat Therapies Go to Washington," *Los Angeles Times*, October 17, 1994; Regan, "Will a Cup of Cow's Whey Keep the Doctor Away?"

87. Jack Rasso, "The Three Faces of Medical Unreason," *Nutrition Forum* 11 (September-October 1994): 43; Marshall, "The Politics of Alternative Medicine."

88. Ibid.; Natalie Angier, "U.S. Head of Alternative Medicine Quits," *New York Times*, August 1, 1994; Budiansky, "Cures or 'Quackery'?"; Silber, "Alternative Medicine Agency Can't Bridge Gap."

89. Budiansky, "Cures or 'Quackery'?"

90. Angier, "U.S. Head of Alternative Medicine Quits."

91. Marshall, "The Politics of Alternative Medicine."

92. "Offbeat Therapies Go to Washington."

93. "OAM Director Outlines Office Mission and Accomplishments," *Complementary and Alternative Medicine at the NIH* 2 (December 1995): 1, 4–5.

94. Office of Alternative Medicine, "Wayne B. Jonas, M.D., Biographical Sketch."

95. Wayne B. Jonas, "Remarks to the D.C. Science Writer's Association," November 2, 1995.

96. "AM Advisory Council Meets New OAM Staff and Reviews Progress," *Complementary and Alternative Medicine at the NIH* 2 (December 1995): 1, 6–7.

97. Jonas, "Remarks to the D.C. Science Writer's Association"; Marshall, "The Poli-

tics of Alternative Medicine."

98. "AM Advisory Council Meets New OAM Staff and Reviews Progress."

99. "OAM Funds Eight Research Centers to Evaluate Alternative Treatments," *Complementary and Alternative Medicine at the NIH* 2 (December 1995): 2, 8.

100. "NIH Panel Endorses Alternative Therapies for Chronic Pain and Insomnia," *Complementary and Alternative Medicine at the NIH* 2 (December 1995): 3, 8.

101. Jonas, "Remarks to the D.C. Writer's Association."

102. "Political Favoritism, Not Merit, Created the NIH Office of Alternative Medicine," *NCAF Newsletter* 15 (September-October 1992): 2; Robert L. Park and Ursula Goodenough, "Buying Snake Oil with Tax Dollars," *New York Times*, January 3, 1996.

103. Wayne B. Jonas, "U.S. Health Agency Isn't Pushing Alternative Medicine," *New York Times*, January 9, 1996.

HAMILTON CRAVENS

# Postmodernist Psychobabble: The Recovery Movement for Individual Self-Esteem in Mental Health Since World War II

By the middle 1990s the recovery movement for personal self-esteem and, thus, mental health for the individual, had reached a new level of penetration into American culture.[1] Many commentators and interpreters of contemporary affairs judged the President of the United States, Bill Clinton, a potential recruit. As the archetypical adult child of an alcoholic parent—the product of a dysfunctional family if there ever was one, according to the movement's clerics—Clinton seemed lacking in self-esteem. His painful childhood was the culprit. And recovery was the solution. In a word, he was too anxious to please his critics—the classic trademark of the adult child of an alcoholic parent. Contemporary therapists taught that such persons were placaters of their critics because of the emotional abuse that their parents had inflicted on them, often for no apparent reason. The damaged child, regardless of his or her chronological age, could not, without appropriate therapy and personal "recovery," ever get over such incidents, which were seared into their psychological and neurophysiological apparatus.

Thus psychotherapy's discourse, or what its critics often dismissed as mere psychobabble, dominated American public culture. For example, television talk shows had reached new heights (or depths) for that kind of personal revelation in public that the movement's champions deemed essential to complete and total psychic health. Indeed, such shows were ideal for these purposes because their format permitted the audience, as well as the everpresent therapist, maximum feasible participation in the recovery process itself. It was as though mental health could become a media event, for all intents and purposes just like religious salvation via the electronic ministry. No longer was the genteel Barbara Walters the most spectacular loosener of tongues and extractor of private secrets on the airwaves. Now talk-show hosts and interviewers routinely had guests whom they and the audience aggressively grilled about their sexual and family relationships. In this way, so the movement's proponents claimed, the afflicted ones would resolve their problems in a shared public confession. That in turn would empower them to attain a full recovery. Thus they would lead better and wiser lives. The recovery movement's motto thus seemed to be, *vox populi, vox Deus.* What had in a different age been one of the most private and intimate aspects of life was now for the broadest possible public consumption. Seemingly the line between private and public had become blurred beyond recognition.

Indeed, recovery and its accompanying therapeutic baggage had a way of turning up in some fairly unpredictable settings. In the 1990s, twenty-eight of the fifty states had enacted laws permitting their citizens to carry concealed weapons. This movement was doubtless testimony both to the growing fear of violent crime and to the increasing conservatism of American politics in the previous decade and a half. The states framed their laws in various ways, but perhaps no legislature was as trendy as the one in Austin, Texas, when it grappled with its new concealed-weapons law. To pack hidden heat in the Lone Star state, a Texan had to pay a fee, have no record of a felony conviction or of mental illness, pass a shooting proficiency test, and—be in touch with his or her "inner child," or collected memory of childhood abuse from one's elders, which, apostles of psychic recovery taught, was the source of most irrational, egotistic, and violent behavior. As amazing as this might sound, it should be understood that Texas had not permitted its citizens to carry concealed weapons for more than a century. Obviously the solons knew what they were doing: bringing the best science they could to address the potential social problems that thoughtless, casual gunplay and violence spawned. Obviously the solons had learned their contemporary psychotherapy well. The recovery movement's champions had taught them that the key to emotional maturity as an adult was "recovering" one's self-esteem from the emotional abuse it had received in childhood, thus healing the pain and the shame that one's inner child had received from one's parents in childhood. Only then would the adult have achieved the necessary self-esteem and psychic serenity to be trusted with a gun.[2]

To show that they were in touch with their inner child and be responsible with a gun, Texans had to complete a twelve-hour course in conflict resolution. The statute mandated an official curriculum which required that all applicants for such permits know about the three ego states champions of emotional recovery insisted existed in everyone: the child, the parent, and the adult. Thus the Texas legislators borrowed from the populist self-help recovery movement in mental health, especially from such gurus as Eric Berne, author of *Games People Play* (1971), and Thomas Harris, author of *I'm O.K.—You're O.K.* (1970), both of whom taught transactional analysis as the underlying method of analyzing human interactions. In this vulgarized and simplified Freudianism for the masses, Berne and Harris insisted that successful interactions were those in which people interacted as individuals equal to one another in power and authority and who worked out their differences without the help (or interference) of a larger network of identities, traditions, assumptions, and the like. In particular, should individuals relate to one another as adults— they should "be in their adult," as the movement's dialect would have it, and not "in their child" or "in their parent." The adult stage was matter of fact, self-assured, and nonjudgmental, whereas that of the child was too selfish and that of the parent too controlling or manipulative. One can see the imprint of Freudian jargon here.

As Mike Myrtoglou, instructor at the Texas Shooters Range in Houston, explained to his class, and getting a laugh in the process, actor Clint Eastwood's famous "Make my day" line in his film *Sudden Impact* (1983) was classic inner-child stuff. "Wrong, wrong, wrong," he exclaimed; inner-child behavior simply would not wash, period. At the Texas Shooters Range, many applicants who were enrolled said they liked very much the minipsychology course. To pass, applicants had to identify the three ego states, list behavior traits of each ego, and answer which was the most effective ego state to resolve a conflict. As Hanan Yadin, an instructor at another school and a former marksman in the Israeli Defense Force, tells his students, when arguments become laced with obscenities, that was powerful evidence that things had degenerated to a dangerous level. "That's people talking child to child," he says. "You want to get to adult to adult. So you might say: 'Sir, we are both in the same unfortunate situation here. Let's see what we can do to resolve the situation together." Satisfaction with the self-help psychologizing seemed to run high among the students.[3]

The postwar recovery movement is the product of a particular cultural and temporal context. As such, its advocates have developed an ideology befitting that larger context. Its champions have often blurred the distinction between the public and private spheres of life. They have insisted that unless we heal our private psychic conflicts and difficulties, we cannot have a wholesome public life among colleagues at work, friends in the neighborhood or church, or even in the nation at large. Recovery seeks to solve more than familial problems, in other words. Recovery is, at bottom, a bundle of therapeutic canards and bromides aimed at the individual. Potentially every individual needs at least some help, for victimization of the child by the parent or other elder is the first important manifestation of oppression in modern life. In that sense, social, economic, and caste oppression and victimization come after parent-child oppression and are less important causes of social problems. The movement's ultimate message, then, is "psychology *ueber Alles*," before racial or religious discrimination, before class privilege, before racism, or any other more traditional social force as detailed by the social and policy sciences. Social problems begin with the individual, and, in a sense, all social problems stem from problems among (and especially between) individuals. This is hardly the interdisciplinary or holistic interpretive causal model of the interwar years. Instead it is the single-factor, single-issue orientation that has long since permeated postwar American culture and society.

According to this logic, since society itself is an aggregate of millions of distinct and unique individuals, the solution of social problems consists of the negotiations of relations among all individuals who "impact upon each other" for each individual's good. In that way will the common good be achieved. This perspective, of course, is that of our own post–World War II epoch. Since World War II, Americans from many walks of life have increasingly moved away from that interpretation of the world around us that Americans embraced between the two world wars. That earlier construction of the world assumed that all the whole was greater than or different from the sum of the parts. Entities were holistic, characterized by dynamic interrelationships among all the discrete parts of the whole. It was possible to integrate radically different kinds of things, to mix, in other words, oil and water. Since World War II, Americans have acted and spoken as if they lived in a world of individuation, fragmentation, of rebellion against larger entities or collectives of any sort whatsoever. The contrast, as we shall see, could not be greater.

In a direct sense, the intellectual parent of our postwar recovery movement is Alcoholics Anonymous (A.A.). For many years after its founding in the late 1930s, A.A. taught its members that to save themselves from a continued life of alcoholism, they must submit to a rigorous twelve-step program of self-discipline. In partaking of that, they understood that they could not control their own lives without surrendering to a vaguely spiritual, quasi-Christian "higher power" that would enable them to resolve the underlying causes of their affliction, which were spiritual and emotional. In that earlier era the group meeting and its various processes were absolutely crucial for the recovering alcoholic. It was in the group that the poor wretch acted out his or her twelve steps for group interpretation

and judgment; without that group context, the individual had no power
and could, in fact, never gain any power whatsoever over his or her life.
Eventually this group regimen would permit recovering alcoholics to take
their place in normal society as stable adults. In the world of American
culture between the world wars, notions of a higher unity, of an entity
that was greater than or different from the sum of its parts, seemingly
pervaded all lines of activity.[4]

But that holistic sense of an entity larger than any or all of its parts
yielded, after World War II, in mental self-help no less than in any other
field of health care, or of anything else, to the notion of a fragmented and
individuated world, as if a giant mosaic had been shattered into an infinite number of shards, as many as any individual might imagine in a particular circumstance. Although twelve-step recovery programs proliferated from their base in A. A. to many other particular causes, what is as
interesting for present purposes is that A.A.'s original group or collective
orientation was changing by the 1950s and 1960s into an individualistic
one. That sense of individualism, of fragmentation from the larger whole,
has been central to the post–World War II era in public health, including
mental health, no less than in any other activity in American culture.[5]

And in our postwar era, we can see this transformation in the scientific
and therapeutic ideology of mental health as well, from the holism of
cultural modernism to the individuation of cultural postmodernism. In
that earlier interpretation of mind and emotions two theories were central—the notions of intelligence as innate and constant at birth, and of
individual development as the automatic maturation of genetically pro-
grammed behavior patterns.[6] Ever since the scaled mental test of the
French psychologist Alfred Binet had been introduced into American
culture in the late 1900s, American mental testers had been inclined to
regard it as a yardstick of innate intelligence. There were numerous reasons for this, some of them seemingly emanating from the work they did,
others apparently the consequence of underlying notions in American
culture than about the organization of natural and social reality.

Most of the technical evidence for the fixity of the intelligence quotient came from the retesting of children six years or older. Some psychologists produced evidence that they used to challenge the notion of
the fixity and innateness of the intelligence quotient, largely from retesting children between the ages of two and six years. These children were
either in preschools or in orphanages, institutions whose professionals
had little stature within the larger worlds of mental science and academic
professionalism. Hence the data that they generated had little currency
among the champions of scientific and psychometric orthodoxy. Belief in

an inherited, fixed intelligence from birth had certain implications for notions about mental health. Probably the most important of these was the assumption that consciousness of any kind was the product of biological inheritance, which in turn was essentially impervious to postnatal intervention. Most professionals in the mental sciences, and in what Christopher Lasch once aptly dubbed the helping and manipulative sciences as well, took this as evidence that unlearned behavior patterns of all sorts, as well as all manner of capacities and skills, were derived, automatically, completely, and perfectly, from structures and processes within the organism.[7]

And the maturation theory reinforced that view. Maturation theorists argued that from birth the development of the infant animal or human was predetermined by the innate structures within the organism which were themselves the product of evolutionary development. Thus children did not learn to walk, or talk, or do anything else before their internal cerebral and emotional structures had "matured" to the time in their development in which they could support such activity. For those who doubted this, the evidence from animal development was rich and detailed—and apparently incontestable. Researchers did all manner of studies of the motor and behavioral development of animals and children in these three decades that seemed to demonstrate that the key to development was the unfolding of patterns of behavior or capacities that were, in a sense, pre-programmed in the innate structures within the organism itself. And there was even a widely accepted scientific method, that of stimulus and response, to explain how maturation "worked." According to this theory, which was behaviorism's legacy to developmental science, there existed within the organism a preset bundle of "responses," embedded within the structures and processes of the cerebral and nervous organs. At certain points in development, an environmental stimulus would "awaken" a particular response, as if a shaft of light could trigger the full-blown articulation of visual capacity in an organism. Thus stimulus-response behaviorism was hereditarian and nativist, not environmentalist and culturist, in orientation.[8]

Taken together, these notions of the fixed IQ and of psychological maturation created a blueprint of human mental life as a holistic system of systems, a network of many distinct yet interrelated structures and functions. Yet by the 1950s there were already signs that this larger model of the human psyche was unraveling.

In American culture and society we can now see that the 1950s marked the beginning of an era of individual protest against larger entities, systems, networks, and structures. The crystallization of the postwar youth

culture makes the point. That youth culture was first and foremost a consumer culture, at least insofar as established institutions, especially commercial and industrial ones, were concerned. Yet there was more. American youth or adolescent culture had begun to take shape after World War
I, but it had thoroughly an ethos of conformity, one that had many parallels with the psychologists' maturation theory.[9] Post–World War II youth
culture was different. It was shot through with interesting contradictions.
Thus, on the one hand, its champions stressed the importance of rebellion against authority, especially adult authority, and also battling against
tradition, including historical tradition. Yet in almost the same breath
there was an insistence on conformity to a collective ethos of individualism, as seen in certain items of attire, such as blue jeans, or artifacts of
popular culture, such as rock and roll music, or the customizing of one's
auto, with various modifications, including throaty mufflers, souped-up
engines, and often extensive changes to the body, as in lowering the roof
line, removing the manufacturer's nameplates and other means of identification, and the like. Thus, within the family the 1950s adolescent seemed
not to conform, to be an individual; yet when 1950s adolescents gathered, as at the local high school, teen hangout, or wherever, all seemed to
have similar attire, listen to the same kind of music, and to drive standard
factory American cars that had nevertheless been customized in complementary ways.[10]

As such films as *Rebel Without a Cause* (1956) made clear, the hero, or
central protagonist, was both an antihero and a victim, chiefly a victim of
not belonging to the right circle of adolescent friends and of having parents who did not understand or appreciate his sensitivity and need for
rebellion, by which was always meant (with no sense of irony) conformity. Yet victimization was a key to popular and political discourse from
the 1950s on. As historians began to discover, for example, that the American immigrant experience was not so much what the immigrants contributed to that larger entity, American civilization, but what that larger (and
discriminatory) civilization did to those blameless immigrants.[11] The list
of victims in American culture grew in the 1950s and later and included
persons of color, the poor, corporate employees, women, and even the
unborn, until American civilization seemed to be a place where none but
victims and victimizers belonged. From that point of view, there was no
longer one America, or a unified American civilization, but a highly op-
pressive system that was oppressing all manner of Americans. The remedy seemed to be to deny one's identification with the larger whole, to
reject public association with one's fellow citizens, and to withdraw, as
individuals, into the safety of one's private space. In some ways, then,

Americans in the 1980s and 1990s seemed to be reinventing the market-oriented, privatized world of the Gilded Age.

And what of the mental disciplines? The science that underlaid them was undergoing a series of shifts beginning in the 1950s that were parallel to these changes in the larger American culture and society. In a word, experience as well as genetic endowment came to matter in the behavioral sciences. In the 1940s, and again in the 1960s, the notion of an innate IQ at birth came under attack, especially by scientists who studied intelligence in very young children, especially those in preschools. Indeed, Head Start as a federal program became a manifestation of society's commitment to the notion that even underprivileged children could be rescued from an unpromising life by being brought up to a middle-class standard of educability and sociability.[12]    Thus belief in the innate IQ, while not vanquished in post-1950s American culture, has become challenged and indeed problematic on scientific and political grounds.[13]    Here the results of a series of studies of early childhood education in nursery schools have mattered a good deal. In 1981 psychologists Irving Lazar and Richard Darlington published a landmark study of twelve longitudinal studies of early childhood education and the effects of intervention in development. They argued that early childhood education did have long-lasting effects, and in particular helped children at risk successfully compete with middle-class children. The need for special education diminished; families of poor children took a far greater interest in their offspring; the children in the preschools developed wholesome values and habits; these were the concrete results of these parallel studies.[14]

And experience mattered also with regard to maturation. Starting in the later 1940s, and continuing into the late 1950s and early 1960s, scientists challenged the argument that maturation was automatic, inevitable, and preprogrammed. One kind of study pointed out that deprivation of stimuli in the developmental processes, or an interruption of a key sequence, could distort development in a serious way. Thus in a study of female rats that had not been allowed to lick themselves in the vaginal area as pups, and thus sense their own vaginal fluid, scientists found that when they became mothers, instead of merely licking their pups so covered with vaginal fluids, they ate them, which suggested that the usual practice of licking the pups at birth was not an instinctual, and therefore fairly automatic, behavior pattern.[15]    A child psychologist who studied orphans in Iran in the 1950s noted that when the children had not been permitted to develop normal methods of locomotion, they did not develop locomotion skills automatically.[16]

But something else was even more important than the demonstration that subtracting or altering experience altered maturational processes. A new general picture of development crystallized in the 1950s. Interestingly enough, it was a portrait of the human brain as a central facility for processing and interpreting information not so different from the emerging concept of the digital computer. Put another way, one part of the whole could control or influence the whole. Instead of arguing, as students of maturation had between the world wars, that the entire body and all its parts were involved in different yet interrelated ways in the development of all behavior traits, the new generation of scientists insisted that behavioral responses often resulted from the mediation of central processes. They made the brain the central organ of behavior and psychic life. In the interwar years, the Gestalt psychologists had insisted that perceptual pictures of the world came to the organism already made, as if they were imprinted in the animal's neural structures. By the early 1950s, everything was changing. Thus in his work with rhesus monkeys, Harry Harlow showed that monkeys learned complex tasks in "learning sets," or series of stimuli and responses. He suggested that there was some kind of central information-processing equipment within the monkey's brain. In this way Harlow and other scientists in the 1950s undercut the traditional view of the brain as a mass of inert specialized tissues that received outside impressions and responded to them. In their construction of natural and social reality, the brain seemed much like a computer. Experience mattered much, then, to the thoughts and deeds of people and the higher animals. But, at the same time, one could not ignore the role of biology and, especially, biologically-based psychology.[17]

Similar notions came to change the technical discourse of psychotherapy as well. Here the work of Wilder Penfield, a neurosurgeon at McGill University in Montreal, was absolutely seminal. In the 1950s he produced new kinds of evidence and studies about how the brain functions and what cells, of the brain's more than 12 billion, constitute the loci of various mental operations. As is often the case, his work was serendipitous, not planned. Penfield began treating patients afflicted with focal epilepsy. He administered a local anesthetic so that he could converse with his patients while exploring their cerebral cortex. Over the next several years he conducted a series of experiments in order to understand more about the brain. In the operating room, he touched each patient's temporal cortex with a weak electric current carried by a probe. Quite to his initial amazement, he discovered that the current could stimulate highly detailed remembrances stored in the patient's subconscious memory. The current itself could be reapplied time after time for more details of the (often) long-forgotten incident. Thus if patients could, with proper stimulation, remember a song, repeated applications at the same point would produce more and more individual fragments of the larger memory, including harmony, melody, or even the room the patient had been in, and the like. Patients could even hum the tune thus remembered through electric stimulation. Penfield concluded —and this was crucial—that the electrode brought forth a single, isolated fact, not an entire picture, of that experience. And the patient's response was involuntary. Even more important for the future ideological development of psychotherapy, Penfield argued that feelings associated with past events were "recorded" in the patient together with the events themselves. Indeed, one could not be invoked without the other.

Nor was this all. Penfield soon realized that all of us "record" such memories in our brains, whether or not we remember them. In this sense the brain was a computer with what amounted to a memory with an infinite capacity for storage and retrieval of past "information"—memories of events, all fragmented, but each with its own distinctive emotional meaning, within the individual's life history, all of them continuous, and all in sequence. Moreover—and this too was crucial—a person could be in the past and in the present at the same time, or, put another way, one could be an adult and still have memories, fully conscious or not, of events earlier in life, including those in one's childhood. Such memories may not be recollections, especially from the early years of childhood or infancy, but Penfield's point was that one could nevertheless be forced to relive the emotions associated with an event, provided there was the right stimulus. And an electrode with a weak electric current was not needed; a stimulus, after all, was carried by a weak electrical current.[18]

The next step in translating this scientific and therapeutic discourse into the recovery movement was taken by the San Francisco therapist Eric Berne, who had been something of a devotee of Freudian psychotherapy himself. First, however, it had been necessary to translate Freud into the American scientific, medical, and popular idioms. Down to the 1920s, Freudian psychiatric ideas were essentially the prisoners of certain doctors of nervous and mental diseases and of certain literary and political radicals.[19] The nonacceptance of Freud's ideas among American scientists and doctors may well have turned, in part, on anti-Semitism, an ideological virus from which the scientific and medical communities was hardly immune before the Holocaust's full horrors were known in the later 1940s. But it was certainly no help to the Freudian cause in America that in so far as American psychiatrists and psychologists were concerned Freud's ideas did not appear to possess any commonly agreed-upon American (and Anglo-American) notions of scientific evidence and logic. It was not until the 1940s that a rising generation of experimental psycholo-

gists began to subject Freud's ideas to verification or falsification. Scientists and psychiatrists opted for retaining a good portion of Freud's specific observations while also dumping many of his theoretical views. In a
very real sense, they extracted Freud's legacy from its time—and from
Freud himself—and dolled it up in contemporary interpretations of the
world.[20] And, indeed, American psychotherapy before the 1940s, as practiced by the mainstream, had happier, more optimistic messages and
sources. Thus Adolph A. Meyer, a Swiss Mennonite who had migrated to
America in the 1890s, became American psychiatrists' and foundation
officials' favorite European guru of psychiatry and of the mental-hygiene
movement. In place of Freud's pessimistic notions about human nature as
beset by seemingly intractable neuroses and psychoses, whose cure might
require years of expensive psychotherapy, Meyer taught that an individual
could, with minimal help, straighten himself or herself out and lead a
good life. What Freud as reconstructed by Americans in the 1940s came
to mean was not so different from Meyer's optimistic message of mental
hygiene.

Berne's contribution was to invent a new unit of analysis for psychotherapy, the transaction. Transactional analysis, as it came to be known
in the 1960s, posited scripts of constructive and destructive "games" that
individuals played with one another, depending on how healthy they were
and how much they had resolved the potentially damaging "memories"
stored in their brain cells from a lifetime of living—and being abused,
victimized, and oppressed. Unfortunately limitations of space prevent a
full discussion of Berne's interesting, not to say hilarious, scripts, or games,
but whether they were first-, second-, or third-degree games, likely to be
socially acceptable, clearly hurtful or, in the last instance, to end up "in
the surgery, the courtroom, or the morgue," all had preordained and specific scripts and outcomes. Whether Berne dubbed these games "Frigid
Woman," or "Alcoholic," or "Now I've Got You, You Son of a Bitch,"
they all had their individual origins and resonances in individual memory
in the distant past of each and every participant—and in each and every
citizen in the world. The key to a pacific resolution was to decode the
script and to avoid disaster.[21]

Then it was left to Berne's most earnest and active disciple, Thomas
Harris, another California champion of mental health, to take transactional analysis and hitch it to the new work on memory, on the one hand,
and to a populistic and individualistic reinterpretation of recovery, on
the other. In his own intellectual development as a mental-health professional, Harris makes it very clear indeed that he was heavily influenced by
Timothy Leary when Leary spoke at a conference in northern California in

1960. Leary had just joined the Harvard faculty. He made an astonishing confession, perhaps not so to those who know his subsequent fame (or notoriety) in American culture, but it was clearly astonishing at the time. Leary confessed before his peers that his realization that he knew nothing, as a psychiatrist, about his patients came in three stages. At first he believed that if he applied a few well-established principles of his science to his cases, he would be able to assist his patients back to mental health. A second stage began when he suddenly realized that he did not know anything about his patients, and probably never would, but they and the world more generally believed he was the authority and always consulted him for advice, thus causing guilt and anxiety on his part for being a fraud. Finally, he declared, " 'the unhappy truth becomes apparent—that although many people may be looking to you and listening to you . . . you begin to think maybe, maybe you don't know what you are talking about.' "[22]

It became Harris's role to synthesize these various strains and to disseminate them throughout American culture. Operating from his clinic in Sacramento, California, Harris ran countless workshops, gave papers, published books and articles, and became perhaps the most celebrated guru of the recovery movement from the 1970s to the present. It is to be noted that although some of his competitors, such as John Bradshaw, may have rivaled him in revenues and public adulation, as with Bradshaw's tapes, books, lectures, and workshops on the abused inner-child syndrome, no other guru equaled Harris and, beyond Harris, Berne for intellectual creativity.[23] In an age of fragmentation and assault on established standards and institutions, mental-health care had become recast as operating in a marketplace of millions of individuals, all equally capable of recovering themselves from their past traumas, none in need of expensive, complicated, and demanding analyses by experts who spouted arcane diagnoses. Neither tradition nor expertise counted for much. Neither, for that matter, did good taste, or the kind of concern for a higher standard of civilization that so often is connected with good taste. How pervasive is the new psychobabble? We cannot answer that question here, but it might be noted that even a casual reading of the work of the W. Edwards Deming, the high priest of Total Quality Management, or T.Q.M., as it is known by its champions, suggests startling if not downright disturbing parallels between T.Q.M. and recovery.[24] And of course T.Q.M. itself has been the management philosophy of choice for private corporations and for public institutions — especially institutions of higher learning — in the 1980s and 1990s. Further discussion would be fascinating and instructive.

*Iowa State University*

# Notes

1. On the recovery movement, see Wendy Kaminer, *I'm Dysfunctional, You're Dysfunctional: The Recovery Movement and Other Self-Help Fashions* (Reading, Mass., 1992). I would like to thank Professors M. Susan Lindee and Charles E. Rosenberg of the History and Sociology of Science Department, University of Pennsylvania, Philadelphia, and Professors Michael Dietrich and James R. Griesemer, of the History and Philosophy of Science Program, University of California, Davis, for inviting me to give early (and crude) versions of this paper and for their hospitality. I would also like to acknowledge, with gratitude, the constructive criticisms and questions that they and their students so graciously offered me.

2. John Bradshaw is the current guru of the inner-child ideology. See, for example, his *Healing the Shame That Binds You* (Deerfield Beach, Fla., 1988).

3. Sam Howe Verhovek, "In Texas, Pistol Packers Must Know Psychology," *New York Times*, November 8, 1995, A1, C23.

4. On Alcoholics Anonymous, see, for example, Alcoholics Anonymous, *The Twelve Steps of Alcoholics Anonymous* (San Francisco, 1987).

5. See Alan I Marcus and Howard P. Segal, *Technology in America: A Brief History* (San Diego, 1989), for a highly creative interpretation of American culture as being constituted of different epoches or eras, each with its own sense of the order of things.

6. Much of the subsequent discussion is based on J. McVicker Hunt, *Intelligence and Experience* (New York, 1960), and on my *Before Head Start: The Iowa Station and America's Children* (Chapel Hill, N.C., 1993).

7. Christopher Lasch, *Haven in a Heartless World: The Family Besieged* (New York, 1977).

8. See my "Behaviorism Revisited: Developmental Science, the Maturation Theory, and the Biological Basis of the Human Mind, 1920s-1950s," in Keith R. Benson, Jane Maienschein, and Ronald Rainger, eds., *The Expansion of American Biology* (New Brunswick, N.J., 1991), 133–63.

9. Paula S. Fass, *The Damned and the Beautiful: American Youth in the 1920s*, (New York, 1977).

10. See, for example, James B. Gilbert, *A Cycle of Outrage: America's Reaction to the Juvenile Delinquent in the 1950s* (New York, 1986); William S. Graebner, *The Age of Doubt: American Thought and Culture in the 1940s* (Boston, 1991); Graebner, *The Engineering of Consent: Democracy and Authority in Twentieth-Century America* (Madison, Wis., 1987); Graebner, *Coming of Age in Buffalo: Youth and Authority in the Postwar Era* (Philadelphia, 1990).

11. See, for example, the contrast between Carl Wittke, *We Who Built America? The Saga of the Immigrant* (New York, 1939), and Oscar Handlin, *The Uprooted: The Epic Story of the Great Migration That Made the American People* (Boston, 1951).

12. Cravens, *Before Head Start*, 151–261; S. J. Gould, *The Mismeasure of Man* (New York, 1981).

13. Richard J. Herrnstein and Charles Murray, *The Bell Curve: Intelligence and Class Structure in American Life* (New York, 1994); Steven Fraser, *The Bell Curve Wars: Race, Intelligence, and the Future of America* (New York, 1995).

14. Irving Lazar and Richard Darlington et al., *Lasting Effects of Early Education: A Report from the Consortium for Longitudinal Studies*, Monographs of the Society for Research in Child Development, vol. 47, nos. 2–3 (Chicago, 1982).

15. H. G. Birch, "Sources of Order in Maternal Behavior of Animals," *American Journal of Orthopsychiatry* 26 (1956): 279–84.

16. Wayne Dennis, "Causes of Retardation Among Institutional Children," *Journal of Genetic Psychology* 96 (1960): 47–59.

17. In general on these points, see Hunt, *Intelligence and Experience*, 35–363; Wolfgang

Koehler, *The Mentality of Apes* (New York, 1925); Harry Harlow, "The Formation of Learning Sets," *Psychological Review* 56 (1949): 51–65; D. O. Hebb, *The Organization of Behavior* (New York, 1949); C. E. Osgood, *Method and Theory in Experimental Psychology* (New York, 1953); A. Newell, J. L. Shaw, and H. A. Simon, "Elements of a Theory of Human Problem-Solving," *Psychological Review* 65 (1958): 151-66.

18. Wilder Penfield, "Memory Mechanisms," *American Medical Association Archives of Neurology and Psychiatry* 67 (1951): 178–98; Thomas Harris, *I'm O.K., You're O.K.* (New York, 1969 [1967]), 11–78.

19. John C. Burnham, "Psychoanalysis in American Civilization Before 1918" (Ph.D. diss., Stanford University, 1958).

20. Robert R. Sears, *Survey of Objective Studies of Psychoanalytic Concepts: Committee on Social Adjustment*, Bulletin no. 51, Social Science Research Council, New York, 1943; Cravens, *Before Head Start*, 237–38.

21. Eric Berne, *Games People Play: The Psychology of Human Relationships* (New York, 1991 [1971]).

22. As cited in Harris, *I'm O.K., You're O.K.*, 34–35.

23. See Bradshaw, *Healing the Shame That Binds You*.

24. W. Edwards Deming, *Out of the Crisis* (Cambridge, Mass., 1989 [1982]).

# Contributors

AMY SUE BIX received her Ph.D. in the history of science and technology from Johns Hopkins University in 1994 and is assistant professor in the history department at Iowa State University. She is currently completing a book about America's Depression-era debate over technological unemployment.

HAMILTON CRAVENS is Professor of History at Iowa State University. His extensive writings on the history of American science and technology coalesce around social policy issues and include *Before Head Start: The Iowa Station and America's Children* (University of North Carolina Press, 1993).

GERALD N. GROB is the Henry E. Sigerist Professor of History and Institute of Health, Health Care Policy and Aging Research at Rutgers University. He has published extensively on the care and treatment of mental illness in America as well as other topics. *The Mad Among Us: A History of the Care of America's Mentally Ill* (Free Press, 1994) is among his most recent publications.

ALAN I MARCUS is Professor of History and Director of the Center for Historical Studies of Technology and Science at Iowa State University. His recent publications include *Cancer from Beef: DES, Federal Food Regulation and Consumer Confidence* (Johns Hopkins University Press, 1994). He is presently completing the second edition of *Technology in America: A Brief History* (Harcourt Brace and Co.).

DIANE B. PAUL is Professor of Political Science and Co-Director of the Program in Science, Technology, and Values at the University of Massachusetts at Boston. She has recently completed a book, *Controlling Human Heredity: 1865 to the Present* (Humanities Press, 1995).

DAVID ROSNER is Distinguished Professor of History at Baruch College and City University Graduate Center, CUNY. GERALD MARKOWITZ is Professor of History at John Jay College and the City University Graduate Center, CUNY. They have collaborated on numerous books and essays exploring American health care, health insurance and labor.  Two of their most germane collaborations are *Deadly Dust: Silicosis and the Politics of Occupational Disease in Twentieth-Century America* (Princeton University Press, 1991) and their edited *Dying for Work: Essays on the History of Workers' Safety and Health in Twentieth-Century America* (Indiana University Press, 1987).

JAMES HARVEY YOUNG is Charles Howard Candler Professor of American Social History Emeritus, Emory University.  He has written extensively on the history of health frauds and regulation and on the history of disease.  Among his recent works is *Pure Food: Securing the Federal Food and Drug Act of 1906* (Princeton, 1989).  Lately he has turned his attention to AIDS and AIDS research.